# HUMAN RELATIONS DEVELOPMENT

## a manual for educators

### second edition

GEORGE M. GAZDA • the university of georgia
and medical college
of georgia

FRANK R. ASBURY • the university of georgia

FRED J. BALZER • institute of human
relations • miami

WILLIAM C. CHILDERS • winthrop college

RICHARD P. WALTERS • life enrichment
center • pine rest
christian hospital •
grand rapids

ALLYN and BACON, Inc.
Boston London Sydney

LIBRARY OF CONGRESS CATALOGING IN PUBLICATION DATA
Main entry under title:

Human relations development.

Includes bibliographies and index.
1. Personnel service in education. 2. Interpersonal
relations. I. Gazda, George Michael, 1931-
LB1027.5.H82      1977          371.4'6       76-40480
ISBN 0-205-05566-4
ISBN 0-205-05558-3 pbk.

# CONTENTS

# PREFACE

We have prepared this manual and the accompanying *Instructor's Guide* to help train educators and prospective educators in the development of human relations skills.

We use the term *human relations development/training* broadly to include skill development in personal and interpersonal relationships. By *skill development* we mean developing expertise in listening and communicating in order to make problem solving easier for those seeking assistance. We also contend that expertise in listening/perceiving and communicating/responding is a potent means of preventing misunderstanding. Therefore, expertise in listening and communicating is essential both in preventing problems and in developing effective strategies or procedures for problem resolution. Throughout the manual we use *helping* and *facilitating* interchangeably. We also use *helpee* very broadly to mean, at times, someone who is actually seeking help and at other times someone with whom we are simply interacting.

By *educators* we are referring primarily to teachers, administrators, teacher aides, special education personnel, and student personnel services specialists such as counselors, school psychologists, school social workers, and the like. The target population is elementary and secondary educators, but with slight modifications in certain exercises, the manual can be used with college and university educators and others engaged in educational endeavors. The manual was developed for use in both preservice and inservice education.

Procedures presented in the manual have been developed over several years with preservice and inservice teachers, administrators, and educational specialists. The manual has been modified and refined in its present form after use with several thousand undergraduate students enrolled in teacher education at The University of Georgia. In addition, input has been received from training several hundred inservice teachers, administrators, and other educational specialists.

The effectiveness of the model employed in this manual is developed in Chapter 1. Additional studies are abstracted in the *Instructor's Guide* and still further research is under way. The basic rationale for the model was developed by Robert R. Carkhuff and his colleagues. Their research on the development and effectiveness of this model is unequaled by any other human relations procedures employed today. As a result, we feel confident that our adaptations of what has become internationally known as the "Carkhuff Model" are theoretically and empirically sound.

This second edition of *Human Relations Development: A Manual for Educators* incorporates a number of changes from the first edition. Decisions on revision of first edition material and addition of new chapters and sections were made, based on several types of feedback: formal reviewers, students' reactions, instructors' responses, and the authors' experiences with the first edition.

The revisions and additions in the second edition include:

1. an updated review of the literature in Chapter 1,
2. a chapter providing a rationale for implementing action strategies,
3. a chapter on attending skills,
4. a chapter on nonverbal behaviors in helping,
5. a chapter on helpee statement types,
6. a chapter on combining empathy and respect in responding,
7. many new stimulus situations including several extended interactions,
8. a revision of rating scales, and
9. sections on communication in employment relationships, responding with action, responding with information, responding to inappropriate communication, dealing with anger, and accepting compliments.

The *Instructor's Guide* to accompany this manual has also been revised. Especially relevant in the *Guide* is a modular outline for a twenty-hour training program that can easily be expanded to forty or fifty hours. The chapter, "Human Relations Training in a Group Setting," is now included in the *Guide* rather than the *Manual* since it is more relevant to trainers than trainees. Additional research abstracts are also included in the *Guide* for the second edition.

The model itself can only be an implement for human relations skill development. Inevitably, the personnel who function as trainers hold the key to the success or failure of this or any other training model. We wish, therefore, to underscore the importance of selecting healthy, high-functioning persons as trainers or educators. We recommend, further, that all potential trainers be trained in the model employed in the manual before they attempt to train others.

We do not pretend that all of the learning or skill development in human relations is contained in the exercises found in this manual and its accompanying guide. The manual and guide are *aids* for the trainer. Trainers should develop audio-visual material of their own to supplement these exercises. We have used audiotapes and videotapes effectively in training, and we recommend their frequent use. We particularly recommend the film/video series, *The Heart of*

*Teaching,* by the Agency for Instructional Television, Box A, Bloomington, Indiana. This manual has been coordinated with The Heart of Teaching programs.

We wish to acknowledge the many individuals who have contributed to the development of this manual and its accompanying guide. First, without the pioneering and tireless efforts of Robert Carkhuff, the basic model would not have been developed. We thank Dr. Carkhuff for permitting us to adapt his model and scales to the educational setting. We wish to recognize the efforts of R. Eric Desselle who contributed to the first edition of this manual but could not participate in its revision. We are grateful to Mark Fawcett, a graduate student at the West Virginia College of Graduate Studies, for helping with the development of stimulus situations for the second edition. We also appreciate the willingness of Dean Joseph Williams and Associate Dean Alex Perrodin of the College of Education, The University of Georgia, to support a human relations training program for prospective teachers. And, finally, we wish to recognize Ina Ruth Scott and Barbara Gazda who typed the final copy of the manual.

G. M. GAZDA

# The Need for Human Relations Training in Teacher Education

# 1

"No limit can be set to the power of a teacher, but this is equally true in the other direction: No career can so nearly approach zero in its effect."

_____ Jacques Barzun

There's an often told story in Georgia about the best math teacher in the state. Year after year, this woman's students gained more on their math achievement test than any other students in the state, so she was considered the best math teacher in the state. A newspaper decided to write a story on this teacher. The journalist followed up some of her ex-students to find out how well they did once out of school. The journalist wanted to find out how many of them had majored in math in college, how many became great mathematicians, how many of them worked in the space program, and how many had made other contributions in math. The journalist found that *none* of the teacher's ex-students had majored in math in college; hence, none had become mathematicians.

Well, the story is very clear. This teacher had taught her students at least one other thing besides math concepts. She had taught them to dislike math or, at least, not to like it to the point of pursuing it further.

Are teachers "disseminators of information" or "facilitators of learning"? If teachers are "facilitators of learning," they must start where the student is *psychologically.* He or she *is* where his or her feelings are. Feelings are the energy source. When students feel negative about their school work, energy is absent or misdirected. Energy is present when teachers relate subject matter in ways which arouse positive feelings. Positive feelings are most likely to occur when students feel good about themselves. This manual places special emphasis on helping teachers understand and build on the feelings of students.

## SELF-CONCEPTS

It is now generally accepted that the vast majority of human behaviors are learned, i.e., they develop as a consequence of persons interacting with their environment. By and large, we *learn* to be the kind of human beings we are. This learning comes about mainly through interacting with other human beings who themselves constitute a principal source of motivations, punishments, and rewards. The quantity and quality of these interpersonal relationships greatly influence each person's unique personality development. It was primarily through people that we grew into what we are today, and it is primarily through our relationships with people that we grow into what we will be tomorrow (Otto, 1970).

Left on their own, newborn children might not live for more than a few hours. In this, their first interpersonal relationship, they must totally depend on their parents or caretakers to survive. In this relationship, infants experience virtually complete oneness with parents, because they have little sense of self.

Numerous terms such as *self-concept, self-perception, self-image,* and *self-structure* have been employed to characterize the organization of beliefs that people hold toward themselves—what they perceive themselves to be. Rogers (1951) describes the evolution of the self as follows: "As a result of interaction with the environment, and particularly as a result of evaluational interaction with others, the structure of self is formed—an organized, fluid, but consistent conceptual pattern of perceptions of characteristics and relationships of the 'I' or the 'me' together with values attached to these concepts" (p. 498).

The way the important people in our lives treat us largely determines our self-perception. These persons help us learn who we are and what we are. The personal evaluations that they make of us become part of our self-structure. From them we learn whether we are capable or incapable, likable or unlikable, lovable or unlovable, valuable or worthless. How they regard us is generally how we come to regard ourselves. The self, then, is partly built of the reflected appraisals of persons important to us. Because these persons have significant effects on our personality development, they are sometimes referred to as *significant others.*

Attitudes, values, and concepts may accrue to the self not only through direct experience but may be taken over unconsciously from other persons. That is, these components of personality may be *introjected,* though the person may perceive them as being experienced directly.

"Once established, the self-concept thereafter provides a screen through which everything else is seen, heard, evaluated, and understood" (Combs et al. 1971, p. 43). This screen serves to perpetuate the self-concept in every aspect of human experience; there is an increased likelihood that our behavior will cause others to respond toward us in ways which validate and support our self-image. If our self-structure is generally positive, it engenders self-respect and confidence, while a generally negative self-image leads to feelings of inadequacy and a lack of confidence. The perception we form of ourselves largely determines what we can do and how we react to life in general. "So the circular effect of the self-concept creates a kind of spiral in which 'the rich get richer and the poor get poorer'" (Combs et al. 1971, p. 46). Thereafter, once the self-concept is firmly established, it is difficult to change.

We have indicated that children come to know themselves largely through interacting with significant others. Children incorporate the attitudes of significant others toward them into their own personality structure; therefore, the attitudes of significant others become the children's own attitudes toward themselves.

The parents or caretakers are the first significant others in the lives of children. If children are fortunate, these persons basically think well of them. If they are unfortunate, they generally think ill of them. In the first case, children "buy a good bill of goods"; in the second case, they are "cheated." In either instance, they have little control over the initial attitudes they develop toward themselves, because children don't choose their parents.

The state of marriage was instituted, in part, to fix responsibility for rearing children. Once children begin to attend school, however, this responsibility is shared with the teacher. And, as Hamachek (1971) observes, "Teachers are quickly established as 'significant' persons in the lives of most students" (p. 194). Children are generally not given the opportunity of choosing their teacher and, once again, they may be either fortunate or unfortunate.

It would seem desirable that teachers try to create a situation in which all students believe that they are fortunate to be taught by the teachers assigned to teach them and look forward to being with their teachers. Students who are eager to attend class are more ready to learn, to grow, and to develop their potentialities fully. A primary purpose of systematic human relations training is to facilitate a healthy teacher-student relationship.

All students deserve to have their total development facilitated by a truly competent human being—their teacher. But one cannot teach well that which one does not know well. Therefore, teachers themselves must grow and live fully if they are to help students learn to do likewise. The authors trust that their readers share this belief. Without acceptance and active participation by trainees, this program will not contribute effectively to the development of their capacities to guide the growth of their students constructively.

In the remaining sections of this chapter we shall sketch briefly how our industrial revolution affected our educational system by dehumanizing it. To humanize education is one of our goals, and we have therefore tried to illustrate through theory and research why this needs to be done and to give examples of research showing that it can and is being done.

## THE ROOTS OF OUR PRESENT SYSTEM—
## INDUSTRIALIZED EDUCATION

As American society became more industrialized, a larger and larger educated labor force was required. The public schools were left with the task of educating personnel to fill these positions. But the highly structured and specialized work world required standardized skills for standardized jobs. Conformity was therefore highly valued and praised, and little attention was paid to developing individual differences and uniqueness. Toffler (1970) points out that the whole design of the school was given an industrial flavor:

> Yet the whole idea of assembling masses of students (raw material) to be processed by teachers (workers) in a centrally located school (factory) was a stroke of industrial genius .... The most criticized features of education today—the regimentation, lack of individualization, the rigid systems of seating, grouping, grading and marking, the authoritarian role of the teacher—are precisely those that made mass public education so effective an instrument of adaptation for its place and time. [p. 400]

Another notable characteristic of this period was the widespread use of harsh methods of discipline. Punishment was believed to be an effective motivator for good learning. Thus, teachers often exercised rigid control over the behavior of their students, forcing them into obedience and submission.

## HUMANIZING THE SCHOOL

In considering where to concentrate our efforts at creating a healthier society, our educational institutions stand out as a fertile audience of millions. To a considerable extent, schools contribute to the total social welfare and play a significant part in shaping the direction of human existence.

As Weinstein (1972) writes, "Children have been called America's most precious natural resource" (p. 46). All children have within them a vast potential for growth and development, and it is the common obligation of the schools to nurture this. Our system of public education has been instituted with the hope that all the children of all the people will receive this nurturance.

Through practical and theoretical research we are constantly discovering new ways and means of providing students with the best possible education. Presently, considerable efforts are being made to humanize education. The prime momentum comes from humanistic psychology, though credit must be given to William James and John Dewey as early contributors to this movement.

When individuals use the humanistic approach, they try to understand people in terms of how they view themselves. Persons are seen as beings who: (1) achieve their uniquely human qualities through interpersonal contact, (2) are aware of themselves and their existence, and (3) are capable of making choices which guide their behavior. Such concepts as love, intimacy, creativity, warmth, and courage are given careful attention in humanistic psychology, as well as individuals, sense of self, personal values and their sense of themselves as changing or "becoming." The positive potentialities of humans are emphasized, and they are approached from an optimistic frame of reference.

Humanistic psychology, called the "third force," (Maslow 1971) is generally viewed as being complementary to the first two forces in psychology, the psychoanalytic and the behaviorist. Each of these approaches uniquely contributes to an understanding of people and their functioning. However, no theoretical system as yet has managed to account fully for all the complexities of our species. Humanistic psychology evolved as an effort to transcend some of the limitations of the first two approaches while building upon their background.

In humanistic education, the goal is to help each student develop his or her positive potentialities and become the best human being each can—one who is fully integrated and fully functioning. The goal is not to mass-produce students so they all come out alike. The focus is on *maximum* development of each student, and not simply statistical normality.

## EDUCATION, LEARNING, AND THE ROLE OF THE SCHOOL

The broad purpose of education, simply stated, is to facilitate the integration of a student's total personality in such a way as to maximize knowledge and skill development for productive living. The process of education is a process of change. "The person who has learned something acts in a different fashion from the person who has not learned this same thing: The first person has been 'educated'; the second person has not" (Grambs 1968, p. 1). When we educate students, we help them develop their own unique personalities by bringing their ideas and feelings into communication with others, breaking down the barriers that produce isolation in a world where, for their own mental health and physical well-being, they must learn to be a part of the human race (Rogers 1961).

Children are thinking, feeling, and physically responsive organisms. Therefore, educating them to be literate or scholarly is simply doing *part* of the job. Children's affective growth needs to be given at least as much consideration as their cognitive growth. From a holistic standpoint, no person can truly live effectively with other human beings if he or she lacks either the necessary cognitive or affective skills. Toffler (1970) writes in *Future Shock,* "For education the lesson is clear: Its prime objective must be to increase the individual's 'cope-ability'—the speed and economy with which he can adapt to continual change" (p. 403). In regard to human relations: "The world each of us personally inhabits grows steadily and rapidly larger. No man today has any choice but to be part of a greater and more diverse community. To forego the opportunity to educate our children faithfully and imaginatively for this larger world will be to fail them tragically and inexcusably" (Fischer 1968, p. 224).

School is one of the major instruments for socializing children in terms of our cultural values, traditions, attitudes, beliefs, knowledge, and skills. Yet while we are engaged in the process of deciding what children should be learning, we sometimes fail to ask them about their learning needs. Rogers (1961), in his chapter, "Significant Learning: In Therapy and in Education," makes the following points: (1) Significant learning is facilitated in a therapeutic relationship, (2) educators interested in significant learning might gain some worthwhile ideas from therapy, and (3) significant learning occurs more readily in reference to situations perceived as problems, and it therefore seems advisable that we allow students to be in actual contact with the problems of their existence— problems they wish to resolve. Similarly, Hopkins (1941) advanced the idea that education is a continuous and lifelong process and should therefore also be concerned with life-coping skills and not just the classroom, books, or academic subjects isolated from the larger world.

Many of our most difficult problems in living are interpersonal in nature. Therefore, it seems reasonable to help students develop the skills necessary for establishing and maintaining effective interpersonal relationships. That is, we must help students become more socially competent, a concept which Barr, Davis, and Johnson (1953) believe is implicit in all statements of broad educational outcome.

## THE ROLE OF THE TEACHER—FACILITATOR OF LEARNING

Clearly, our schools have a tremendously important role to perform in our culture. Within each school, the basic unit is the classroom, which is under the guidance and direction of a teacher. The individual teacher appears to be the single most vital factor in the system; few people would deny the importance of the influence a teacher may have on a student's behavior and personality development. Unfortunately, we have not always provided our teachers with the proper training in human relations that would help to ensure that the influence teachers have on a student's personality formation is indeed in the student's best interest. Considerable attention must be given to the relationship between teachers and students if our schools are going to help to develop fully functioning persons who together might constitute a healthier society.

In order to contribute to the total well-being of children, teachers must attend to as many of the students' basic needs as possible. Traditionally, as has been pointed out, the cognitive needs of students have been given noteworthy attention. However, a teacher might coerce a student to reach high levels of cognitive achievement to the detriment of the student's total development. This may be the case where teachers are primarily subject-centered or where they place the intellectual needs of the student above all others. This restricted view can be costly to the child. The child may be left with a one-sided personality; the child may become an academic success but an affective failure. "This is perhaps the greatest indictment of the contemporary Western intellectual: He lives almost completely within his own head and is proud of this disability. By his excessive emphasis on the rational and intellectual processes he becomes progressively less human and more dehumanized, for life is feelings" (Otto 1970, p. 139).

Students learn all sorts of things in school, some of them useful and some useless. If a child learns to associate either the school or the teacher with strong feelings of anxiety, guilt, frustration, aggression, inadequacy, or worthlessness, then, plainly, that school or teacher is not effective.

It is important to note that the relationship between teacher and student is really one of interdependency, because neither can enact his/her role without the participation of the other. This point was well illustrated by Dewey, who suggested that a teacher could no more teach without a learner than a seller could sell without a buyer (Mouly 1960).

Axline (1947) observed that learning requires the participation of the student. This simple principle is easily overlooked. As Turberville (1965) advises, "In the last analysis the instructor cannot 'learn' the pupil anything" (p. 82). If this point of view is accepted, it follows logically that a teacher's primary role is to *facilitate* student learning of academic subject matter as well as other life-coping skills.

In conclusion, for a teacher to be effective in facilitating the total growth and development of students, at least three primary conditions need to be met: (1) The teacher must be adequately prepared in the subject or course to be taught, (2) the teacher must have some general knowledge of learning theory and the technical skills to present the material in a learnable fashion, and (3) the teacher must have a well-developed repertory of interpersonal skills through which to establish, maintain, and promote effective interpersonal relationships in the classroom. Some writers consider the third condition to be the most significant. Weigand (1971) writes, "How we interact, relate and transact with others, and the reciprocal impact of this phenomenon, forms the single most important aspect of our existence" (p. 247).

## HUMAN RELATIONS AND DISCIPLINE

Good discipline in a classroom involves helping students learn to take responsibility for behaving in an acceptable manner, a manner which does not infringe upon the rights of other students or the teacher and, of course, a manner which increases the probability that learning will take place. Teachers who understand and care for students and who can communicate this to the students tend to have good relationships, and students who know that teachers care for them, tend to care about what teachers think about their behavior. Therefore, they tend to behave in more acceptable ways when they are with teachers who care about them. In other words, students tend to reflect back to the teacher the respect that they get from the teacher. Good human relations is one of the keys to having good discipline.

Harbach and Asbury (1976) found that negative behaviors decreased when teachers responded facilitatively to students with behavior problems. Eleven high school and middle school teachers each identified the student he/she considered his/her most difficult problem. Each teacher specified the behavior he/she would like to change. Base-line data were collected for one week. During the next two weeks each teacher contacted the problem student at least once per day, initiated a facilitative conversation and communicated empathic understanding. Postdata collected the following week revealed that negative behaviors had decreased from 212 occasions during the base-line week to eighty-nine occasions during the posttest week.

Each of the eleven teachers in the above study had an interesting story to tell about his or her facilitative responses and the changing relationships. Several teachers reported that they found it extremely difficult to try to understand these problem students and to respond facilitatively to them. On the first day or two, problem students seemed to be skeptical of teachers behaving in this manner. All teachers reported that, following the experiment, they understood their students better and that the relationships improved. One female teacher was amazed that her attitude had become much more positive toward her student. She said, "I thought *his* attitude was supposed to change, not *mine*." After completing the project, a second female teacher immediately started an identical project with another student indicating that she couldn't wait to help another student with a problem. Her second treatment was also effective.

Much has been learned in the last twenty years about maintaining good classroom management or discipline through behavior modification methods. Of course, behavior modification methods which are most effective are those which are based on positive reinforcement rather than punishment. The problem for some teachers is finding ways to give positive reinforcement, but if a teacher has good relationships with students and a large repertoire of interpersonal skills, then the teacher has more potential for giving positive reinforcement. In fact, the good teacher becomes a personal reinforcer of behavior. A smile, a pat, a glance by the teacher are positive reinforcers to some students. Teachers who do not have potential for reinforcing students positively through their verbal and nonverbal behavior must resort to M&M's or authoritarian tactics and more punishment-oriented methods in order to maintain control. One of the most important objectives of this manual is to help future teachers and inservice teachers become more effective reinforcers of positive behavior.

## A GENERAL REVIEW OF RELATED RESEARCH LITERATURE

The highlights of a rather comprehensive review of teacher effectiveness and competency research are outlined below. The studies were chosen from among hundreds that were carefully examined. Particular attention was given to studies which have demonstrated the importance of good human relations for effective teaching. Many of the studies reported were well designed and skillfully implemented, and their contributions to the field of education are well recognized. Some of the lesser known studies are imperfect in design; nevertheless, they help to validate what is known about effective teachers.

## Students' Attitudes toward Their Teacher

Kratz (1896) asked more than 2,000 young school children to describe the best teacher they ever had. The most frequently mentioned characteristics were: (1) help in studies, (2) personal appearance, and (3) goodness or kindness. Hart (1934) obtained the opinions of nearly 4,000 high school seniors in regard to best-liked and least-liked teachers. Students listed forty-three different reasons for liking one particular teacher the most. The four most frequently mentioned reasons were that the teacher was: (1) helpful in schoolwork, (2) cheerful, happy, good natured, (3) human, friendly, "one of us," and (4) interested in and understanding of students. Students listed thirty different reasons for liking one particular teacher the least. The four most frequently mentioned reasons were that the teacher was: (1) too cross, grouchy, unsmiling, sarcastic, loses temper, (2) not helpful with schoolwork, (3) partial, favoring some students and picking on certain others, and (4) superior, aloof, overbearing, does not know you out of class. Along similar lines of investigation, Witty (1947) solicited, through radio broadcasts, letters from 12,000 students on the theme, "The Teacher Who Helped Me Most." Some qualities referred to most often were: (1) cooperative and democratic attitudes, (2) kindliness and consideration for each individual, (3) patience, (4) wide interests, (5) personal appearance and pleasant manner, (6) fairness and impartiality, and (7) sense of humor.

Evans (1962) reviewed eight studies conducted between 1900 and 1946. He concluded that:

> Children, apparently, know quite clearly what they like and what they dislike in their teachers, and different generations of school children have held the same opinions for a period of over fifty years. They like teachers who are kind, friendly, cheerful, patient, helpful, fair, have a sense of humor, show an understanding of children's problems, allow plenty of pupil activity and at the same time maintain order. They dislike teachers who use sarcasm and ridicule, are domineering and have favourites, who punish to secure discipline, fail to provide for the needs of individual pupils, and have disagreeable personality peculiarities. [p. 112]

## Classroom Emotional Climate

Interpersonal relations in the classroom determine what has been called the social-emotional atmosphere, classroom climate, classroom atmosphere, or group climate. The emotional tone of the classroom is of vital importance. Students learn best when they are emotionally involved. However, the specific emotion and its intensity may either facilitate, distract from, or inhibit learning. As Mouly (1960) writes, "A certain amount of emotional tension (e.g., motivation) is beneficial if the individual utilizes the energy which is generated to further the attainment of his goals. However, when the tension is too great . . . the individual becomes so concerned with the tension itself that he is no longer able to devote himself to dealing with the problem confronting him" (pp. 139–140).

Satisfying students' emotional needs is an important factor contributing to their total growth and development. In regard to the learning process, Jenkins (1951) suggests that greater learning will occur in the classroom to the extent that students are also able to satisfy their emotional needs there. The more fully their emotional needs are satisfied, the more they will be able to participate in their own learning. If students are free from disruptive anxieties, fears, or stages of anger or depression, then they are more likely to make the desirable cognitive and affective gains.

A comprehensive series of studies under the direction of Anderson (Anderson and Brewer 1946; Anderson, Brewer, and Reed 1946) was conducted on the subject of classroom climate. From a number of follow-up studies on teachers, the researchers concluded that the teacher, more than any other person, sets the emotional climate in the classroom. That is, the general behavior of children is a response to that of their teacher rather than vice versa. They observed that over a given period of time the teachers' behavior remained essentially unchanged, but students adapted to, and their behavior corresponded with, that of their new teacher. Similarly, Withall (1952) demonstrated that different psychological climates were produced by different teachers with the same group of seventh-grade students.

A large number of studies have been conducted in the area of classroom climate. Pooling the findings of Withall (1949), Flanders (1951), Perkins (1951), Kearney and Rocchio (1955), and Withall and Lewis (1963), the following propositions can be made: (1) The teacher's behavior largely determines the quality of emotionality in the classroom, (2) teacher-pupil relationships may affect pupils at deep psychological levels, and (3) the way a teacher behaves in interacting with students affects how students come to view others (social attitudes) and how they will treat others (human relations).

## Classroom Interaction Styles

A number of investigations have focused on the way teachers interact with their students. Flanders (1965) found that teachers who tend to dominate, force, and command also tend to elicit similar behaviors from their students. Teachers who are socially integrative, offer choices, and acknowledge and encourage students to express their feelings and opinions stimulate their students to behave likewise.

Students who were exposed to the dominating teachers displayed greater compliance to, as well as rejection of, teacher domination. The students of teachers who demonstrated more integrative behavior were more spontaneous, volunteered to contribute more often, and did more problem solving. Significant achievement differences in mathematics and social studies followed as a consequence of the teaching method used, and indirect methods of influence yielded greater gains than did direct methods of influence.

In another study, Flanders (1951) conducted teacher-pupil interaction research in a laboratory-type setting where students were exposed to different teacher behaviors. Dominating teacher patterns were disliked by the students, produced disruptive anxiety (as measured by galvanic skin responses and accelerated heartbeats), and interfered with memory (recall). When the teachers were integrative, the opposite trends were noted.

In general, Flanders found that indirect teacher influence fostered learning and resulted in the most favorable attitudes. But, more specifically, he observed that the students who learned the most and scored the highest on classroom attitude scales had teachers who were *flexible* in their patterns of influence— they could be direct or indirect depending on the particular situation encountered. The teachers who demonstrated less latitude in shifting interaction styles to meet the needs of students were judged unsuccessful. These two styles of behavior might aptly be described as *authoritarian* and *democratic*. The former makes use of such things as orders and commands and generally restricts the student's freedom of action while increasing dependency on the teacher. The latter style generally expands freedom of action while decreasing dependency on the teacher. The latter style also allows more student autonomy. Obviously, a democratic society can best be developed through the use of democratic means.

## Personal Characteristics of Effective Teachers

The focus in the preceding sections has been broad in reviewing the studies on the emotional climate of the classroom and the basic interaction style of the teacher. We will now review studies where the investigators narrowed their focus to more personal characteristics of teachers.

One of the most comprehensive studies of teacher characteristics was made by Ryans (1960). The project involved over 100 separate research investigations of some 6,000 teachers from 1,700 schools. For the purposes of this chapter, only selected findings from the total project will be presented.

The Teacher Characteristics Schedule (TCS) is a 300-item, self-report inventory that was developed and used extensively in Ryans's project. Through factor analyzing numerous assessments of elementary and secondary teachers, three major patterns of teacher classroom behavior were identified (Ryans 1964, p. 76). These were as follows:

TCS pattern X:    warm, understanding, friendly versus aloof, egocentric, restricted behavior.

TCS pattern Y:    responsible, businesslike, systematic versus evading, unplanned, slipshod behavior.

TCS pattern Z:    stimulating, imaginative versus dull, routine behavior.

In one study in Ryans's project, school principals were asked to nominate outstandingly good and poor teachers. These teachers then completed the TCS. The good group attained significantly higher mean scores with respect to friendly and understanding behavior, organized and businesslike behavior, and stimulating behavior. The good teachers expressed a liking for personal contacts and were generous in their appraisal of others. The characteristics which distinguished the poor teachers suggested self-centeredness, anxiety, and restriction.

Several things were observed about the relationship between teacher behavior and student behavior in the classroom. Productive pupil behavior was related to the following teacher behaviors and characteristics: (1) understanding-friendly teacher behavior, (2) systematic-businesslike teacher behavior, (3) stimulating-imaginative teacher behavior, (4) child-centered educational viewpoint, (5) emotional adjustment, and (6) favorable attitudes toward pupils and democratic classroom procedures (Ryans 1964).

Increasing numbers of schools are seeing their primary role as one of providing children with opportunities to grow and develop in ways that contribute to sound mental health and effective living (Tryon 1950). In this regard, several investigators point out the positive correlation between teachers' mental health and their effectiveness in the classroom. Heil et al. (1960) compared several different teacher-pupil personality combinations and reported that the healthy and well-integrated teachers were the most effective with the various types of students in the study. Gowan (1957) reported that emotional stability, responsibility, and interest in personal relations were characteristics related to being an effective teacher. Axline (1947) writes, "It seems to the writer that the most important single factor in establishing sound mental health is the relationship that is built up between the teacher and his or her pupils" (p. 142). Likewise, Biber (1961) reported a circular relationship between a healthy personality and effective learning.

## Research Based on the Systematic Human Relations Training Development Model for a Helping Relationship

In order for the reader to understand most clearly the frame of reference in which the following group of studies was conducted, a basic proposition of the comprehensive helping model is here presented: "All effective interpersonal processes share a common core of conditions conducive to facilitative human experiences" (Carkhuff 1969, p. 7). The core conditions which receive the most impressive backing from the research are empathy, respect, warmth, genuineness, self-disclosure, concreteness, confrontation, and immediacy of relationship. Research investigations indicate that a teacher may especially either facilitate or retard the emotional and cognitive growth of students and that the teacher's level of functioning on core interpersonal conditions significantly influences student emotional and cognitive growth.

One of the early investigations of the effects of teacher-offered conditions upon students was conducted by Aspy (1969). The study involved 120 third-grade children and their teachers. Aspy found that the students of teachers functioning at high levels of interpersonal skills achieved at significantly higher levels than the students of teachers functioning at low levels. More specifically, the children whose teachers were rated at high levels of empathy, congruence, and positive regard attained the highest achievement test results. Aspy and Hadlock (1967) also found that pupils of teachers functioning at the highest levels of warmth, empathy, and genuineness demonstrated higher levels of academic achievement than pupils of teachers functioning at the lowest levels. They reported that, over the course of one academic year, the students of the highest level teacher gained an average of two and one-half academic *years,* while the students of the lowest level teacher gained an average of six academic *months.* They also discovered that pupils of teachers functioning at low levels in these three dimensions were significantly more truant than pupils of high-level teachers.

In another study reported by Aspy (1972), a group of seventeen first-grade teachers took part in a training program designed to increase their levels of interpersonal skills. Before their training began, twenty-five students were randomly selected from among their classes and were administered the Stanford-Binet Intelligence Test. This test was again administered after the teacher training. The students gained an average of nine IQ points, an increase which was found to be statistically significant. In addition, the inferred self-concepts of the students were positively related to the improved interpersonal functioning of the teachers.

The cumulative effects of parent- and teacher-offered conditions upon indexes of the students' physical, emotional, and cognitive functioning were investigated by Kratochvil, et al. (1969). They established that while some of the high-level teachers had immediate positive effects upon pupil functioning, these effects tended to "wash out" after a series of neutral or debilitating experiences with other teachers. In terms of learning theory, we might speculate that the students were no longer being reinforced for behaviors they had exhibited while interacting with the high-level teachers. That is, high-level teachers are more likely to reward students for such things are responsible and autonomous behavior while low-level teachers are more likely to reward students for such things as behaving in submissive, dependent, or conforming ways. As in the Aspy and Hadlock study, it was found that the students of the highest level teacher obtained an average of twenty-two months academic growth, while the students of the lowest level teacher obtained an average of nine months academic growth, both measured over a period of one academic year.

Research investigations contributing to the development of a comprehensive human relations model for helping have dealt with a variety of student populations. Truax and Tatum (1966) studied the effects of empathy, positive regard, and genuineness communicated to preschool children by their teachers. They concluded that empathy and positive regard were significantly related to positive changes in the children's adjustment to school, to teachers, and to peers. Griffin and Banks (1969) conducted systematic human relations training for teachers working with inner-city students. Following training, the teachers demonstrated high levels of interpersonal skill, and the elementary students were unanimous in evaluating the learning experience as the best in their school years. Carkhuff (1970a) directed a study in which separate human relations training groups were conducted for inner-city school children who were experiencing difficulty in self-expression. The student group was also given some additional training in systematic desensitization to lower their anxiety levels. The end result of this project was that the students received exceptionally high ratings in regard to expressing themselves openly in the classroom. Hefele (1971) studied the effects upon deaf students' academic achievement of teachers who received systematic human relations training and teachers who did not receive such training. Both the primary and secondary students of the trained teachers attained significantly higher levels of performance in language skills, reading skills, motivation for learning, and general achievement than the students of the untrained teachers. Stoffer (1970) examined the relationship between the levels of empathy and regard offered by teacher-counselors and measures of elementary student achievement and classroom behavior. He reported a significant positive relationship between these variables.

A study of student teachers by Berenson (1971) compared a human relations training group, a didactic training control group, a Hawthorne Effect control group, and a control group on their levels of interpersonal functioning. Following training, the human relations training group demonstrated the highest levels of interpersonal functioning. Classroom supervisors rated this group significantly higher than the other groups in total competency, classroom management, understanding children, and understanding the learning process. In addition, this group of student teachers was significantly more indirect (democratic) in their approach to motivation and control and used less extended patterns of direct influence. They also demonstrated greater use of positive reinforcement in relating to their students. In the final analysis, the human relations training group evidenced clear superiority over the other groups on a total of thirty-one different indexes of teacher competency and pupil learning. This direct effect on teacher competency and effectiveness makes clear the need to incorporate training in human relations skills into the conventional curriculum for teacher education.

Childers (1973) compared student teaching practices of preservice teachers who had participated in systematic human relations training with student teachers who had not participated in such training. Childers found that those who had taken part in the training gave more indirect responses to students as opposed to direct responses. They also gave significantly less criticism to students and stimulated more student talk and involvement.

In a study of effects of systematic human relations training on fourth graders, Desselle (1974) found that students who received human relations training were observed to be more cooperative in class and were rated more positively by their teachers than students in the control group.

## Traditional Courses of Study in Teacher Education

Historically, the curriculum in teacher training institutions has adequately prepared teachers to deal with the academic aspects of instruction. However, as Gazda (1971) suggests, "Mastering the academic subject matter is a prerequisite to good teaching but is no guarantee of it" (p. 49). Unfortunately, teacher education programs—both preservice and inservice—have generally given insufficient attention to the human relations aspects of teaching. Although there are usually a number of courses dealing with human behavior, these are commonly taught in a didactic manner. The emphasis is placed on theory rather than direct application to the classroom. In other words, the focus is on the *discrimination* of desirable teaching behaviors rather than the *communication* of these behaviors (Berenson 1971). Thus, the deliberate modeling and other experiential sources of learning are largely neglected and, as a result, the attitudinal, emotional, physical, and behavioral changes are not maximized.

## WHERE DO WE GO FROM HERE?

We have written at length of the benefits students are likely to enjoy as a consequence of interacting with facilitative teachers. We have also reviewed the research literature and demonstrated the efficacy of a systematic human relations training program in developing such teachers. Now we shall review briefly some of the benefits a teacher or prospective teacher is likely to gain from human relations training.

A number of contemporary social scientists (Mead, Rogers, Allport, Maslow, Fromm, Otto, and others) have hypothesized that the average "healthy" human being is functioning at 10 percent or less of his/her potential (Otto 1970). The human relations training program described herein is designed to help develop one's vast capacities for improved functioning. The major theme of this type of program is skills acquisition.

We will concentrate on the development of a fundamental group of personal and interpersonal skills, that is, skills that facilitate living effectively with one's self and others. We will be working in small, supportive groups designed to accelerate the acquisition of these human relations skills through a "series of step-by-step reinforcement experiences" (Carkhuff 1970b, p. 81). However, to gain the most from this program, each trainee must regularly practice these behaviors in daily interactions. These behaviors may seem mechanical, awkward, and perhaps phoney at first. This is true of learning most difficult skills. For example, learning skills in golf, public speaking, piano, and typewriting all involve awkward stages.

Through one's own efforts, the facilitative skills that are developed may be carried into one's relations with one's students and their parents, one's classmates, one's peer group of teachers, principals, and other school personnel, "the man on the street," friends, and loved ones. In short, these abilities may be employed in relating to all human beings. As individuals become more proficient in the art of helping, they may find that they move from a condition of "techniquing it" to one of living it—helping may become a way of life!

The top two priorities voted on by the delegates to the 1971 White House Conference on Children were: "(1) Provide opportunities for every child to learn, grow, and live creatively by reordering national priorities. (2) Redesign education to achieve individualized, humanized, child-centered learning" (Close 1971, p. 47). The Education Commission of the States (1975) has also proposed a program for life-coping skills training, including among these skills, interpersonal relationship skills. Thus, the program outlined in this manual is congruent with what appears to be a national trend to teach children to be human by behaving humanly toward those children. In the next chapter we will take a closer look at the model that we will use in order to bring about this condition.

# REFERENCES

Anderson, H. H., and J. E. Brewer. 1946. "Studies of teachers' classroom personalities. II. Effects of teachers' dominative and integrative contacts on children's classroom behavior." *Applied Psychological Monographs* no. 8.

Anderson, H. H., J. E. Brewer, and M. F. Reed. 1946. "Studies of teachers' classroom personalities. III. Follow-up studies of the effects of dominative and integrative contacts on children's behavior." *Applied Psychological Monographs* no. 11.

Aspy, D. N. 1969. "The effect of teacher-offered conditions of empathy, congruence, and positive regard upon student achievement." *Florida Journal of Educational Research* 11, no. 1, 39–48.

Aspy, D. N. 1972. "Reaction to Carkhuff's articles." *Counseling Psychologist* 3, no. 3, 35–41.

Aspy, D. N., and W. Hadlock. 1967. "The effects of high and low functioning teachers upon student performance." In R. R. Carkhuff and B. G. Berenson, *Beyond Counseling and Therapy.* New York: Holt, Rinehart & Winston, p. 297.

Axline, V. M. 1947. *Play Therapy.* Boston: Houghton Mifflin.

Barr, A. S., R. A. Davis, and P. O. Johnson. 1953. *Educational Research and Appraisal.* Philadelphia: J. B. Lippincott.

Berenson, D. H. 1971. "The effects of systematic human relations training upon the classroom performance of elementary school teachers." *Journal of Research and Development in Education* 4, no. 2, 70–85.

References

Biber, B. 1961. "Effective learning and healthy personality." *National Elementary Principals* 41, no. 1, 45–48.

Carkhuff, R. R. 1969. *Helping and Human Relations: A Primer for Lay and Professional Helpers.* Vol. 2: *Practice and Research.* New York: Holt, Rinehart & Winston.

Carkhuff, R. R. 1970a. "The development of effective courses of action for ghetto children." *Psychology in the Schools* 7, 272–274.

Carkhuff, R. R. 1970b. "Systematic human relations training." In G. M. Gazda and T. L. Porter (Eds.). *Proceedings of a Symposium on Training Groups.* Athens: College of Education, University of Georgia, pp. 77–110.

Childers, W. C. "An evaluation of the effectiveness of a human relations training model using in-class student teacher observation and interaction analysis." Unpublished doctoral dissertation, University of Georgia, 1973.

Close, K. 1971. "Selecting priorities at the White House Conference on Children," *Children* 18, no. 1, 42–48.

Combs, A. W., D. L. Avila, and W. W. Purkey. 1971. *Helping Relationships: Basic Concepts for the Helping Professions.* Boston: Allyn and Bacon.

Desselle, R. E. "Experimental learning program effects on classroom behaviors." Unpublished doctoral dissertation, University of Georgia, 1974.

Education Commission of the States and National Assessment of Educational Progress. Lay and subject matter reviews of National Assessment. Basic Skills Objectives Conferences, June 18–25, 1975. Denver, Colo.

Evans, K. M. 1962. *Sociometry and Education.* London: Routledge & Kegan Paul.

Fischer, J. H. 1968. "The inclusive school." In "Editorial Boards of the Teachers College Record and of the Harvard Educational Review," *Problems and Issues in Contemporary Education.* Glenview, Ill.: Scott, Foresman.

Flanders, N. A. 1951. "Personal-social anxiety as a factor in experimental learning situations." *Journal of Educational Research* 45, 100–110.

Flanders, N. A. 1965. "Teacher influence, pupil attitudes, and achievement." Cooperative Research Monograph No. 12. Washington, D.C.: U.S. Government Printing Office.

Gazda, G. M. 1971. "Systematic human relations training in teacher preparation and in-service education." *Journal of Research and Development in Education* 4, no. 2, 47–51.

Gowan, J. C. 1957. "A summary of the intensive study of twenty highly selected elementary women teachers." *Journal of Experimental Education* 26, 115–124.

Grambs, J. D. 1968. *Intergroup Education.* Englewood Cliffs, N. J.: Prentice-Hall.

Griffin, A. H., and G. Banks. 1969. "Inner-city workshop for better schools." *American International College Alumni Magazine,* Fall.

Hamachek, D. E. 1971. Encounters with the self. New York: Holt, Rinehart & Winston.

Harbach, R., and F. R. Asbury. "Some effects of empathetic understanding on negative student behaviors." *The Humanistic Educator,* September, 1976.

Hart, F. W. 1934. *Teachers and Teaching.* New York: Macmillan, p. 18.

Hefele, T. J. 1971. "The effects of systematic human relations training upon student achievement." *Journal of Research and Development in Education* 4, no. 2, 52–69.

Heil, L. M., M. Powell, and I. Feifer. 1960. *Characteristics of Teacher Behavior Related to the Achievement of Children in Several Elementary Grades.* Washington, D.C.: U.S. Office of Education, Cooperative Branch.

Hopkins, L. T. 1941. *Interaction: The Democratic Process.* Boston: D. C. Heath.

Jenkins, D. H. 1951. "Interdependence in the classroom." *Journal of Educational Research* 45, 61.

Kearney, N. C., and P. D. Rocchio. 1955. "Relation between a teacher-attitude inventory and pupils' ratings of teachers." *The School Review,* November, 443–445.

Kratochvil, D., R. R. Carkhuff, and B. G. Berenson. 1969. "Cumulative effects of parent and teacher-offered levels of facilitative conditions upon indices of student physical, emotional and intellectual functioning." *Journal of Educational Research* 63, no. 4, 161–164.

Kratz, H. E. 1896. "Characteristics of the teacher as recognized by children." *Pedagogical Seminary* 3, 413–418.

Maslow, A. H. 1971. *The Farther Reaches of Human Nature*. New York: Viking Press.

Mouly, G. J. 1960. *Psychology for Effective Teaching*. New York: Holt, Rinehart & Winston.

Otto, H. A. 1970. *Group Methods to Actualize Human Potential: A Handbook*. Beverly Hills: Holistic Press.

Perkins, H. V. 1951. "Climate influences group learning." Journal of Educational Research 45, 115–119.

Rogers, C. R. 1951. *Client-Centered Therapy: Its Current Practice, Implications, and Theory*. Boston: Houghton Mifflin.

Rogers, C. R. 1961. *On Becoming a Person*. Boston: Houghton Mifflin.

Ryans, D. G. 1960. *Characteristics of Teachers*. Washington, D.C.: American Council on Education.

Ryans, D. G. 1964. "Research on teacher behavior in the context of the Teacher Characteristics Study." In B. J. Biddle and W. J. Ellena (Eds.), *Contemporary Research on Teacher Effectiveness*. New York: Holt, Rinehart & Winston.

Stoffer, D. L. 1970. "Investigation of positive behavioral change as a function of genuineness, non-possessive warmth and empathic understanding." *Journal of Educational Research* 63, 225–228.

Toffler, A. 1970. *Future Shock*. New York: Random House.

Truax, C. B., and C. Tatum. 1966. "An extension from the effective psychotherapeutic model to constructive personality change in pre-school children." *Childhood Education*, 42, 456–462.

Tryon, C. M. 1950. *Fostering Mental Health in Our Schools*. 1950 Yearbook. Washington, D.C.: Association for Supervision and Curriculum Development, National Education Association.

Turberville, G. 1965. "A teacher rating scale." *Peabody Journal of Education* 43, no. 2, 78–88.

Weigand, J. E. (Ed.). 1971. *Developing Teacher Competencies*. Englewood Cliffs, N.J.: Prentice-Hall.

Weinstein, G. W. 1972. "Communities that care." *Parents' Magazine,* May.

Withall, J. G. 1949. "The development of a technique for the measurement of social-emotional climate in classrooms." *Journal of Experimental Education* 17, 347–361.

Withall, J. G. 1952. "Assessment of the social-emotional climates experienced by a group of seventh graders as they moved from class to class." *Educational and Psychological Measurement* 12, no. 3, 440–451.

Withall, J., and W. W. Lewis. 1963. "Social interaction in the classroom." In N. L. Gage (Ed.), *Handbook of Research on Teaching*. Chicago: Rand McNally.

Witty, P. 1947. "An analysis of the personality traits of the effective teacher." *Journal of Educational Research* 40, 662–671.

# The Model for
# Human Relations
# Training

# 2

The model for human relations training, which shall be described in this chapter and operationalized throughout the remainder of this manual, has evolved from hundreds of studies based on the research of numerous counselors and psychotherapists. From the many studies of divergent theories and therapies, a common thread was discovered. Truax and Carkhuff (1967) have carefully traced this thread, and they describe it as consisting of certain particular characteristics of the therapist. The characteristics first described were termed *accurate empathy, nonpossessive warmth,* and *genuineness.* Rogers et al. (1957) served as the impetus to focus renewed interest on these and similar characteristics.

Working with Rogers at the University of Wisconsin, Truax, Carkhuff, and a host of others began to investigate the effect of the presence of the "common thread" in the therapist-client relationship. They did indeed discover that certain conditions or dimensions offered by the therapist, when present at high levels, led to growth on the part of the client and, when absent or present only at low levels, led to deterioration of the client. The accumulated evidence of the validity of the "core" conditions, or dimensions, as they were to be called, can be found in several volumes, especially in Rogers et al. (1967), Truax and Carkhuff (1967), Carkhuff and Berenson (1967), Berenson and Carkhuff (1967), Carkhuff (1969a 1969b), Carkhuff (1971b), and Berenson and Mitchell (1974).

As the research progressed, several new dimensions were discovered and scales for rating these dimensions were developed (Carkhuff 1969a 1969b; Carkhuff and Berenson 1967; Truax and Carkhuff 1967). Eventually Carkhuff (1969a, 1969b) refined, renamed, and standardized the scales of the core dimensions and added a rationale which seemed to complete the model for a helping relationship. Although further refinement of existing dimensions and scales and the search for new dimensions continues, there is now available a substantial body of research and knowledge to support a preferred mode of helping.

We know of no other model for human relations training which has been so thoroughly researched and so carefully developed, and we therefore offer it to the trainer and trainee with considerable confidence in its validity. The credit for the model in its present form, however, goes to Robert Carkhuff, and we shall present the outline of his rationale as we interpret it from personal contacts, from his research and writings, and from our own application of the constructs to preservice and inservice training of teachers and other educators.

## THE GOALS OF HELPING

Generally speaking, the universally accepted goal of helping is to generate more appropriate behavior. The specific goals for a given helpee[1] will be determined by the helper and helpee collaboratively as they interact in the helping relationship. The nature of the interaction must be controlled by the helper. The helper is the expert on the conditions necessary for change to occur and, therefore, must control his/her own behavior and create an atmosphere of security and trust that is a prerequisite for the first step or goal in helping. The conditions, necessary for healthy, productive interpersonal relationships can be taught, systematically practiced, and incorporated into one's life style.

Carkhuff (1971a) has outlined (and the authors have adapted) the three goals of helping as follows:

### Helpee Self-Exploration

The first goal of helping is to facilitate helpee self-exploration. Before helpers can be of any assistance to a helpee, they must understand the helpee's problem in depth. Likewise, helpees must know their own problems in all their ramifications if they are to be fully involved in their solution.

Untrained lay "helpers" frequently miss their first opportunity to help by being too willing to accept helpees' initial statement of their problems as the primary concern. The helper then often gives advice on how the helpee should handle the problem. This is what we call "cheap and dirty" advice because it is "off the top of the head" of the helper and based on too little information. It is typically the kind of advice that the helpee has already considered and probably even tried but was still unsuccessful in solving the problem. Anything the helper can conclude spontaneously and on very sparse information

1. Helpee(s) is used throughout this manual to designate the person(s) seeking some kind of assistance at a given moment of time. The authors do not wish to imply that the helpee is the kind of person who is continuously in a state of emotional turmoil or some other difficulty. The authors have simply chosen this term as a succinct means of referring to a person on the help-seeking or help-receiving end of a continuum at a given moment. In other words, the helpee may be showing a very positive behavior in actively seeking assistance and understanding that in every respect is prevention oriented, whereas at other times the helpee may, in fact, be the passive recipient of the helper's action. Whether the helpee is the seeker or passive-recipient of help, the goal of the model is the same—to provide the conditions that enable the helpee to be actively involved in the solution of his/her problems in such a manner that he/she may also be willing to accept responsibility for his/her actions.

from the helpee is usually something the helpee has already considered and tried but has found to be ineffective.

### Helpee Understanding and Commitment

When helpees are permitted to explore or are helped to explore their problems in depth, they are likely to understand them and themselves better. The role of helpers is to assist helpees in making some kind of sense out of the many pieces of their puzzle. Typically, helpees have thought about their problems a great deal, but because they did not have the necessary skills or responses, or because they could not put them together in the proper combination, they were unable to change their behavior and so remained problem ridden.

Although self-understanding is generally considered to be a prerequisite condition for most types of problem solving, it is a well-accepted fact among professional helpers that understanding alone is frequently insufficient in changing behavior. Witness, for example, the many people who know cognitively that smoking is harmful to their physical health, yet they persist in smoking. What is missing from the persons who know what is best for them and do not act to change in that direction, is *commitment.* Therefore, during the second phase of helping, the helpees must not only understand their problems in depth, but they must also make a cognitive and visceral decision to follow through with a plan or program designed to correct their deficits.

### Helpee Action

Often the most difficult step in problem solving is taking the necessary action to correct the identified problem. The helper and helpee must devise a plan of action which helpees must follow to resolve their problems. It must be a plan that is possible to complete. That is, helpees must be capable of taking the first of a series of steps or actions that will ensure the success of the next step and ultimately the successful resolution of the problem itself. In the process of arriving at a given course of action, helper and helpee consider alternate plans and the possible consequences of different plans before selecting one (see Chapter 21 for a more complete description of program planning).

It is important to understand that that not all teachers and educators will always be able to develop a sequence of actions that will lead to a desired outcome. Often, the helper will be just one link in the chain of life of a helpee. The helper may simply be the person who assists in developing a few key responses in the helpee's total repertory of responses that can be used in the future to help solve problems or enrich his/her life.

## THE CYCLE OF HELPING

If helpees will *self-explore,* this usually leads to a better understanding of their concerns and a commitment to change which, in turn, makes possible a more successful course of action. The action itself provides the ultimate feedback to helpees. Often they will need to refine or to alter their responses to arrive at the preferred behavioral outcome. Helpees repeat the cycle as often as necessary to lead them toward their goals.

The three-phase cycle that Carkhuff has outlined (and that we have adapted) for problem solving—*self exploration* → *better self-understanding and a commitment to change* → *more appropriate action or direction*—works for most people; however, there are exceptions. With individuals who are not in good contact with reality, it is usually necessary to reverse the cycle and first do something to get them back in contact with reality before understanding can occur. We are, at this point, generally describing the emotionally and mentally disturbed, and since educators are not expected to deal extensively with this population, this type of helping will not be considered in this manual.

## THE PROCESS OF HELPING

Table 2.1 on page 23 contains the key concepts in the helping model developed by Carkhuff (1969a 1969b, 1971b, 1972). (See the Global Scale on page 102 for a description of the levels of responses.) We begin with the procedural goals for basically normal individuals of all age levels. Of course, when dealing with a very young child, the adult communicates through direct action. For example, the adult communicates to the young child directly by cuddling, squeezing, feeding, cleansing, hugging, rocking, slapping, spanking, and so on. Often the adult adds words to describe the action even when the child cannot understand the words, and also responds with verbal and nonverbal expressions that express the way the adult feels about the child at the moment.

The first phase of helping is directed toward establishing a base, or building a good relationship with the helpee. It might entail verbal expression, nonverbal expression, direct physical action, or a combination of all of these modes depending upon the age, intelligence, and degree of contact with reality of the helpee.

Preparing for a space shot and firing the rocket is analogous to the two basic phases of helping: facilitation and action. Before a rocket can be fired, many preparations must be made. First, a very strong base must be built under the rocket to hold it and to sustain the backward thrust when it is fired. Similarly, in a helping relationship, the helper must first use the less threatening (facilitative) dimensions to prepare and sustain the helpee for the more threatening but often necessary action or initiative dimensions. If helpers will carefully build their base with helpees, they will help ensure their success when they become conditional with helpees at a later action period. Carkhuff (1971a) succinctly stated the importance of the facilitation phase of helping when he said, "Even if you have just fifteen minutes to help, you must use five minutes or so responding [facilitating] to the helpee in order to find out for sure where the helpee is before starting to put the picture together [initiating] and acting upon that picture."

## Table 2.1. PHASES OF THE HELPING RELATIONSHIP

| DIMENSIONS | FACILITATION | TRANSITION | ACTION |
|---|---|---|---|
| Empathy | Level 3 (reflective interchangeable affect/meaning) | Level 4 (interpretation of underlying feelings/meaning) | Level 4 (emphasizes periodic feedback) |
| Respect | Level 3 (belief in helpee's worth and potential) | Level 4 (deep valuing and commitment to helpee's growth) | Level 4 (deep valuing and commitment to helpee's growth) |
| Warmth | Level 3 (shows attention and interest clearly) | Level 4 (wholly, intensely attentive and supportive) | Level 4 (wholly, intensely attentive and supportive) |
| Concreteness | Level 3 (specific, concrete expressions) | Level 4 (Concreteness may be deemphasized; abstract exploration is sometimes necessary) | Level 4 (specificity plus solicitation of specificity for plans and programs of action) |
| Genuineness | Level 3 (controlled expression of feelings; absence of phoniness) | Level 3 (controlled expression of feeling; absence of phoniness) and Level 4 (congruence between verbal and nonverbal messages; spontaneity) | Level 4 (congruence between verbal and nonverbal messages; spontaneity) |
| Self-Disclosure | | Level 3 (volunteers own general material) and Level 4 (volunteers own specific material) | Level 4 (volunteers own specific material, and may risk exposing own fear; hang-ups, etc.) |
| Confrontation | | Level 3 (tentative expression of discrepancy) | Level 4 (explicit expression of discrepancy) |
| Immediacy | | Level 3 (discusses relationship in a general way) | Level 4 (discusses relationship in a specific way) |

Self-Exploration → Self-Understanding and Commitment → Action

The helper's communication, having these dimensions, serves as a stimulus and elicits

these behaviors from the helpee in response

Helper-offered levels of the core dimensions and helpee behaviors in the phases of helping. (This represents an extension of the figure by Carkhuff, 1969b, p 101. Prepared by Fred J. Balzer.) Adapted from G. M. Gazda, R. P. Walters, and W. C. Childers, *Human Relations Development: A Manual for Health Sciences* (Boston: Allyn and Bacon, 1975.) Reproduced by permission.

## FACILITATION DIMENSIONS

Helpers begin to build their base with helpees by first responding with *empathy, respect,* and *warmth.* Figure 2.1 shows how this leads to increased helpee exploration (the first goal of helping).

To achieve success in the first goal of helping, helpers must be able to refrain from acting on their judgments about helpees. Virtually no one can refrain from making evaluations or judgments about others, but we have found that helpers can refrain from *acting* on their judgments. This is especially important if their early evaluations or judgments are negative. For example, helpers may initially be repulsed by helpees for a number of good reasons; nevertheless, if they can suspend acting on these feelings, they can usually discover something good or likeable about the helpees and at that point begin to invest in the helpees and build a base from which to work.

"Putting oneself in the shoes of another" and "seeing through the eyes of another" are ways of describing empathy. Empathy appears to be the most important dimension in the helping process (Carkhuff 1969a, p. 202). If we cannot understand—empathize with—the helpee, we cannot help him.

Another facilitative dimension is respect. We cannot help someone if we have no faith in his/her ability to solve his/her own problems. Respect develops as we learn about the uniqueness and the capabilities of helpees. It grows as we observe their efforts in many aspects of their lives. Respect can usually be demonstrated by good helpers' attending behavior and a belief in the capacity of helpees to help themselves, as exemplified by not doing something for them when they can do it for themselves, but rather supporting them in their efforts.

Warmth or caring is closely related to empathy and respect. We tend to love or have concern for those we know (understand) and believe in (respect). It is difficult to conceive of being able to help someone for whom we do not care. ("Help" here means to "make a significant investment in.") In this model, warmth is communicated primarily through nonverbal means, such as a smile, caress, touch, hug, and so on.

## FACILITATION/ACTION DIMENSIONS— HELPER-ORIENTED

As the helper begins to develop a base with the helpee through empathy, respect, and warmth, the helpee self-explores in greater and greater depth. In fact, the clue to whether or not the helper is being successful in the early phase of helping is based on the degree to which the helpee uses helper responses to make deeper and more thorough self-explorations.

With repeated, interchangeable (level 3.0) helper responses—responses that give back to helpees essentially that which they have given to helpers—

helpees often begin to repeat themselves and "spin their wheels" or reach a plateau of self-exploration and understanding. It is at this point that helpers need to draw upon some new dimensions to encourage helpees to risk more self-exploration. The dimensions of *concreteness, genuineness,* and *self-disclosure* are next carefully implemented. When helpers press for greater concreteness or specificity on the part of the helpees, they introduce a certain degree of threat. The same thing occurs when helpers become more genuine and set the stage—model—for the helpees to become more genuine. Helpers' self-disclosure encourages greater intimacy in the relationship, which can lead to increased threat to the helpees. In other words, these three dimensions increase the threat level for the helpee, and they are thus *action-oriented* as well as facilitative. In addition to the relationship between level of threat and the action phase, these three dimensions are also involved in the problem-solving or planning stages of the action phase.

Specifically, *concreteness* refers to the helpees' pinpointing or accurately labeling feelings and experiences. Helpers facilitate this by being specific themselves, or at least as specific as the helpees have been (Level 3). When helpers are more specific than helpees, they are going beyond where the helpees are—they are *additive*. If helpers' *timing* of their use of additive concreteness is correct, the helpees can achieve greater understanding because their concerns were made more explicit.

*Genuineness* refers to the ability of helpers to be real or honest with the helpees. Their verbalizations are congruent with their inner feelings. Whether or not the helpers' genuineness is useful to helpees will often depend upon the helpers' ability to time their level of honesty so as to lead to greater trust and understanding. As Carkhuff (1971a, p. 21) has said, "Helping is for the helpee." And if the helpee cannot utilize the helper genuineness, it may be useless or even hurtful. The saying, "Honesty is the best policy," is not always correct, especially if brutal honesty is employed and the recipients are not capable of dealing with it to improve themselves. To illustrate, encounter groups are often harmful to certain persons, especially when, as is sometimes the case, frankness precedes the establishment of a solid base or relationship.

*Self-disclosure* by helpers, *if it is appropriate* or relevant to the helpee's problem, can lead to greater closeness between helpers and helpees. If the helper has had a concern similar to that of the helpee and has found a solution to the problem, this can be reassuring to the helpee. Furthermore, the helpee's solution may even be similar to the one which was used by the helper. The success of Alcoholics Anonymous and other self-help groups is related to this dimension. Drinking alcoholics, for example, look to the "dry alcoholics" of AA for the solution to their own problems. The "speaker" phase of AA thus uses the self-disclosure dimension.

When helper self-disclosure is premature or irrelevant to the helpee's problem, it tends to confuse the helpee or put the focus on the helper. There is a danger of stealing the spotlight when the helper self-discloses prematurely.

# FACILITATION/ACTION DIMENSIONS— HELPEE-ORIENTED

The facilitation-action dimensions of concreteness, genuineness, and self-disclosure can be used to predict the degree of success of the *helpee's help seeking*. The degree to which helpees can be concrete about their problems (can label them accurately, for instance), can be honest and open with helpers, and can self-disclose at high levels will determine whether or not the helpees will, in fact, receive help. Of course, the other important factor in the help-seeking equation is the helpers. If helpees choose to be concrete, genuine, and to self-disclose to persons who are incapable of helping them, helpees may become disillusioned or, worse still, hurt. Helping can be for better or for worse (Truax and Carkhuff 1967, p. 143).

Prospective helpers (educators) can predict the relative success that they might achieve with a given student helpee. For example, helpers can rate student helpees on the scale for help seeking, e.g., their ability to be concrete about their needs and problems, their ability to be genuine with the helper, and their ability to disclose personally relevant material. These dimensions and others for rating helpees' potential for receiving help can be found in Appendix C. Also, in predicting whether or not helpees are amenable to receiving help, helpers may observe the degree to which helpees employ the basic defense mechanisms described in Chapter 3.

If prospective helpees talk about their concerns in vague and general terms (not concrete), are observed to be playing a role or relate in a superficial or phony manner (not genuine), and do not make personally relevant disclosures, helpers are relatively safe in predicting that these helpees will be difficult to help. Also, the process might require a relatively long period of time to develop the base—the first phase of helping—before any positive action may occur.

# ACTION DIMENSIONS

The action or initiative phase of helping may be considered as the most important phase. It is in this phase that tough decisions are made and the hard work must be done. It is the ultimate test of whether or not the helper is, in fact, the "more knowing" individual and is tough and confident enough to believe both in his or her own and the helpee's ability to devise a plan of action (strategy) and follow through when the work gets difficult. The helper must be capable of helping develop a plan or strategy for the helpee that will lead to the successful resolution of the helpee's current problem and provide the helpee at the same time with a method for attacking future problems. Since teachers usually do not have the time nor, perhaps, the special training in behavior problem solving, they should not expect to carry the primary burden of developing strategies for behavioral problem solving, but they should be partners in efforts developed by specialists.

If helpers have not resolved the particular problem or concern in question, it is highly unlikely they can assist their helpees with the problem. That you cannot help someone else solve a problem you have not resolved yourself is a maxim every helper must use to guide all helping attempts. If helpers know themselves, they will be unlikely to enter into a helping relationship in a problem area that remains unresolved for them.

There is another cardinal rule in helping: One does not confront nor emphasize the action dimensions until one has earned the right, that is, has built the base. We often hear, especially from young people, "Tell it like it is." Telling it like it is often is tantamount to confronting someone. We must emphasize once more that one can be most punitive or harmful when one is being brutally honest and confronting. *Confrontation,* a key action dimension, can be helpful when the helpee has learned, from earlier experience, that the helper is concerned about his/her welfare and cares enough even to risk the relationship by "leveling."

Frequently, confrontation refers to dealing with a discrepancy between what helpees have been saying about themselves and what they have, in fact, been doing. A common confrontation is assisting helpees to face the reality of a situation. The most threatening type of confrontation is one that does not allow helpees to "save face." This is the type of confrontation that deals with the here and now. When you catch helpees behaving contrary to the way they claim to behave, and you confront them directly with it, it is difficult for them to deny it. They have few good means of defense and may use denial and other inappropriate short-term mechanisms that have long-term disadvantages. For example, if a mother catches her son in the cookie jar and accuses him of stealing cookies, the child may actually deny that he was taking a cookie. This often happens; the child often denies reality when the external threat is great enough. Parents and teachers often unknowingly teach children to lie and deny reality by their use of threats.

Berenson and Mitchell's (1974) extensive research on the effects of the use of confrontation is quite sobering. They contend that confrontation is never necessary, but that it can be effective and efficient when used by highly functioning persons. Jacobs (1975) reported that in a series of eleven studies on verbal feedback in groups, no evidence was found where negative feedback (one might consider this a form of confrontation of deficits) was advantageous to the group or recipient. Positive feedback (confrontation of one's potential) was rated as more believable, desirable, and impactful by recipients and donors with various populations of participants, types of leaders, manners and styles of delivery, and types and amounts of information exchanged. Jacobs furthermore contends that believability of information seems likely to be a necessary, although perhaps not always a sufficient, condition for attitudinal and behavioral change. In other words, the evidence is beginning to suggest that confrontation of one's deficits (negative feedback) must only be used by highly functioning sensitive helpers. Even then, the evidence suggests that the risk may be too great for potential benefits derived.

The last dimension, *immediacy,* is often related to confrontation. It refers to what is really going on between helper and helpee. When helpees are unaware of their reactions toward helpers, helpers may need to describe or explain them. It includes "telling it like it is" between helper and helpee in the here and now. Helpees can gain a better understanding of themselves, especially how they affect others (in this case the helper), when helpers appropriately use the immediacy dimension. Once again, the helper must time the employment of immediacy so that the helpee can use it productively.

The productive use of the action dimensions of confrontation and immediacy can be guaranteed by taking the position that "the customer (helpee) is always right." By this we simply mean that regardless of how brilliant and creative the responses of a helper may appear to be, if helpees cannot use them in solving their problems they are worthless—if not harmful—to them.


## Implementing a Course of Action

The courses of action that may be developed for helpees to achieve their goals or to give them direction may be many and varied. They may involve the physical, psychosocial, cognitive, vocational, or moral domains or, for some, all five of them.

### Table 2.2  THE STAGES OF IMPLEMENTING A COURSE OF ACTION IN HELPING

I. The definition and description of problem area(s)

II. The definition and description of direction(s) and/or goal(s) dictated by the problem area(s)

III. An analysis of the critical dimensions of these direction(s) and/or goal(s)

IV. A consideration of the alternative courses of action available for attaining the dimensions of the direction(s) and/or goal(s)

V. A consideration of the advantages and disadvantages of the alternative courses of action

VI. The development of physical, emotional-interpersonal, and intellectual programs for achieving that course with the most advantages and fewest disadvantages in terms of ultimate success in goal achievement

VII. The development of progressive gradations of the programs involved

From *Helping and Human Relations: A Primer for Lay and Professional Helpers,* vol. 1, *Selection and Training,* by Robert R. Carkhuff. Copyright © 1969 by Holt Rinehart & Winston, Inc. Reprinted by permission of Holt, Rinehart & Winston, Inc.

The principles involved in implementing a course of action recommended by Carkhuff (1969a, p. 243) are summarized as follows: (1) The helper must check with the helpee at all stages of development and implementation to be sure that what is planned or performed is relevant to the helpee's functioning. (2) The focus of change should usually be on the helpee first and only secondarily on the helpee's relationships with others. (3) Only those measures or procedures that ensure the highest probability of constructive change are employed.

(4) The emphasis is on outcomes and the achievement of attainable goals. The helper and helpee must be shaped by the feedback that they receive.

Often the real test of helpers, as stated earlier in this chapter, will be whether or not they can develop appropriate plans of action for their helpees. Frequently helpees will be unable to develop their own course of action and will require help in structuring their program. When helpees cannot participate fully in the program planning, Carkhuff (1969a) cautions helpers to develop programs that will "enable the helpee to carry some of the burden of responsibility for his own life" (p. 243).

If teachers and other educators can master the basic dimensions of the helping relationship that we have outlined in this chapter, they will prevent the development of many potential problem children and problem adults. Even with higher level functioning teachers in the classrooms, other external factors such as the home, school, and community environment will produce child casualties. The teacher will need the assistance of educational experts such as school counselors and school psychologists, reading experts, and special education experts working as a team in problem prevention and resolution.

## Helping Involves Teaching and Learning

As helpers show empathy, respect, and warmth, helpees explore themselves and their problems. As helpers continue to show empathy, respect, and warmth, and display appropriate levels of concreteness, genuineness, and confrontation, helpees begin to understand themselves and their problems. After the base is built, helpers use high levels of confrontation and immediacy to help the helpees take action or find direction.

This description (as shown in Figure 2.1) is oversimplified, but this is generally the pattern of helping. An important understanding is that during this process the helper is really reinforcing certain behaviors and extinguishing others. Showing empathy, respect, and warmth generally reinforces whatever helpees say or do, which increases the probability of self-exploration and problem exploration.

Responding with appropriate levels of concreteness, genuineness, and Level 3.0 confrontation results in more selective reinforcement. Helpers are no longer speaking strictly from the helpees' point of view. They begin to focus on aspects of helpee behavior that they think will be more productive, they begin to relate more of their own feelings which reinforce in a certain direction, and they point out discrepancies in helpee behavior. These helper behaviors increase the probability that helpees will understand themselves and their problems.

If an adequate relationship has been established, high levels of confrontation clearly reinforce certain kinds of behavior and extinguish others. These helper responses increase the probability that helpees will act on their problems and try to find some direction to follow which may solve their problems.

The art of helping includes first knowing *how* to respond helpfully and then knowing *when* to seek higher levels on various dimensions or *when* to use interchangeable responses. Many beginning helpers learn to show interchangeable empathy, respect, and warmth but never become capable of displaying other, more action-oriented dimensions. They often say, "I don't want to be responsible if she makes the wrong decision so I always make sure it's her decision," or "I don't want her to become dependent on others to make her decisions." These are legitimate concerns but they must be kept in perspective.

Helpers who display only interchangeable levels of empathy, respect, and warmth are not very selective in what they reinforce. This often results in helpees accepting their problems as a permanent part of themselves instead of solving them. If helpees are rewarded for discussing their problems over and over without moving toward some goal, they become desensitized to the problem and begin to think it's normal to have that problem.

It is extremely important for helpers to be aware of what behaviors they are reinforcing. The art of helping, therefore, includes knowing what behaviors to reinforce at a given time and how to do it. The next chapter provides the theoretical rationale for assisting the helper to attend to and focus on helpee behavior and respond appropriately to it.

# REFERENCES

Berenson, B. B., and R. R. Carkhuff. 1967. *Sources of Gain in Counseling and Psychotherapy: Readings and Commentary.* New York: Holt, Rinehart & Winston.

Berenson, B. G., and K. M. Mitchell. 1974. *Confrontation: For Better or Worse!* Amherst, Mass.: Human Resource Development Press.

Carkhuff, R. R. 1969a. *Helping and Human Relations: A Primer for Lay and Professional Helpers.* Vol. 1: *Selection and Training.* New York: Holt, Rinehart & Winston.

Carkhuff, R. R. 1969b. *Helping and Human Relations: A Primer for Lay and Professional Helpers.* Vol. 2: *Practice and Research.* New York: Holt, Rinehart & Winston.

Carkhuff, R. R. 1971a. "Helping and human relations: A brief guide for training lay helpers." *Journal of Research and Development in Education* 4, no. 2, 17–27.

Carkhuff, R. R. 1971b. *The Development of Human Resources: Education, Psychology, and Social Change.* New York: Holt, Rinehart & Winston.

Carkhuff, R. R. 1972. *The Art of Helping.* Amherst, Mass.: Human Resources Development Press.

Carkhuff, R. R., and B. G. Berenson. 1967. *Beyond Counseling and Therapy.* New York: Holt, Rinehart & Winston.

Jacobs, A. April, 1975. "Research on methods of social intervention: The study of the exchange of personal information in brief personal growth groups." Paper presented at the Invited Conference on Small Group Research, Indiana University, Bloomington.

Rogers, C. R. 1957. "The necessary and sufficient conditions of therapeutic personality change." *Journal of Consulting Psychology* 21 95–103.

Rogers, C. R., E. T. Gendlin, D. J. Kiesler, and C. B. Truax. 1967. *The Therapeutic Relationship and Its Impact: A Study of Psychotherapy with Schizophrenics.* Madison: University of Wisconsin Press.

Truax, C. G., and R. R. Carkhuff. 1967. *Toward Effective Counseling and Psychotherapy: Training and Practice.* Chicago: Aldine.

# PeRceiviNg aNd Responding

## 3

## THE ACT OF PERCEIVING

A universally accepted definition of perception is not available, but because of the emphasis on interpersonal relations in this manual we shall focus on interpersonal perception—the process whereby one person discerns both the overt and the covert or disguised behavior of another person. Carkhuff (1969a, 1969b) has referred to the same process as "discrimination." Hargrove and Porter (1971) contend that the process might better be labeled "discriminative learning." Discriminative learning is defined by English and English (1958) as "the learning to note those particular cues or clues in a situation needed to evoke one response rather than another" (p. 290).

In order to be interpersonally effective, one must accurately be able to perceive the behavior of others. However, one's ability to do this is influenced by several factors, such as one's own needs, preferences, expectations, defense mechanisms, prejudices, or fears, as well as the same factors operating in the other person. For example, a person who feels "self-conscious" may well perceive others as "singling him/her out" when, in fact, they are not. In this case, feeling self-conscious hinders accurate and objective perception. Faulty perceptions can get a person into considerable interpersonal conflict and create interpersonal barriers. One who fails to perceive accurately may miss important parts of the message (or the entire message) that others transmit.

While processing messages communicated by others, one generally begins to form beliefs concerning their personalities, that is, one begins to form other-concepts. However, because of the complexity of the perceptual process, it is often difficult to arrive at other-concepts that are free from distortion. As Jourard (1963) points out, "Other-concepts probably enjoy the unique advantage of being the last of the theories which an individual will test, much less abandon. By some curious quirk of vanity, each man believes he is an expert psychologist and that his other-concepts are accurate and irrefutable. Never has so much been believed about people, by people, on so little evidence" (p. 321).

An obvious first step in improving one's perceptual skills is to achieve a more comprehensive understanding of one's self. This can be accomplished to some degree by introspection (observing and analyzing one's own behavior) and by participating in a counseling or training-group experience where this is the main point of emphasis. In such groups, one may enter into relationships with others where feedback is given and received.

## Feedback

Nylen et al. (1967) define feedback as "communication which gives back to another individual information about how he has affected us and how he stands with us in relation to his goals or intentions" (p. 75). Feedback itself may be either positive or negative in nature.

As stated earlier in Chapter 2, Jacobs (1975) reported that positive verbal feedback was found to be believable, desirable, and impactful for the recipient, and he found no evidence that negative feedback was advantageous to the group recipient. Positive feedback delivered in a manner similar to strength bombardment, i.e., where each group member gives some positive feedback to a target person, was found to lead to increased group cohesion. He found similar results with intermittent positive feedback when, after the first group session, each member makes a positive statement to the person next to him/her at the beginning of a group session.

In an attempt to find a means of utilizing negative feedback, Jacobs (1975), based on preliminary research results, recommends the detoxification of negative feedback. He suggests three methods of detoxifying negative feedback: (1) present information referring to desired improvement in a positive behavioral statement in association with positive affect. (2) Increase the credibility of the feedback by emphasizing in its delivery its origin in the deliverer and/or its repugnance to him/her. (3) Give positive feedback just prior to the negative feedback.

## Change

Nylen et al. (1967) contend that the tendency to live by habit and to be comfortable with the familiar makes it difficult for us to adjust to new circumstances. We try to create a stable view of the world so that we will feel in control. Attempts are made to "freeze" reality, denying that the world is full of change and that our mental and physical selves are constantly changing. Often, we simply fail to notice ourselves!

In order to live effectively, one must be aware of changes in one's self and must incorporate these new meanings within the old framework, thus better comprehending and experiencing one's own person. But because of the tendency for perceptual processes to work in a selective way, it is not easy to remain open to one's experiences. That is, one perceives that which favors one's

32

frame of reference and denies realities that are incongruent. Thus, one generally *perceives* himself or herself as functioning in ways that make sense and are reasonable. Selective perception, while minimizing anxiety, can often be a barrier to learning more effective behaviors.

## Defense Mechanisms

To perceive one's own and another's disguised feelings accurately, one must be aware of the nature of defense mechanisms and the most common types of patterns of defense. (It may be helpful to remember that the more facilitative the environment, the less will be the need for such defensiveness.)

Most of us suffer to some degree from feelings of inadequacy, guilt, or fears of punishment that can cripple our effectiveness. Such feelings are sometimes disguised through our defense mechanisms which operate in an attempt to protect one's self-image and control the level of anxiety. "Defense mechanisms are not acquired deliberately. For the most part, they are unconscious and un-verbalized.... Defensive behavior develops through blind learning and does not involve conscious choice" (Shaffer and Shoben 1956, pp. 169-170). "The mechanisms offer useful descriptions of typical adjustments and valuable insights into the ways in which drives are reduced" (ibid.). The reduction of drives (usually anxiety or tension) is the primary goal of any defense.

When defense mechanisms are used appropriately, they usually allay anxiety and promote a feeling of well-being. If these mechanisms fail to work, a person who is living effectively is capable of using other methods to achieve the same end. However, attempts to adjust or relieve tension through defense mechanisms are often nonintegrative because one drive is overemphasized at the expense of others and results in unevenness of satisfaction. Also, the defense mechanisms employed may be harmful to other people and ultimately to the user if they are exaggerated. "A defensive person is so intensely engaged in proving his adequacy that he does not attend to the satisfaction of broader motives of self-realization. Another shortcoming of defensive behavior is that it limits social interaction. With the exception of identification, all defense mechanisms increase the social distance between a person and his fellow men" (Shaffer and Shoben 1956, pp. 184-185).

Although the mechanisms are generally defined as though they represent clear and distinct forms of behavior, they are not usually found in pure form. Often they overlap, or several may be involved in a given behavior. We now turn attention to the basic defense mechanisms.

### Identification

Identification involves anxiety reduction through ascribing to one's self the accomplishments and other valued characteristics of another person, group or object. Identification typically occurs early in life between a child and the parent of the same sex. Individuals also identify with groups such as neighborhoods,

33

professional organizations, teams or schools, and objects such as cars or homes. Identification is the result of trial-and-error learning, but for most people it is a constructive and integrative adjustment.

Some examples of identification are:

1. "I get furious when I hear students talk about other teachers the way they do. They are not the way they describe them at all."
2. "I admire Miss Jones, our fourth-grade teacher. We have many things in common."
3. "You should have seen my son outrun the whole team as he scored the winning touchdown!"

## Rationalization

Rationalization is a defense mechanism in which a person gives socially acceptable reasons for behavior that was motivated by socially unacceptable impulses. There are several types of rationalization. Blaming the incidental cause, sour grapes, and sweet lemon are common mechanisms.

Examples of each of these in the order cited above are:

1. "I won't ever make an 'A' in this course, because Miss Jones doesn't like me."
2. "I'm glad that Jim has found himself a new girl; he's kind of square anyway."
3. "I wouldn't want to be as slim as Mary Jane. My plump figure suits my personality just fine!"

## Compensation

A person who compensates reduces tension by accepting and developing a less preferred but more attainable objective for a more preferred but less attainable objective. Compensatory behavior also is often characterized by extreme preoccupation. The adjustment occurs because the substitute goal may be an adequate substitute for the preferred objective and because success in the achievement of the substitute goal diverts attention from other personal shortcomings.

Some examples of compensation are:

1. "I would rather spend all my evening working on my lesson plans than anything else I can think of."
2. "I try to be first in everything I do."
3. (A teacher describes a situation where a child is compensating for his low ability): "Billy has flunked two grades and is just bullying everyone in my fifth grade."

### Projection

Projection involves attributing one's own motives and characteristics to others, especially when these motives are a source of great anxiety.

Some examples of projection are:

1. "The only things girls in our sorority are interested in are men."
2. "Everybody will cheat on an exam if given the chance."
3. "I'm disgusted with the money-grabbing, nonprofessional attitude of every teacher in my school!'

### Reaction Formation

Reaction formation is the adoption of an exaggerated attitude that is the opposite of one that produces tension and anxiety. In effect, this reduces tension by concealing one's true motives from one's self and others.

Some examples of reaction formation are:

1. "I have never had to punish any of my students!"
2. "I love everyone—black and white—alike!"
3. "I am horrified by the immorality in all our movies today!"

The defense mechanisms have been described to assist trainees in perceiving and labeling responses that are unconsciously motivated to reduce anxiety. By being able to recognize these defensive behaviors, trainees will also be in a better position to time their responses to produce the least defensiveness and the greatest impact for positive change. (Since the teacher and typical educator do not deal with the more disturbed personality, defenses such as acute withdrawal or dissociation, repression, regression, and the like were omitted from our discussion.)

In Chapter 5 we describe and illustrate nine ineffective communication styles. One can relate the overuse of the defense mechanisms to these ineffective communication styles. If a particular helper behavior or verbal response is confusing, classifying the response according to a defense mechanism could assist the trainee in better understanding the helpee.

Although we have no established validity to our relating the defense mechanisms to our list of ineffective communication styles, we believe, nevertheless, that these associations can be utilized effectively in sharpening the trainees' perceptual skills. Examples of the relationships as ineffective responder types to the defense mechanism are described below.

The ineffective communication style that may be related to *identification* is the *florist-type responder*. The florist-responder tries to hide problems under flowery phrases and bouquets of optimism. This could be the result of over-identification with the helpee, leading to an overly protective attitude. Conversely, the ineffective *judge-responder* might respond to the negative feelings aroused through identification with the helpee and be quite critical of the helpee.

35

The defense mechanism of *rationalization* may be expressed through *swami-type responders* who predict unhappy futures for themselves because of the behavior of someone else or who account for predicted future failure because of some intervention over which they will have no control. The *guru-type responder* also may be illustrating the defense mechanism of rationalization. Gurus illustrate rationalization when they provide cliches to account for behavior: "You can lead a horse to water, but you can't make him drink."

The *magician-type responder* probably best illustrates the *compensation* defense mechanism. Overcompensation would be the magician-responder's attempt to have the problem ameliorated through denial of its seriousness: "It really can't be *that* bad." The *drill sergeant-responder* who "barks" orders and bosses others around may be responding (compensating) for feelings of inadequacy. The *foreman-responder* who keeps everyone else busy with authoritative responses may also be compensating for his/her own tendency to be nonproductive.

The defense mechanism of *projection* is probably illustrated by several ineffective responder types. The *sign painter-responder* illustrates projection by putting certain kinds of labels on behaviors. The judge-type responders may also be evaluating others based on projections of their own motives.

*Reaction-formation* may be used to understand the florist-type responder who actually has an overriding fear that the worst will happen but responds as though everything will turn out fine. The opposite response may be conveyed by the *detective-type responders* who are very suspicious because of a fear of their own naiveté. The judge-type responders could also be employing the defense mechanism of reaction-formation by being either overly critical or very uncritical.

## THE ACT OF RESPONDING

To respond means, among other things, to answer, reply, act, behave. As used in this chapter and manual, it includes both verbal and nonverbal behavior as well as direct physical activities such as embracing, touching, striking, and so forth. We have chosen to substitute *responding* for Carkhuff's concept of *communication* because we feel responding conveys a more complete type of interaction than that often inferred from the term communication. For the most part, we mean what Carkhuff (1969a, 1969b) intended through his choice of "communication."

Just as gains or losses in a trainee's level of perception are dependent upon the trainee and trainer, so it is with responding. If trainers are not capable of responding at high levels, they are not capable of providing the conditions that would raise trainees to high levels of responding and functioning. "The evidence is consistent, indicating that trainees of high-level communicating [responding] trainers improve while those of low-level communicators demonstrate negative change in communication [responding]" (Carkhuff 1969a, p. 197).

36

Carkhuff (1969a) found that training in human relations skills, in general, is best accomplished through a three-pronged approach: (1) experiential, (2) didactic, and (3) trainer modeling. The solid experiential base is developed if the circumstances surrounding the training are facilitative. Specifically, trainers must be perceiving and responding at high levels, and they must manage the group of trainees so that they provide experiences that are facilitative to one another. Trainees must experience an atmosphere where they are understood and accepted and where they can practice extending themselves through experimenting with varying behaviors.

If trainers are successful in creating a facilitative experiential base, they will be in a position to teach trainees in a didactic fashion also. There are many occasions where structured teaching is appropriate in this training model. Often when the trainees have experienced a facilitative base, trainers can best instruct by sharing their understandings of the constructs they use. In so doing, they also allow the trainees to question and search with them for more and more effective means of helping.

Regarding the importance of modeling by the trainer, Carkhuff is unequivocal. He states, *"Finally, the trainer is the key ingredient insofar as he offers a model of a person who is living effectively.* Without such a person there is no program" (Carkhuff 1969a, p. 201, emphasis Carkhuff's). In other words, the training can be only as good as the trainers. If the trainers have not been able to apply the core conditions to their own lives so that they are living effectively, they will be unable to teach or train others to do so.

## Interpersonal Dynamics

The processes of perceiving and responding are closely related. When persons send messages, receivers respond to the messages as they perceive them. This manual is designed to aid persons in systematically increasing both the quality and the quantity of their perceptual and responsive skills. Along with this manual, the trainer will have access to a number of exercises in the *Instructor's Guide* that are designed to increase group feedback. This allows each person the opportunity to develop a more complete understanding of self, as we have described above. One may then wish to consider the possibility of behavioral changes that would result in greater interpersonal effectiveness.

But in order to improve understanding of self and others we must also understand the dynamics involved in communicating (responding). Some basic propositions should be understood:

*Proposition 1. Both parties involved in an interaction are modified by the interaction.* In this proposition, we are simply referring to a fundamental law of learning which, generally stated, means that the response produced by person A from person B will affect the next response of person A. That is to say that we are being influenced while we are influencing others.

*Proposition 2. Responses may be nonverbal, verbal, or a combination of both.*

*Proposition 3. Nonverbal responses are more likely to transmit the real message, since they are often involuntary reactions transmitted from the autonomic nervous system.* Mehrabian (1968) has shown that facial expression alone transmits over 55 percent of the meaning of a message. Often, one communicates more than he/she may intend by his/her body posture, gestures, tone of voice, eye contact, and the like. Nonverbal communications may distort or even negate one's verbal messages. That is, one's nonverbal behavior may "speak" so loudly that one's verbal messages are scarcely heard.

*Proposition 4. Verbal responses or messages are generally composed of two parts: content and affect.* Content refers to the topic under discussion, whereas affect tells how one feels about the topic. For example, a child who has just been struck and hurt by a playmate says, "Sally hit me; I hate her!" The topic is Sally's hitting. The affect or feeling expressed is hurt combined with anger.

In the first three chapters we have presented the basic rationale for the practice exercises that are to follow in the remaining chapters. Our primary emphasis in the remaining chapters, then, will be to operationalize the theoretical model.

# REFERENCES

Carkhuff, R. R. 1969a. *Helping and Human Relations: A Primer for Lay and Professional Helpers.* Vol. 1: *Selection and Training.* New York: Holt, Rinehart & Winston.

Carkhuff, R. R. 1969b. *Helping and Human Relations: A Primer for Lay and Professional Helpers.* Vol. 2: *Practice and Research.* New York: Holt, Rinehart & Winston.

English, H. B., and A. English. 1958. *A Comprehensive Dictionary of Psychological and Psychoanalytical Terms.* New York: Longmans Green.

Hargrove, D. S., and T. L. Porter. 1971. "Discrimination: An aspect of the helping process." *Journal of Research and Development in Education* 4, no. 2, 28–35.

Jacobs, A. April, 1975. "Research on methods of social intervention: The study of the exchange of personal information in brief personal growth groups." Paper presented at the Invited Conference on Small Group Research, Indiana University, Bloomington.

Jourard, S. M. 1963. *Personal Adjustment: An Approach through the Study of Healthy Personality.* New York: Macmillan.

Mehrabian, A. 1968. "Communication without words." *Psychology Today* 2, 52–55.

Nylen, D., J. Mitchell, and A. Stout. 1967. *Handbook of Staff Development and Human Relations Training: Materials Developed for Use in Africa.* Washington, D.C.: National Training Laboratories Institute for Applied Behavioral Science.

Shaffer, L. F., and J. J. Shoben, Jr. 1952. *The Psychology of Adjustment.* (2nd Ed.) Boston: Houghton Mifflin.

# Helpee Statement Types

# 4

Beginning with this chapter and throughout the remaining chapters of this manual we have included various exercises for the trainee. *We also speak more directly to the trainee in an attempt to personalize the material.*

> Behavioral Objective: *The trainee should be able to classify helpee requests for assistance according to the four areas outlined in this chapter: (1) requests for information, (2) requests for action, (3) requests for inappropriate interaction, and (4) requests for understanding/involvement.*

As soon as a helpee speaks to you, you begin to assess his/her situation. Even though you may not be aware of it, in your mind you seek answers to such questions as: "What does this person need? What does this person want from me? What can I do for this person?" Your answers to those questions determine the way in which you respond to the helpee.

When you assess the helpee's immediate needs, you draw upon several kinds of expertise. Your professional training in your educational specialty is an important part of the process; you also draw upon your life experiences and "common sense," and upon your grasp of interpersonal dynamics. Because you have considerable expertise in your field, this book does not attempt to provide more technical information about your specialty. Similarly, you already possess a wealth of life experience that can be utilized in helping other persons. The objective of this book is to help you understand the dynamics of interpersonal relationships and acquire communication skills that are essential in helping. When those are combined with the professional training, experience, and your personal characteristics, you will be able to help other persons in the ways that research shows are productive and effective, as cited in Chapter 1.

Helpee statements can be classified into four categories based upon what the helpee is seeking: (1) request for action, (2) request for information, (3) inappropriate interaction, and (4) request for understanding/involvement. For each of the four types there is a helper response mode that is proper and effective, as shown diagramatically in Figure 4.1. While the helper's response differs for each of the four kinds of helpee statements, there are components of communication that are common to all, shown on the diagram as "facilitative dimensions used in all communication." Training in this book covers responses to each type of helpee statement, with main emphasis on the "request for understanding/involvement." As the diagram indicates, the first task is for the helper to classify the helpee's statement into one of the four types, which are defined and illustrated below.

## REQUEST FOR ACTION

The helpee may ask you, the helper, to do something for him/her—to perform a physical act. For example, a teacher in the lounge might say, "Would you please hand me that test booklet next to your chair? I have my lap full of papers." This request is simple and straightforward; its meaning is obvious. An appropriate helper response would be to hand the test booklet to the teacher.

Requests for action may be as explicit as the example above, but often the request is only implied. The statement, "I don't have a ride home," may mean, "Would you please give me a ride?" In the latter case, the helpee may be *thinking*, "I have a favor to ask you, but I'm a little afraid you might not say 'yes.' I wish I didn't have to ask. Maybe if I tell you my need, you will offer to help. That would be a lot easier than asking." As the helper, you must be aware of what is *not* said, and its significance, as well as what has been put into words.

Other requests, while simple to fulfill, require knowledge of the situation before they can be implemented. For example, a student might make a request that is in conflict with instructions from another teacher. When you are the helper, you must know whether or not *fulfilling* the requested action is in the best interest of the helpee. Helping sometimes means doing, and sometimes it means not doing the things requested by the helpee. You use your professional training and other data to decide what is appropriate under the circumstances. (In Chapter 22 you will learn how to respond to requests for action.)

## REQUEST FOR INFORMATION

This type of request is similar in dynamics to the request for action, because the helpee is asking the helper for something. For example, a student might ask, "Will you give me some ideas about what subject I might use for my term paper?" Information involves a verbal response only, whereas action involves some physical movement on the part of the helper.

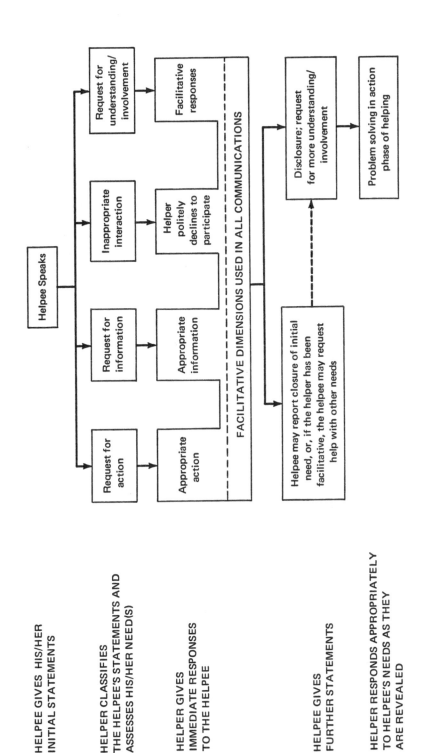

HELPEE GIVES HIS/HER
INITIAL STATEMENTS

HELPER CLASSIFIES
THE HELPEE'S STATEMENTS AND
ASSESSES HIS/HER NEED(S)

HELPER GIVES
IMMEDIATE RESPONSES
TO THE HELPEE

HELPEE GIVES
FURTHER STATEMENTS

HELPER RESPONDS APPROPRIATELY
TO HELPEE'S NEEDS AS THEY
ARE REVEALED

Figure 4.1

41

# REQUEST FOR UNDERSTANDING/
## INVOLVEMENT

This category represents conversations in which the helpee's feelings are of major importance. It is so called because the helpee is generally seeking a *relationship* with another person, rather than direct answers. A request for understanding/involvement may be explicit: "There's something that is really bothering me; I wonder if I could talk with you about it." Or, for example, a student might say, "I thought that I really had a great relationship with my parents, but recently I have started to wonder." This student has verbalized a real concern and the most appropriate response at this point is to listen fully and to respond to that concern with understanding and caring. The major part of this book (Chapters 4 through 23) deals with communicating with persons about matters as intimate as the one in the latter example. In the process of learning to deal with such highly personal situations, you will acquire skills that will help you in all other kinds of interactions and relationships with other persons.

What may appear to be a simple request for action or for information may be the helpee's device for steering the conversation toward a substantive concern that he/she is not able to express directly. Most persons have occasions when they wish to talk with others about matters that are important to them. It is not uncommon for helpees to approach sensitive topics gradually, to avoid the possible painful experience of being ignored or rebuffed by the helper. For example, a student might say, "Will basketball practice go past five o'clock this year?" Taken at face value, this is a request for information that can be answered with a word or two, but there may be much more on the helpee's mind than just the answer. The student may be wanting to say, "I can't work and be on the team at the same time."

You must always be alert for needs that are not verbalized. To be fully effective as an educator, you must be able to examine every helpee statement to see if it might be masking needs that go beyond the literal message.


# INAPPROPRIATE COMMUNICATION

There are several kinds of conversations that are potentially damaging to the persons talking, to persons not present, or to the organization. At best, such interaction is inappropriate, and it *can* become destructive and disruptive. Included in this category are (1) gossip, (2) inordinate griping, (3) rumor, (4) solicitation of a dependency relationship, and (5) encouragement of activities that are counter to the benefit of other persons or the organization, e.g., a student's attempts to turn one staff member against another.

For example, a tenth grader might say, "I'm always glad when fourth period rolls around. Those teachers in the morning are pitiful!" Engaging in a conversation such as this could lead to either talking negatively about a person or persons not present or to defending others, perhaps without first-hand knowledge. Either way of responding would be ineffective. To disparage your co-workers is to decrease the students' confidence in the organization or to encourage them to hold in their feelings about things they do not like. Attempting to defend the person or persons referred to in the inappropriate interaction is to deny prematurely the students' perception of the situation.

Generally, then, the best response to an inappropriate helpee statement is to communicate your preference by not reinforcing that kind of conversation. This response must be given in a way that does not offend a friend and helper. This is much more easily proposed than practiced! When helpees' comments are inappropriate, they usually know it, and when another person does anything but go along with them, the helpees are likely to feel some degree of embarrassment. Still, there is no basis for a helper to encourage inappropriate behavior, even by passivity. Even the act of listening without comment to inappropriate communication reinforces the speaker's behavior positively, and he/she may infer that you agree with him/her. *If you encourage inappropriate behaviors, even by silence, you may lose your opportunity to be a helper.* An example of a response to a person who is trying to involve you in gossip is as follows: Helpee: "I'm sure glad to see that Gloria is getting chewed out for being late again. Did you know she's been slipping out to lunch with Mr. X and he's a married man with five children?" Helper: "I can see you've been irritated with Gloria for being late and for meeting with Mr. X, but I prefer not to get into a discussion about Gloria. I must admit that it sounds kind of juicy, but I've found I feel bad after I indulge in this kind of talk." A detailed discussion and training exercise in the skills for responding to inappropriate communication appears in Chapter 23.

Chapter 5 presents examples of ineffective communication styles frequently employed by untrained individuals. Trainees are encouraged to compare their own responses with those in Chapter 5 and to avoid the use of such ineffective responses if they are in their repertoire.

## CLASSIFYING COMMUNICATION TYPES

Behavioral Objective: The trainee shall classify accurately twenty-five out of thirty exercises on communication types.

In this exercise you will practice classifying helpee statements. After carefully studying the examples of the four types of helpee statements, write in the space in front of each interaction the type of communication it illustrates. Use RA for request for action, RI for request for information, II for inappropriate interaction and RUI for request for understanding/involvement. In some instances categories overlap; therefore, more than one category may be used to classify one interaction. Check your answers with the Answer Key at the end of the chapter.

## Helpee Situations

_____ 1. Principal to teacher: "Mrs. Johnson is not here today. Will you take her bus duty?"

_____ 2. Teacher to teacher: "Sometimes John Smith [student] really irritates me with his questions."

_____ 3. Student to teacher: "You know, you're a really neat teacher. You're so much different from Mr. Jones. He always gives us too much homework to do. Do the other teachers like him?"

_____ 4. Student to teacher: "I just can't figure out this geometry. I'm so stupid when it comes to math. I'll never be able to pass the test tomorrow."

_____ 5. Student to teacher: "I just don't understand these algebra problems. Would you do an example and explain it for me?"

_____ 6. Student to teacher: "Would you sign this class excuse for me? I have to study for a test tomorrow and don't have time to sit in Mrs. Haynes's class and listen to her babble."

_____ 7. Teacher to teacher: "I just cannot stand to sit beside the students in the lunch room. They're so foul-mouthed these days. The kids today are certainly going downhill if you ask me."

_____ 8. Principal to teacher: "I seem to make all the wrong decisions. Every time I try to please someone, it makes someone else angry."

_____ 9. Teacher to teacher: "Do you have a lot of students in your classes this year? It seems like I have twice as many as usual."

_____ 10. Student to counselor: "I have this application form for the State University. Would you get my records for me so I can fill in the academic information?"

_____ 11. Teacher to counselor: "I hear that Johnny's mother is divorced and is going to have another man's baby. Isn't that just disgusting? It's no wonder Johnny's so bad in his schoolwork."

_____ 12. Teacher to counselor: "Cheryl [student] and I had a real confrontation in my second period class today. Could you talk to her and help her see how upset she has made me today?"

44

___ 13. Teacher to counselor: "When are you going to do the state achievement tests this year? I've had several students ask me about it, and I didn't know what to tell them."

___ 14. Student to counselor: "Hey, man, I hear you've been doing some counseling with Stevie [student]. He's really a messed-up kid, isn't he? What kinds of problems does he have?"

___ 15. Student to counselor: "I hear you're having a group counseling session every Friday after school. What do you all do in there?"

___ 16. Student to teacher: "I'm lost in this big school. Where's the cafeteria?"

___ 17. Student to counselor: "My family is going to be moving to the other side of town, and I'll have to go to East High School. Can you find out what courses they offer over there?"

___ 18. Teacher to teacher: "It seems I'm really alienating a lot of the teachers here. I'm just trying to be as helpful as possible when I offer to help them plan their classes."

___ 19. Teacher to teacher: "Did you find that Billy [student] wasn't able to relate to the other students in the class when you had him last year?"

___ 20. Teacher to custodian: "Can you get me a new chair for my desk? The one I have is just too short for me."

___ 21. Teacher to student: "Tommy, when are you going to turn in that special project you've been working on? It sounds very interesting."

___ 22. Teacher to principal: "How do you expect the teachers to work under such awful conditions? There's absolutely no control in this school. You seem to just sit around in your office."

___ 23. Teacher to counselor: "I don't really understand these test scores. Can you explain them to me?"

___ 24. Teacher to teacher: "There is going to be a big fight in the faculty meeting tomorrow. If you want to help us plan it, you're invited to meet at John's [teacher] house tonight. We're really going to get Mr. Jackson [principal] for the way he told us all off last week "

___25. Student to counselor: "There really isn't much time for me to study at home. My mother and dad are separated and I have to work after school to help Mom. It was so much nicer when Mom and Dad were together and happy."

___26. Student to teacher: "Miss Hale, what do I do about Harold [her boyfriend]? I love him so much but he doesn't want to get married."

___27. Custodian to teacher: "I wish you'd ask your kids to keep their chairs in the lines. Why are the chairs always in a circle after the last period?"

___28. Student to counselor: "I've decided to go to college but haven't been able to decide which ones to apply to. Can you tell me some stuff about the ones around here?"

___29. Principal to counselor: "There seems to be a real problem between the teachers and me this year. I don't know what caused it and it really bothers me to think that I did something to make them angry at me."

___30. Student to counselor: "I've been thinking lately about the kind of job I want to get when I graduate this year. I really don't know anything about the jobs available here, or even what they're like. Is there some way to find out about what my interests in careers are? The whole situation has me really confused and I don't even know where to start looking."

## Answers to Examples of Communication Types

| | | |
|---|---|---|
| 1. RA | 11. II | 21. RI |
| 2. RUI | 12. RUI, RA | 22. II |
| 3. II | 13. RI | 23. RI, RA |
| 4. RUI | 14. II | 24. II |
| 5. RA, RI | 15. RI, RUI | 25. RUI |
| 6. II, RA | 16. RI | 26. RUI |
| 7. II | 17. RA | 27. RA, RI |
| 8. RUI | 18. RUI | 28. RI |
| 9. RI, RUI | 19. RUI | 29. RUI |
| 10. RA | 20. RA | 30. RUI, RA, RI. |

# Ineffective Communication Styles

*Behavioral Objective: The trainee should become aware that many common ways of responding are not helpful and should recognize the major characteristics of good responses.*

There are many ways of responding to any helpee situation, and some are more effective than others. This section gives examples of some of the ways of responding that are generally not helpful and which may even be harmful. Notice that none of the ineffective responses attends to the feelings or emotions of the helpee. These are only a few of the many common response styles that are not facilitative.

As you read through these situations, think of occasions when someone responded to you in these ways, or in similar ways that were not helpful, and try to recall how you felt at that time. Each situation is followed by a response that follows the model outlined in this manual. The helpful response illustrates a natural style that might be given on an actual occasion.

## Helpee Situation 1

Fourth grader coming in from recess, to teacher: "They wouldn't let me in their game!"

HELPER RESPONSES THAT ARE NOT HELPFUL:

1.  Detective: "Who wouldn't?"

    The Detective is eager to track down the facts of the case. He/she grills the helpee about the details of what happened and responds to this factual content instead of giving attention to feelings. The Detective controls the flow of the conversation, which often puts the helpee on the defensive.

2. Magician: "Recess is over so it doesn't matter now, does it?"

The Magician tries to make the problem disappear by telling the helpee it isn't there. This illusion is not lasting. Denying the existence of a problem is not respectful because it denies helpees the validity of their own experience and perception.

3. Foreman: "Would you help me pass out these papers?"

The Foreman believes that if a person can be kept too busy to think about a problem, there will be no problem. Doing this has the effect of telling helpees that the assigned task is more important than their problems, which is disrespectful even if true. Effective helpers communicate their awareness of the magnitude given by the helpee to any particular problem.

4. Judge: "Remember yesterday when you didn't play fair? Of course they wouldn't want to play with you today!"

The Judge gives rational explanations to show the helpee that his/her past actions have caused the present situation—that the helpee is the guilty party. Although such responses may be accurate, they are rarely helpful because they are premature—given before the helpee is ready to accept and use them. A helper does not punish.

HELPER RESPONSE THAT FOLLOWS THE MODEL: "It hurts to be turned down!" or "That hurt!"


## Helpee Situation 2

Teacher to another teacher: "Consultants! Consultants! They keep sending these people around with their impractical ideas!"

HELPER RESPONSES THAT ARE NOT HELPFUL:

1. Swami: "You better make them think you follow their suggestions. If you don't, it will get back to the principal."

The Swami knows and predicts exactly what is going to happen. By declaring the forecast, the Swami relieves himself/herself of responsibility and sits back to let his/her prophecy come true.

2. Judge: "Sounds like your attitude may have kept you from giving their ideas a fair chance."

3. Sign Painter: "You're just a complainer! You don't seem to like anything that happens!"

The Sign Painter thinks a problem can be solved by being named. The Sign Painter has an unlimited inventory of labels to affix to persons and their problems.

4. Drill Sergeant: "You need to adapt their ideas to your own situations. Try thinking of it that way next time they come."

Drill Sergeants give orders and expect them to be obeyed. Because they know just what the helpee should do, they see no need to give explanations or listen to the helpee's feelings, or to explain their commands to the helpee.

HELPER RESPONSE THAT FOLLOWS THE MODEL: "It annoys you to get interrupted."

## Helpee Situation 3

Eighth-grade student to teacher after class: "You asked me to be chairman of the panel discussion next week, but I can't do that. Please get somebody else. Anybody in the class would be better than me."

HELPER RESPONSES THAT ARE NOT HELPFUL:

1. Drill Sergeant: "When you get home tonight, figure out what each panel member will do. Give them assignments and make sure they work on it some each day. Get organized now and it will come out fine."

2. Guru: "You won't find out what you can do if you don't try new things. It's better to try and fail than not to try at all."

   Gurus dispense proverbs and cliches on every occasion as though they were the sole possessors of the accumulated wisdom of the ages. Unfortunately, their words are too impersonal and general to apply to any individual's situation with force or accuracy, and often are too trite to be noticed at all.

3. Magician: "You don't *really* mean that do you?"

HELPER RESPONSE THAT FOLLOWS THE MODEL: "You're sort of afraid to accept this responsibility—it looks like more than you can handle."

## Helpee Situation 4

Parents to teacher: "You told us at our last meeting that if we worked with Johnny at home his grades should improve. We've spent more than enough time with him, but his grades aren't any better."

HELPER RESPONSES THAT ARE NOT HELPFUL:

1. Detective: "Let's talk about what you are doing at home and how you go about it."

2. Florist: "Oh, I think your extra effort is going to pay off in the long run. These things take time, you know, but he has been trying harder in class. I think things are working out."

   The Florists are uncomfortable talking about anything unpleasant, so they gush flowery phrases to keep the helpee's problem at a safe distance. The florist mistakenly thinks that the way to be helpful is to hide the problem under bouquets of optimism.

3. Guru: "Well, you know what they say about leading a horse to water. It could be that we're pushing Johnny too hard at this time. According to some developmental theories I've read . . . ."

HELPER RESPONSE THAT FOLLOWS THE MODEL: "All the extra work doesn't seem to be paying off—that discourages you!"


## Helpee Situation 5

Teacher to another teacher: "Things today are all so confusing. My work seems to pile up and there's never enough time to get it done. I'm afraid I'm just getting so far behind that I'll never catch up."

1. Guru: "Hard work never killed anybody. Just hang in there. Things could be worse."

2. Detective: "What do you mean? Do you have it more difficult than anyone else? Tell me *exactly* what is bothering you?"

3. Sign Painter: "Come on now. You don't want to be known as a quitter. You're just discouraged."

4. Swami: "You're working yourself into a nervous breakdown if you take all this so seriously."

5. Drill Sergeant: "Stop complaining! Get organized and just plan to do one thing at a time."

6. Judge: "Look, as I see it, you're the one responsible for this mess. You volunteered for the extra work."

7. Magician: "Things aren't that bad, you're just tired. Everything will be better tomorrow."

8. Florist: "Dedicated people such as you are often feel this way. If we didn't have you people, nothing would ever be accomplished around here."

9. Foreman: "Look, we've got other things to worry about. This project we selected is right up your alley and I need your help."

HELPER RESPONSE THAT FOLLOWS THE MODEL: "You're confused and you feel discouraged because your work is piling up on you. And right now you don't see any way out."

# THOUGHTS THAT LIE BEHIND THE HELPEE'S WORDS

*Behavioral Objective: The trainee will learn the effect that nonhelpful communication styles have upon persons.*

Everything a helper says has an effect on the helpee. This effect can be for better or for worse.

Sometimes we know what the effect of our communication is; often we do not. When we respond in an effective way, the helpee will often be more pleased than he/she is able or willing to express.

It is when we have been hurtful and/or inaccurate that we get the least helpful response from the helpee. When the helpee feels disappointment or anger as a result of our response, he/she may not be able to express his/her disappointment or anger in a way that alerts us to our failure to be helpful. If we say something to a helpee that is not helpful, he/she will usually be polite, but superficial in his/her reply. Often he/she will say something that relates to the conversation but will not reveal his/her feelings. We often interpret the absence of negative remarks or obvious resistance by the helpee as evidence that our communication has been good. But the truth is that most helpees are too timid or too polite to say everything they think and feel. Also, if we have been ineffective in responding to what they have already said, why should they bother to say more? Most persons would rather close the conversation.

The conversations below show what might be going through a helpee's mind as he/she replies to various helper responses. You will notice that what the helpee thinks is different from what he/she says. Because of social sanctions on expressing our feelings and attitudes in their entirety, this is a frequent condition. As you read these conversations, ask youself the question, "Is the helpee better off after this conversation?"

## Helpee Situation 1

Student to teacher: "I know I'm behind in my work. It's all these technical terms you said we had to learn. It's all I can do to pronounce them, let alone learn what they mean."

HELPER RESPONSES THAT ARE NOT HELPFUL:

1. Instructor (Detective): "Are there any words in particular that are giving you trouble?"

   *Student says:* "I don't know where to begin."
   *Student thinks:* "You don't realize how big the problem is. I wish it was just a word or two. Are you going to be angry with me when you find out how much trouble I'm having? Maybe I shouldn't have said anything about it."

2. Instructor (Swami): "You better hit it pretty hard with the exam coming up next week. You know what happens if you fail that test."

*Student says:* "Oh, I *am* studying as much as I have time to!"
*Student thinks:* "Of course I know I should study. The thing is I have been, and I'm *still* having trouble. *That's* what's worrying me, and that's why I'm talking to you, but you're just not hearing me!"

3. Instructor (foreman): "That's going to work out OK. Say, I'm glad you stopped by. I know you're interested in dramatics and I wondered if you would like to help me with the senior play?"

*Student says:* "Yes."
*Student thinks:* "You're right, I *do* like dramatics, but I won't be around for that if I don't pass biology. I've *got* to get some help with that, but it looks like it won't be from you."

HELPER RESPONSE THAT FOLLOWS THE MODEL:

4. Instructor: "Yes, there are a lot of words here that you've never heard before. Some people compare it with learning a foreign language. Right now it looks like learning them all would be an impossible job."

*Student says:* "It seems like as soon as I learn one, I forget another one."
*Student thinks:* "That's *exactly* how I feel—it's *impossible.* It sounds like she really does understand what I'm going through. Maybe I'm not the only person who has felt this way."


## Helpee Situation 2

School secretary to principal: "I need a raise. I think it must be time for one. If food prices keep going up, I won't even be able to feed my family."

HELPER RESPONSES THAT ARE NOT HELPFUL:

1. Principal (Sign Painter): "You're overreacting. You must be a worry-wart. The government is taking care of the price situation—your children aren't going to starve."

*Secretary says, apologetically:* "Well, I guess we've gotten by so far."
*Secretary thinks:* "If he had to face what I've had to face, he'd worry plenty."

2. Principal (Drill Sergeant): "Do you budget your money?" First, keep track of how you spend your money for a month. Then, see where

you can improve your habits. Stick to a careful plan of how you spend your money and you'll come out OK."

*Secretary says:* "I don't do that. I guess it would be a good idea."
*Secretary thinks:* "He's one to talk with *his* fat salary. I'd like to see him manage with what I make! By the time I pay the rent and buy the food, there's nothing left!"

3. Principal (Magician): "Oh, come on now, it couldn't be as bad as you say. I know how much you make. There are other people working here who make a lot less than you and are getting along fine. You're fortunate!"

*Secretary says:* "I don't know of anybody who's in a worse financial situation than I'm in."
*Secretary thinks:* "He's just giving me the runaround."

HELPER RESPONSE THAT FOLLOWS THE MODEL:

4. Principal: "It sounds like your situation is pretty difficult. You think you can't make ends meet without a raise."

*Secretary says:* "I really hated to come to you like this, but I had to tell *somebody* about it."
*Secretary thinks:* "It sounds like he cares about what's happening to me."

In the next chapter the trainee will be provided with a rationale and need for training in attending behavior. Exercises for improving attending behavior are included.

# Training in
# Attending Skills

Attending skills are the physical behaviors you use while listening to another person. These behaviors—such as posture, eye contact, and facial expression—carry messages to persons with whom you talk. They communicate without the use of words. This kind of communication is called nonverbal communication and you will learn more about it in Chapter 12. In this section we will consider the behaviors that are especially important in the facilitation phase.

Attending skills may be effective or ineffective. Effective attending skills communicate that you are interested in the other person. If attending skills are ineffective, it is unlikely that a helping relationship can develop.

There are no exact rules to follow in using attending skills. There are some general principles that will help you use behaviors that are effective and avoid those that are ineffective. Just as the communication model gives you general principles to follow and allows you to adapt those principles to your own personal style, the guidelines for attending skills will allow you to express your own uniqueness as a person.

Table 6.1 lists a number of modalities of communication and describes, in general terms, behaviors in those modalities that may be either effective or ineffective. There are several important benefits of using good attending skills:

1. They make it easier for you to listen and remember. Listening can be hard work. Good attending skills are behaviors that are physically comfortable. Being natural and comfortable makes it easier to stay emotionally and intellectually alert over a period of time.

2. They enhance the self-respect of helpees. They encourage them to feel better about themselves because you are giving fully of your own energy, time, and attention. This helps build a good base relationship.

3. They facilitate self-exploration. By making it worthwhile for the helpee to talk, they reinforce the helpee's openness and self-disclosure.

4. They model behavior that is appropriate. Your example teaches the helpee useful skills.

Ineffective attending behaviors tend to close off conversation or prohibit a helping relationship from developing. If your attention begins to lapse after you have been listening to a person talk for a few minutes, you will probably notice some changes in his/her behavior. When the speaker suspects that your attention is beginning to drop, he/she is likely to try to recapture your attention. He/she may do this by talking more loudly or in a more animated way, by talking faster, by changing the subject to something that he/she thinks may be

### Table 6.1 ATTENDING SKILLS

| INEFFECTIVE USE | NONVERBAL MODES OF COMMUNICATION | EFFECTIVE USE |
|---|---|---|
| *Doing any of these things will probably close off or slow down the conversation.* | | *These behaviors encourage talk because they show acceptance and respect for the other person.* |
| Distant: very close | Space | approximate arms-length |
| away | Movement | toward |
| slouching; rigid; seated leaning away | Posture | relaxed, but attentive; seated leaning slightly toward |
| absent; defiant; jittery | Eye contact | regular |
| you continue with what you are doing before responding; in a hurry | Time | respond at first opportunity; share time with them |
| used to keep distance between the persons | Feet and legs (in sitting) | unobtrusive |
| used as a barrier | Furniture | used to draw persons together |
| does not match feelings; scowl; blank look | Facial expression | matches your own or other's feelings; smile |
| compete for attention with your words | Gestures | highlight your words; unobtrusive; smooth |
| obvious; distracting | Mannerisms | none, or unobtrusive |
| very loud or very soft | Voice: volume | clearly audible |
| impatient or staccato; very slow or hesitant | Voice: rate | average, or a bit slower |
| apathetic; sleepy; jumpy; pushy | Energy level | alert; stays alert throughout a long conversation |

From *The Amity Book: Exercises in Friendship and Helping Skills*, p. 53. Copyright 1975 by Richard P. Walters. Reproduced by permission.

of more interest to you, by moving closer to you, or, if you are looking in another direction, he/she may move into your field of view so you will be forced to look at him/her. These are signs that your attending skills are deficient at that time and indicate that the speaker is not satisfied with the level of attention that you are offering.

## Exercise in Attending Skills

*Behavioral Objective: The trainee should be able to demonstrate consistent use, as judged by the trainer and another trainee, of effective attending skills in a three-minute interaction.*

Work in triads. One partner should talk freely for three minutes about any topic of interest. The other partner will mostly listen, although he or she may ask questions or otherwise encourage the speaker to continue. The third person will rate the helper (listener) on attending skills using the items in Table 9.1.

Each member of the triad will rotate through each of the three roles: speaker, helper-listener, and observer-rater. The observer-rater should be careful to give positive feedback first before citing areas in need of improvement. Additional practice in attending skills will be provided in future exercises in chapters focusing on nonverbal behavior and the warmth dimension.

In Chapter 7, the trainee will be provided with exercises on perceiving feelings, both surface and underlying.

# Training in Perceiving Feelings

# 7

*Behavioral Objective: The trainee should learn to perceive accurately surface and underlying feelings from written helpee situations.*

The first step in communicating helpfully is identifying the helpee's feelings, a process we call perceiving. The examples of "not helpful" communication in Chapter 5 were characterized by ignoring or denying the helpee's feelings; the helpers seemed to be unaware of how the helpees felt.

In our communication model we will learn to respond to the helpee's feelings, as well as to the content of his/her situation. Before we respond, we must perceive; that is, we must decide what the helpee is feeling and think of words to express those feelings.

The following section provides practice in perceiving feelings. Examine helpee situation 1 which has already been completed. Notice that there are many words that can be used to describe the feelings of the helpee. Often, no single word will summarize all the feelings the helpee has expressed.

These exercises will help build your repertory of words to use when describing emotions, and they will sharpen your analysis of helpee feelings so that you can be more accurate in responding. To be effective, a helper must be accurate in perceiving feelings and spontaneous in responding. This involves judgment and practice. Helpee situation 1 is offered as an example. For helpee situations 2 through 11, write down several words to describe how the helpee might have been feeling in that situation.

In order to assist you in selecting the most appropriate feeling word, the following five steps proposed by Cash, Scherba, and Mills[1] are recommended.

1. Identify the general category/mood—positive or negative.
2. Identify the specific kind of feeling—unhappy, fearful, elated, and so forth.

1. R. W. Cash, D. S. Scherba, and S. S. Mills, *Human Resources Development: A Competency Based Training Program* (Trainer's Manual) (Long Beach, Calif.: Authors, 1975).

3. Decide on the intensity level of the feeling—high, moderate, low.
4. Select a word that means the same as those feeling words used by the helpee.
5. Verbalize (write) the word that would be meaningful to the helpee, i.e., in the helpee's vocabulary range.

Refer to Appendix A—Vocabulary of Affective Adjectives, if necessary, in order to add to your description of the helpee's feelings. List as many words as you can before referring to Appendix A.

## Helpee Situation 1

Teacher to teacher: "I'm so mad at myself! I was upset and tired and I blew up at my class for no reason. I know some of them felt hurt."

*Feelings present:* _upset, mad, angry, tired, guilty, ashamed_

## Helpee Situation 2

Student to math teacher: "I can't bring my friends home from school because my dad said they're not our kind of people."

*Feelings present:* _____

## Helpee Situation 3

Student to teacher: "All of my friends smoke and I don't. I like to think my parents believe me when I say I don't smoke, but they just look at me funny—kind of like they are saying to themselves, 'sure'."

*Feelings present:* _____

## Helpee Situation 4

Student to teacher: "Like, everybody is always wanting to know what I'm going to do when I grow up. How do I know! That's a long way off."

*Feelings present:* _____

## Helpee Situation 5

Student to homeroom teacher: "I feel great! The chemistry teacher said I was the best student she'd had all year."

*Feelings present:* _____

## Helpee Situation 6

Student to math teacher: "Some students here are down on us football players because they think the teachers aren't as hard on us as they are on the other students. That just isn't true."

*Feelings present:* _____

## Helpee Situation 7

Student to student: "I don't think we should be *required* to take physical education. It's going to ruin my average this semester."

*Feelings present:* _____

## Helpee Situation 8

Student to teacher: "Sometimes when people ask me questions, I want to help but I don't know what to say."

*Feelings present:* _____

## Helpee Situation 9

Student to faculty advisor: "I wish my mother wasn't going to be a chaperon on the Senior Trip."

*Feelings present:* _____

## Helpee Situation 10

Student to student: "All Ed thinks about is sports. He expects me to be interested in everything he's interested in, but I'm not."

*Feelings present:* _____

## Helpee Situation 11

Student to teacher: "Betty found out I was going on vacation with my family this summer and she hit the ceiling. She thinks I should stay home alone so we can be together more."

*Feelings present:* _____

Some of the feelings a helpee experiences are obvious from the words used and the way they are said. These feelings are clearly related to the situation being discussed. We call these *surface feelings.*

Other feelings must be inferred from the helpee's statements. For example, in helpee situation 1, that the teacher is feeling guilty or ashamed is less obvious than mad or angry. We inferred that the helpee may be ashamed for blowing up for no reason, or that the helpee may feel guilty for hurting the feelings of some of the children.

We also determine feelings by interpreting the way portions of the conversation are put together—the familiar "reading between the lines." We will call these inferred and interpreted feelings *underlying feelings.* These feelings are more abstract than surface feelings and may not relate directly to the content of the situation being discussed.

When we begin responding, we will use only words which refer to the surface feelings, but we want to be aware of the underlying feelings and keep them in mind for possible use later. We form tentative ideas about the helpee and the nature of his situation from the underlying feelings, but we keep these words in reserve.

Look over the feelings you have perceived in helpee situations 2 through 5 and classify them as surface or underlying. Then, for situations 6 through 11, circle the words that describe the helpee's underlying feelings.

In helpee situations 12 through 19, list as many surface and underlying feeling words that you can think of for each situation. (Use the five-step process described for use with situations 2 through 11.)

Having exhausted your supply of feeling words, turn to Appendix A and locate and record additional feeling words that are synonymous with your list.

## Helpee Situation 12

"Since I lost the weight, I feel like a million dollars. It's great!"

Surface: _____

Underlying: _____

## Helpee Situation 13

"I thought you'd never get here! What took you so long?"

Surface: _____

Underlying: _____

## Helpee Situation 14

"Sure, I could get ahead too, if I pulled the kind of tricks *she* does."

Surface: _____

Underlying: _____

## Helpee Situation 15

"How can I *ever* face them again? They will be laughing about my mistake for *years.*"

*Surface:* _____

*Underlying:* _____

## Helpee Situation 16

"Everyone else is having fun after class, but I always seem to go home by myself."

*Surface:* _____

*Underlying:* _____

## Helpee Situation 17

"Whenever you work as hard as I worked toward a goal and then something like this happens, it's enough to make you want to give up."

*Surface:* _____

*Underlying:* _____

## Helpee Situation 18

"Don't crowd me!"

*Surface:* _____

*Underlying:* _____

## Helpee Situation 19

"When we had children in the house, it seemed there weren't enough hours in the day. Now that they are gone, it's just the opposite."

*Surface:* _____

*Underlying:* _____

Beginning with Chapter 8, and including Chapters 9, 11, 15, 16, 17, 19, and 20, the trainee will be introduced to each of the *core conditions* of the helping relationship. Chapter 8 includes exercises in perceiving and responding with empathy. Each chapter focusing on a core condition is arranged similarly to Chapter 8.

# Perceiving and Responding with Empathy

# 8

Empathy was shown in Chapters 1 and 2 to be the key condition in developing helpful communication with another person. We will use scales to rate the effectiveness of responses on each of the eight dimensions of our communication model. The process of rating your responses will be of great value in helping you improve your level of helpfulness during training and later.

Each scale has four levels. Levels 1.0 and 2.0 are not helpful; level 3.0 is minimally helpful. Level 4.0 is more intense than level 3.0 and, when used appropriately, is more helpful.

## EMPATHY—ITS MEANING AND VALUE

Helpees' feelings must not only be understood, but this understanding must be put into words. The first step in communicating with empathy is to listen carefully to what helpees are saying about how they feel because of what is happening to them. The second step is thinking of words that represent the helpees' feelings and the helpees' situation. The third step is to use those words to tell helpees that you understand their feelings and their situation. This process is not easy. To succeed, you must listen while the helpee is talking and not spend that time thinking about what you are going to say in response.

Empathy and sympathy are different. Sympathy means that the helper experiences the same emotions as the helpee. If the helpee is sad, the helper feels sad; if the helpee is afraid, the helper also experiences fear and perhaps also the physical sensations that may accompany fear (such as trembling, sweaty palms, and upset stomach). Fortunately, it is not necessary to experience the helpee's feelings to be helpful. You can help if you can understand how the other person feels, and that is what is meant by empathy.

All persons have, at one time or another, experienced the same emotions, even though it may have been under different circumstances. I have been afraid and you have been afraid. The thing that made me afraid may not cause you to be afraid but, if I talk about fear and if I describe how I feel when I am afraid, you can understand that because you can remember how it felt when you were afraid. Feelings are universal—they are the same among all peoples throughout the world—even though the things that cause us to experience a particular emotion may be quite different from one culture to another.

When we respond with empathy, we prove to the persons that we understand, as best we can, what they are saying about their feelings. Some persons try to take a shortcut and say, "I know what you mean," or "I understand." Probably something like that has been said to you, and when it was, you may have realized that the person telling you that he/she understood had no idea what you were talking about. Those phrases are overused and as a result they lose their meaning.

What is the effect on helpees when you respond to them with empathy? Helpees will realize that you are listening to them with full attention and that you really understand what they wish you to understand about them. Giving another person your full attention is the greatest compliment you can give, because it shows to that person that you think he/she is important and worth your time. This is a compliment that is made all the more meaningful because there is no way that giving time and attention can be faked.

The helpfulness of empathic responding is not limited to severe problems. It can be a part of everyday life that will help bring about more meaningful relationships. If your response shows others that you are seeking to understand their point of view, they will be attracted to you and will seek to understand your needs, interests, and feelings. Helpful responses beget helpful interaction.

Table 8.1 sets the requirements for each level of empathy. The short "Key Words" scale will help you recall the longer, more precise scale.

The helpee situation below illustrates the four levels of responses of the Empathy Scale, with an explanation of why each response is rated as it is. Keep in mind that these are rated on the basis of the Empathy Scale alone.

## ILLUSTRATION OF EMPATHY SCALE

Teacher to teacher: "The harder I try to get along with the new math teacher, the more I feel that he just wants to be left alone."

Level 1.0. "If the handwriting is on the wall, why don't you just leave him alone. Don't butt in where you are not wanted."

*Discussion:* This response is rated level 1 because it ignores surface feelings, it is criticizing, and although the helper might have the right idea, it is too early to present this to the helpee. Remember that there is not a strong base between the helper and helpee at this point.

Level 1.0. "Don't you have a minor in math?"

## Table 8.1. EMPATHY SCALE

| 1.0 | 1.5 | 2.0 | 2.5 | 3.0 | 3.5 | 4.0 |
|---|---|---|---|---|---|---|
| An irrelevant or hurtful response that does not appropriately attend to the surface feelings of the helpee. However, in instances where content is communicated accurately, it may raise the level of the response. | | A response that only partially communicates an awareness of the surface feelings of the helpee. When content is communicated accurately it may raise the level of the response; conversely, it may lower the level of the response when communicated inaccurately. | | A response conveying that the helpee is understood at the level he/she is expressing himself/herself; surface feelings are accurately reflected. Content is not essential, but, when included, it must be accurate. If it is inaccurate, the level of the response may be lowered. | | A response conveying that the helpee is understood beyond his/her level of immediate awareness; underlying feelings are identified. Content is used to complement affect in adding deeper meaning. If content is inaccurate, the level of the response may be lowered. |

KEY WORDS—Empathy Scale

Level 4.0—underlying feelings; additive
Level 3.0—surface feelings reflected
Level 2.0—subtractive
Level 1.0—irrelevant; hurtful

*Discussion:* This response ignores the helpee's feelings and is irrelevant. The response is not related to the stimulus statement in any significant way.

Level 2.0. "That's too bad."

*Discussion:* This response is rated level 2.0—subtractive—because it is only a partial awareness of the helpee as a person. The response ignores most of what the helpee said and sounds mechanical.

Level 3.0. "I guess it's kind of disappointing when you make an effort to be friendly and it's not accepted."

*Discussion:* This response is rated level 3.0 because (1) it includes a communication of a primary surface feeling (disappointment); (2) it includes the essence of the content; and (3) it neither adds to nor subtracts from the helpee's statement.

A level 3.0 empathic response communicates to the helpee that you heard what he/she said (content) and you are attempting to understand how he/she feels (affect). In the early stages of the helping process the task is to establish a relationship and gather information. By doing this, the helper and helpee can make more realistic decisions later. In this model the helper must *earn* the right to be judgmental.

Level 4.0. "It's upsetting not to be responded to positively. Although you are only referring to this one incident, it sounds like maybe you are questioning your ability *in general* to get along with people."

*Discussion:* This response is rated level 4.0 because it goes beyond the present awareness, or at least the present verbalization, of the helpee. In order to be rated level 4.0, however, a response must be validated by the helpee. For example, if the helpee responded, "I guess maybe things have not been going well in that area for quite some time," the underlying idea of the helper would have been validated. An attempt at level 4.0 that is not validated is generally a level 2.0. For example, if the helpee had responded, "No! This is the first time anything like this has ever happened," the helper has attempted to go beyond, but the response was not accepted by the helpee. Consequently, the response would be rated level 2.0.

In training groups or classes, the helpee response to an attempted level 4.0 response is frequently not known. When the situation exists, a rating of 2.0 to 4.0 is generally assigned.

# PERCEIVING EMPATHY

*Behavioral Objective: The trainee should be able to rate helper responses on the Empathy Scale with an average discrepancy score of 0.5 or less.* (The discrepancy score is obtained by subtracting the trainee score and the Answer Key score, adding the absolute differences and dividing by the number of items—N = 16 for the following situations.)

Several helper responses are given to the helpee situations. Rate each on the Empathy Scale. Place your rating (1.0, 1.5, 2.0, 2.5, 3.0, 3.5, or 4.0) in the blank to the left of each helper response, and then check your choices against the Answer Key at the end of the chapter.

## Helpee Situation 1

School secretary to teacher: "I really like my job here and I like the people I work with, but I can't seem to please the principal. The harder I work, it seems, the more she expects me to do."

_____ 1. "I know how you feel. I've been living with that for six years!"

_____ 2. "You really are concerned about your job, but right now you're confused about just what you have to do to satisfy your boss."

_____ 3. "The thing to do is stand up to her. If you let her push you around now, things will never be any better."

_____ 4. "That's a real bummer!"

_____ 5. "You like being here, but right now the situation is pretty discouraging for you."

_____ 6. "As a professional teacher in this school, I don't think it's my place to become involved with disputes at the clerical level."

_____ 7. "Research indicates that our principal's personality reflects a deep-seated feeling of inferiority. In order to keep herself feeling okay, she has to put other people down and maintain a tight control. You either learn to put up with her neurotic behavior or leave. It's as simple as that."

_____ 8. "Underneath your frustration I can sense a great deal of anger. You're giving her 100 percent and instead of appreciating that she expects even more. That's pretty hard to take."

## Helpee Situation 2

Educator to educator: "I really feel like my family is being short-changed. With graduate school at night, plus all the other things I have to do around the house, I don't have much time at all to just be with my family."

9. "You seem pretty perplexed because you feel that you are short-changing your family due to your responsibility of working

all day and going to school at night. This doesn't allow enough time with your family."

____ 10. "You feel like you are spreading yourself too thin, taking on too much and missing out on your family life."

____ 11. "You feel down because you're not with your family as much as you want because of school and activities around the house."

____ 12. "I am sure your family realizes your feelings and your situation— they probably understand more than you realize and, in fact, appreciate the fact that you're going to school to better your position in life and make it easier for them."

____ 13. "You seem concerned that your relationship with your family is not all it could be due to your many activities."

____ 14. "It seems hard to sit still and enjoy anybody else when there are so many things to be done."

____ 15. "You feel inadequate and not really a part of the family as you don't seem to have enough personal time to spend with them."

____ 16. "Rearrange your activities so you can let some things go."

# RESPONDING WITH EMPATHY

*Behavioral Objective: The trainee should be able to write helper responses in a natural style at level 3.0 or above on the Empathy Scale.*

In this exercise you will apply the principles you have learned by writing responses to helpee statements. When responding, we wish to reflect back to the helpee the feelings and content he/she has expressed. This shows the helpee that we have attempted to hear and understand what he/she said. Read the stimulus situation carefully, perceiving the surface and underlying feelings. Choose a word or two which best summarizes the feelings and content, and fill in the blanks in the sentence below the situation. These responses tend to sound mechanical, but beginning this way will help you concentrate on choosing words that accurately reflect the feelings and content. With practice, it becomes easier to state the response with spontaneity and freshness. The formula response and the natural response would technically get the same rating, but in the future we will always strive for natural and stimulating ways to respond.

When you have written formula responses for each situation, write a natural response for each. The natural response should contain the same elements as the formula response but should express them in good conversational style. You may use Appendix A "Vocabulary of Affective Adjectives," for finding words to express the feelings you perceived in the helpee's statement.

## Helpee Situation 1

Student to student: "I used to really enjoy going to the coffee house and sitting around talking with the people there. But it all seems so trivial to me now."

HELPER RESPONSES

*Formula:* You feel _____ because _____

*Natural:* _____

## Helpee Situation 2

Student to teacher: "Miss Johnson, I really like you and I like history, but couldn't you do something besides read to us in class?"

HELPER RESPONSES

*Formula:* You feel _____ because _____

*Natural:* _____

## Helpee Situation 3

Teacher to teacher: "I really dread coming to work in the mornings. Teaching isn't fun anymore."

HELPER RESPONSES

*Formula:* You feel _____ because _____

*Natural:* _____

## Helpee Situation 4

Student to teacher: "I work so hard to get an A in your class, but you don't like me enough to give it to me."

HELPER RESPONSES

*Formula:* You feel _____ because _____

*Natural:* _____

## Helpee Situation 5

Teacher to principal: "That Sanders girl is really driving me up the wall. I don't know how to deal with her attitude."

HELPER RESPONSES

*Formula:* You feel _____ because _____

*Natural:* _____

## Helpee Situation 6

Teacher to teacher: "My grade book is gone. I don't know what I'm going to do."

HELPER RESPONSES

*Formula:* You feel _____ because _____

*Natural:* _____

## Helpee Situation 7

College student to other student: "I'm really in trouble. My parents are coming to visit me and I have a guy living with me."

HELPER RESPONSES

*Formula:* You feel _____ because _____

*Natural:* _____

## Helpee Situation 8

Teacher to teacher: "I'm worried about how well I'm doing with my classes. I haven't had any experience before, and I'm not quite sure I'm doing it right."

HELPER RESPONSES

*Formula:* You feel _____ because _____

*Natural:* _____

## Helpee Situation 9

Parent to teacher: "Jane seems so afraid of coming to school in the morning. She actually gets physically ill at times to avoid coming."

HELPER RESPONSES

*Formula:* You feel _____ because _____

*Natural:* _____

## Helpee Situation 10

Student to student: "Man I'm really having fun at college. Sometimes, though, I feel that it's not fair to my parents for me to have such a good time when they're paying for my education."

HELPER RESPONSES

*Formula:* You feel _____ because _____

*Natural:* _____

**Answer Key**

| | | |
|---|---|---|
| 1.  2.0 | 6.  1.0 | 11.  3.0 |
| 2.  3.0 | 7.  1.0 | 12.  1.5 |
| 3.  1.0 | 8.  4.0 | 13.  3.0 |
| 4.  3.0 | 9.  3.0 | 14.  2.5 |
| 5.  3.0 | 10.  2.0 | 15.  3.5 |
| | | 16.  1.0 |

# Perceiving and Responding with Respect

In this chapter you will learn to use a scale for rating helper statements on the dimension of respect. Respect was described in Chapter 2. As with the Empathy Scale, levels 1.0 and 2.0 are not helpful, level 3.0 is minimally helpful, and the appropriate use of level 4.0 for this and the other dimensions is the most helpful method of communication presented in this manual. Study the Respect Scale and the situations which illustrate it.

## ILLUSTRATION OF THE RESPECT SCALE

The helpee situation below illustrates the four levels of the Respect Scale. Ratings are based on the Respect Scale alone; they might be rated differently on other dimensions or on the Global Scale.

## RESPECT SCALE—ILLUSTRATION OF LEVELS

Senior student to teacher: "Some of the kids don't seem to care at all about keeping the cafeteria clean. It's not our class; we really care about the school. It's mostly the freshman class."

Level 1.0. "Well, John, what more can we do? I think you should just leave that problem up to the cafeteria monitors and the janitors."

*Discussion:* This response is an overt attempt on the part of the helper to impose his/her values onto the helpee, while completely ignoring what the helpee had to say. It seems to make the assumption that: "What I think, you should think also," which, of course, is an irrational assumption.

## Table 9.1 RESPECT SCALE

| 1.0 | 1.5 | 2.0 | 2.5 | 3.0 | 3.5 | 4.0 |
|---|---|---|---|---|---|---|
| A response that overtly communicates disrespect. The helper may attempt to impose his/her own beliefs and values onto the helpee, seek to focus attention on himself/herself by dominating the conversation, instantly challenge the accuracy of the helpee's perception, or devaluate the worth of the helpee as an individual by communicating that the helpee is not able to function appropriately on his/her own. These responses leave the helpee wishing that he/she had not talked to the helper, and probably preclude future interactions. | | A response in which the helper withholds himself/herself from involvement with the helpee. This may be communicated by declining to enter a helping relationship, by ignoring what the helpee is saying, or by responding in a casual or mechanical way. Such responses tend to terminate the interaction. | | A response that communicates that the helper is open to or will consider entering a helping relationship. It communicates recognition of the helpee as a person of worth, capable of thinking and expressing himself/herself and able to act constructively. The helper suspends acting on his/her judgment of the helpee in his/her situation. | | A response that demonstrates the helper's willingness to make sacrifices and bear the risk of being hurt in order to further the helping relationship. This results in the helpee experiencing himself/herself as a valued individual and stimulates deeper interaction by allowing the helpee to feel free to be himself/herself. |

---

KEY WORDS—Respect Scale

Level 4.0—involved, committed
Level 3.0—open
Level 2.0—withholds
Level 1.0—imposes, dominates, devaluates

Level 1.0. "I'm a teacher, not a disciplinarian or a policeman. I have to put all of my attention on the classroom."

*Discussion:* This response is rated level 1.0 because it devaluates the worth of the helpee as a person. It sets up a definite, more knowing/less knowing dichotomy that communicates to the helpee, "I am more important than you—leave me alone."

Level 1.0. "Oh, come on, John, it can't be as bad as you say!"

*Discussion:* This response is rated level 1.0 because it challenges the accuracy of the helpee's perception of the situation. This kind of response communicates to the helpee, "I know more about you and what you believe than you know about yourself." The helpee is *very* unlikely to accept your assessment when it is in conflict with a real feeling he is having. As a consequence, the response is hurtful. It will have a real tendency to terminate the relationship.

Level 2.0. "Please don't ask me to get mixed up in this—I'd like to help you but I can't. I've had to work very hard this year to get along with the freshmen. If I mention this, it might undo all that I've done."

*Discussion:* In this response, the helper declines to help. He/she offers his/her regrets and a rational reason for withholding himself/herself from the helping relationship. Though intended to be a neutral response so as not to lose face with the helpee, in practice this kind of response discourages the helpee from seeking help in the future.

Level 3.0. "It makes you mad to see other kids messing up the cafeteria. Let's talk about what we might be able to do."

*Discussion:* This response represents an openness to involvement with the helpee, which is the minimally helpful level of respect. The experienced helper enters a helping relationship cautiously, with the knowledge that involvement takes a commitment, can be time-consuming, and has the potential of bringing hurt and disappointment to the helper. It is respectful of the helper, then, to weigh carefully the decision to help, and not to enter into it half-heartedly or carelessly, or to enter a situation in which he cannot be effective.

Level 4.0 "It hurts you very much to see a school you like very much be abused. I'll do what I can to help and I'll start by talking to the principal about some more teacher supervision of the cafeteria."

*Discussion:* This response is rated level 4.0 because it is a commitment to involvement by the helper. Timing is important in making this kind of commitment, and a good relationship between helper and helpee is essential. A level 4.0 respect response that comes before the relationship is well established, is very likely to communicate phoniness rather than concern.

# PERCEIVING RESPECT

Behavioral Objective: *The trainee should be able to rate helper responses on the Respect Scale with an average discrepancy score of 0.5 or less.* (see page 66 for the method to compute the discrepancy score).

Rate each of the helper responses on the Respect Scale, putting the number (1.0, 1.5, 2.0, 2.5, 3.0, 3.5, or 4.0) in the blank to the left of the helper response. Use the Answer Key at the end of the chapter to check your choices.

## Helpee Situation 1

Teacher to principal: "Mrs. Bigley is really furious with me. She claims that I'm ruining her child's education. I don't even know what I'm supposed to have done."

HELPER RESPONSES

_1_ 1. "Why is she mad at you?"
_2_ 2. "Mrs. Bigley is really angry at you."
_3_ 3. "You're really confused by Mrs. Bigley's anger at you."
_4_ 4. "You're afraid that you really have done something wrong with Mrs. Bigley's son."
_1_ 5. "I'm sorry but I've got to answer a telephone call."
_1_ 6. "Tell her to get off your back."
_2_ 7. "It's really something the way parents react to their kids' teachers."
_2_ 8. "I've had that happen to me before."
_3_ 9. "It would be very confusing to be attacked for a reason you're not aware of."
_4_ 10. "You're wondering about your ability as a teacher as a result of this attack by Mrs. Bigley."
_1_ 11. "Don't let the old woman bother you."
_1_ 12. "Mrs. Jackson did the same thing to me and it really made me furious. Let me tell you about it. . . ."
_3_ 13. "This attack by Mrs. Bigley has really upset and confused you."

## Helpee Situation 2

Teenager to parent: "I really wish you'd treat me like I'm eighteen instead of like I'm six. You don't give me credit for having any sense at all. You just tell me everything to do and then become furious when I don't want to do it."

HELPER RESPONSES

_1_ 14. "Don't talk to me that way."

_2_ 15. "Maybe you're right."

_3_ 16. "You're really angry with me for treating you like a child."

_1_ 17. "Well, you act like a six-year-old."

_2_ 18. "You're really upset."

_4_ 19. "It must be very demeaning to you to be treated that way."

_1_ 20. "You have no right to complain about the way I've raised you."

_1_ 21. "You're just trying to start an argument."

_2_ 22. "You want me to treat you like an adult?"

_4_ 23. "You feel that I'm being unfair in treating you like a child, and it makes you feel inferior."

_3_ 24. "It is unfair for me to treat you this way, and I can see it makes you very unhappy."

_1_ 25. "I'm not going to discuss it with you now. See me when you cool off."

## RESPONDING WITH RESPECT

Behavioral Objective: *The trainee should be able to write helper responses in a natural style at level 3.0 on the Respect Scale.*

Read each helpee situation and develop your response as though you were speaking to the helpee. Write it down as quickly as possible to retain the conversational style. Check your response with the criteria of a level 3.0 response on the Respect Sacle. If it does not reach a level 3.0, rework it to meet the criteria.

### Helpee Situation 1

Teacher to teacher: "I never seem to catch up. I'm so far behind I don't know what I'm going to do."

HELPER RESPONSE _____

_____

### Helpee Situation 2

Student to student: "I wish I knew why my mom and dad always argue over money. It really bothers me when they scream at each other."

HELPER RESPONSE _____

_____

## Helpee Situation 3

Parent to teacher: "I'm concerned that Sam is not learning his spelling. He never studies at home and his grades are not good."

HELPER RESPONSE _____

_____

## Helpee Situation 4

Neighbor to neighbor: "Mona is drinking again. I could just shoot her when she goes on these binges. She's so disgusting."

HELPER RESPONSE _____

_____

## Helpee Situation 5

Parent to teacher: "It seems to me that this school is doing nothing for my child."

HELPER RESPONSE _____

_____

Because empathy and respect are frequently closely related in a response, the next chapter provides exercises in combining empathy and respect in responding.

**Answer Key**

*Helpee Situation 1*

1. 1.0
2. 2.0
3. 3.0

4. 4.0
5. 1.0
6. 1.0
7. 2.0
8. 2.0
9. 3.0
10. 4.0
11. 1.0
12. 1.0
13. 3.0

*Helpee Situation 2*

14. 1.0
15. 2.0
16. 3.0
17. 1.0
18. 2.0
19. 4.0
20. 1.0
21. 1.0
22. 2.0
23. 4.0
24. 3.0
25. 1.0

# Combining Empathy and Respect in Responding

# 10

Many trainees find it difficult to distinguish a level 3.0 empathy response from a level 3.0 respect response. There is quite a bit of similarity, by definition, and it is easy to become confused. For a respect response, we can define a minimally helpful level as more what the helper *does not* do than what he/she does. That is, a level 3.0 respect response is defined as an openness to involvement. This can be communicated overtly (as in telling the helpee that you are open to helping), or implied by listening in a nonjudgmental way. The latter respect response is identical to a level 3.0 empathy response.

In the following example, a mother who is emotionally upset because of her daughter's problems in the classroom visits the teacher, who has combined empathy and respect in her responses. In some of the responses the respect is overt, but in most it is implied. When completing examples 2 and 3, try to write examples of both types.

> *Behavioral Objective: The trainee shall be able to write responses to examples 2 and 3 that include level 3.0 empathy and respect.*

## EXAMPLE 1

Bee Bryant is a first grader whose socioeconomic status is much higher than most other students in her class. Her father is a professor of economics and her mother is a socially active housewife. Most of her classmates are from working class homes. Bee has two sisters in high school. Bee is not achieving as well in school as her sisters, and her parents are very much concerned. The parents ask Ms. Holt, Bee's teacher, what they can do to help their daughter. Ms. Holt states that Bee spends much time in school playing with and bragging about her bracelets and rings and that perhaps Bee should not be allowed to wear jewelry to school.

Example 1

Bee continues to wear her jewelry to school and also begins to talk more and more about her trips to various parts of the United States. Some of the working class students begin to resent Bee, and one girl hits Bee every chance she gets.

Ms. Bryant visits Ms. Holt and says, in a high-pitched voice, "What's going on in that classroom? Bee is being beaten up and she's learning nothing. What are you going to do about it?"

Ms. Holt realizes that she must help Ms. Bryant before she can help Bee. She responds with empathy and respect: "You're mad at me because you want so much for Bee to do well and you think I may be at fault."

> Ms. Bryant (calms down a little and continues): "Yes, I'm upset! I'm not sure who's at fault. I just know something must be done to help Bee."

> Ms. Holt (knows it's too early yet to try to give advice): "You know, there must be a solution to this problem and you and I together can find that solution."

> Ms. Bryant (settles down a little more and reflects on the situation): "I know Bee is a little flighty and that she's very proud of her jewelry and life style, but isn't that normal for a six-year-old child?"

> Ms. Holt: "Perhaps it is, but I wish we could discourage her from bragging around the other students who have much less than Bee."

> Ms. Bryant: "That doesn't give them a right to hit Bee, and it doesn't give you a reason to give her low grades."

> Ms. Holt (realized that she had put Ms. Bryant on the defense; empathy and respect reduce ego defensive behavior): "It's irritating because it seems to you that Bee can't be proud of her possessions without being picked on."

> Ms. Bryant: "Yes, Dr. Bryant and I have always wanted the best for our children and now it almost seems like a handicap for them to have advantages."

> Ms. Holt (knew she very much needed to understand Ms. Bryant and to help Ms. Bryant understand her own attitude more fully): "I guess it's difficult for you to understand why other kids don't appreciate Bee's advantages."

> Ms. Bryant: "Of course, they don't appreciate her advantages, they resent her. I guess it's only normal to have some negative feelings when others have more of everything than you."

> Ms. Holt: "I think you are right. How can we help Bee to understand how the other kids feel?"

Ms. Bryant: "I don't know, but I'm going to work on it. I am also going to restrict her jewelry. Thanks for talking with me about this."

Ms. Holt: "Thanks for coming in, Ms. Bryant."

The example which follows concerns a junior high school youth who, though doing well in his academic work, is rebelling against his teachers and the principal. Both empathy and respect are shown by his history instructor in the responses given.

## EXAMPLE 2

Jack is a seventeen-year-old junior who has been sent to the principal twelve times during the past month. Jack, who is black, lives with his mother and two brothers and a sister. He was an above average student last year and was an honor student before the schools were integrated. In eleven of the twelve cases he was sent to the office by white teachers. Black teachers generally reported that he was a good student.

Mr. York has him in American History class. Jack questions the value of teaching American History.

Jack: "What's the use of teaching history? I want to know more about what's going on now!"

Mr. York knew he must try to understand Jack and respect his right to speak. Before reading Mr. York's response, write what you would say to Jack in the space that follows: _____
_____

Mr. York: "You see no value in studying history, but you would like to learn more about the world today."

Jack: "Yeah, we need to know about politics and social movements, especially us black people."

Before reading Mr. York's response, write what you would say in the following space: _____
_____
_____

Mr. York: "Blacks especially?"

Jack: "Yeah! If we don't look out for ourselves, no one else will look out for us."

Example 3

Write your response: _____

_____

_____


Mr. York: "In order to be prepared one must be educated. What are some topics you would like to study?"

Jack: "Open housing, school integration, job discrimination, educational discrimination against minority groups, and prejudice against minority groups."

Write your response: _____

_____

_____


Mr. York: "Sounds interesting to me. What do you think, class?"

Mr. York listened and understood Jack. He communicated that he was open to modifying the curriculum. How do you think students would respond to this attitude? How would the administration respond?


## EXAMPLE 3. RESPONDING WITH EMPATHY AND RESPECT TO SAM, A "PROBLEM" STUDENT

Sam is a tall, slender high school junior with a big nose, and he would probably be considered homely by most Americans. Sam had a B average through the eighth grade; since eighth grade his grades have become lower. Most high school teachers consider Sam to be a problem. He often talks to teachers with sarcasm in his voice, telling them that he does not like school and that high school teachers are lousy. Sam stops by Ms. Ball's room after school and says: "High school teachers are all the same. They don't make you learn anything. You all should take some lessons from elementary teachers."

Before reading Ms. Ball's response, write what you would say to Sam in the space that follows: _____

_____

Ms. Ball is happy to see Sam come by. She knows his attitude toward school is negative and that he needs to talk. Ms. Ball knows that when a teacher communicates empathy and respect, students are encouraged to explore their situation and attitudes.

Ms. Ball: "You are disappointed with us. You want us to make you learn."

Sam: "High school teachers aren't strict like elementary teachers. I haven't worked hard since the eighth grade."

Before reading Ms. Ball's response, write what you would say to Sam in the space that follows: _____

_____

Ms. Ball: "If we were tougher on you, you would make better grades."

Sam: "I don't want you to get tougher, but most teacher don't seem to care whether we learn or not.

Before reading Ms. Ball's response, write what you would say to Sam in the space that follows: _____

_____

Ms. Ball: "High school teachers are sort of impersonal compared with elementary teachers."

Sam: "Right! This isn't true of you, but most of my teachers never talk to me like I'm a human being. They just give orders and criticism and I lose all my desire to learn.

Before reading Ms. Ball's response, write what you would say to Sam in the space that follows: _____

_____

Ms. Ball: "You're dissatisfied because it seems to you that your teachers don't like you."

Sam: "Yeah! That's the way it seems. But, I guess it may be partly my fault. I let them know I don't like them."

Before reading Ms. Ball's response, write what you would say to Sam in the space that follows: _____

_____

Ms. Ball: "You may be contributing to the problem, but it sounds like you would like to improve your relationships."

Sam: "Yes, can you tell me what to do?"

Ms. Ball allowed Sam to explore and understand himself and his problem. Sam asked for help.

# Perceiving and Communicating Warmth

# 11

The dimension of warmth, to be considered in this chapter, is the third of the facilitative conditions that are essential for establishing a helping relationship. Warmth is the degree to which helpers communicate their caring about the helpee. Warmth is seldom communicated by itself; it is most often included in communications of empathy and respect. Warmth alone is insufficient for relationship building, for the development of mutual respect, or for problem solving, but appropriate communication of warmth enhances these processes.

Warmth is communicated primarily through a wide variety of behaviors such as gestures, posture, tone of voice, touch, or facial expression. These behaviors, for the most part, do not include words, so they are referred to as "nonverbal communication." These nonverbal messages are received by others and given meaning, just as words are, and their impact can be just as strong as that of verbal messages. Consider common expressions about the use of the eyes: "an icy look, a piercing stare, a look that could kill." Or think about the rage that can be expressed by a shaking fist. These examples only suggest the powerful impact nonverbal behaviors can have. This chapter presents the nonverbal mode of communication as it relates to warmth. A more general treatment of nonverbal communication appears in the following chapter.

It is chiefly through nonverbal messages that the helper's caring for the helpee is communicated. But warmth can also be expressed in words, such as, "If this is important to you, it's important to me. Let's talk about it some more." Or, "You're in a bind, and I'd like to help out if there's any way I can."

The level of warmth the helper communicates can be rated, just as you have rated helpers on their communication of empathy and respect (see Table 11.1.). Examples of nonverbal behaviors at different levels of the scale appear below.

## BEHAVIORS ON THE WARMTH SCALE

Level 1.0

Does not respond when approached or spoken to.
Laughs when helpee is sad or frightened.

## Table 11.1. WARMTH SCALE

| 1.0 | 1.5 | 2.0 | 2.5 | 3.0 | 3.5 | 4.0 |
|-----|-----|-----|-----|-----|-----|-----|
| The helper has disapproving facial expression or appears disinterested. He/she turns away or does other tasks while the helpee is talking. Affect is not congruent with the helpee's affect. | | Expressions and gestures are absent or neutral; responses sound mechanical or rehearsed. | | Clearly shows attention and interest; nonverbal behaviors vary appropriately as helpee's emotions vary. | | The helper is wholly and intensely attentive to the interaction, resulting in the helpee's feeling complete acceptance and significance. The helper is physically closer to the helpee than at level 3, and may make physical contact. |

---

### KEY WORDS—WARMTH SCALE

Level 4.0—intense nonverbal communication
Level 3.0—clear nonverbal response
Level 2.0—gestures absent or neutral, voice sounds
　　　　　　mechanical
Level 1.0—visibly disapproving or disinterested

Frequently uses ineffective attending skills described in Chapter 6.

Mumbles or does not speak loudly enough to be heard.

Appears impatient for helpee to go away, as communicated by fidgeting, frequently looking at watch, drumming fingers on desk, etc.

Uses "baby talk" or patronizing tone of voice.

Is ingratiating or overly familiar.

Makes physical contact to which helpee responds negatively.

## Level 2.0

Is apathetic in level of energy.

Faces helpee, but slouches.

Does not change behavior with changes in helpee's affect, e.g., does not laugh out loud.

Uses ineffective attending skills only occasionally.

## Level 3.0

Consistently uses most effective attending skills.

## Level 4.0

Has high level of alertness.

All attending behaviors are effective.

May make physical contact in a way acceptable to helpee.

Facial expression congruent with helpee's affect.

A high rating on nonverbal warmth does not automatically follow high levels of empathy or respect. A helper may have and attempt to communicate high levels of empathy and respect but, because he/she has unexpressive nonverbal behaviors, he/she may be perceived by the helpee as uncaring. This type of helper may find that it takes more time to build a base than it takes a helper whose nonverbal behaviors are more clearly warm. Helpers who do not nonverbally communicate warmth must demonstrate their caring through words and deeds and be careful that their nonverbal behaviors are not harmful to the development of the relationship. On the other hand, high-level warmth behavior may occur with low-level empathy or respect, as in a person who presents interested, responsive nonverbal communication but who gives low-level empathy or respect.

Warmth that is not genuine can usually be detected by the helpee. When verbal and nonverbal messages do not agree, the helpee usually believes the nonverbal message, even though he/she may not be consciously aware of having received it. For example, if a helper says he/she is interested in talking, but is frequently glancing at his/her watch, the helpee will probably conclude that the helper doesn't mean what he/she says.

The way warmth is expressed varies. When a helper with low-level warmth talks with a helpee who has been accustomed to high-level warmth, the base-building process will probably be lengthened. On the other hand, warmth and intimacy cannot be forced. Helpers should allow helpees to exercise their right to maintain distance in the relationship if this is their preference. High levels of warmth during the early stages of a relationship can harm the base-building process with helpees who have received little or no warmth in the past, or who have been "taken advantage of."

## PRACTICE IN PERCEIVING AND RESPONDING WITH WARMTH

*Behavioral Objective: The trainee should be able to rate nonverbal communication with a discrepancy score of 0.5 or less from the consensus rating given by the group and respond with warmth at level 3.0 or higher.*

Because the communication of warmth is primarily nonverbal, written exercises are almost without value. Use the group exercise below to learn and practice communication of warmth at helpful levels. You may find it useful to read the next chapter before doing this exercise.

For each of the following stimulus situations, choose a helper and a helpee. The helpee will read the statement and the helper will respond, attempting to attain high levels of warmth. Continue the dialogue in a role-playing fashion for as long as you wish. After each stimulus situation the other group members should discuss specific aspects of the helpee's nonverbal behaviors and assign a rating on the Warmth Scale. They should then determine the consensus rating for that stimulus situation. An individual rating within 0.5 of the consensus rating is acceptable. Continue this exercise until all members of the group have a chance to play the role of the helper and achieve a warmth level of 3.0.

### Helpee Situations

1. Teacher to teacher: "These kids are just getting to be too much for me. I've been teaching for twenty years, and it looks like I just can't keep up with the pace of things. I don't understand the ideas these kids come up with today. To me that's a sign I should quit, but I don't want to."

2. Student to teacher: "I'm glad we'll be getting into biology soon. I really love cats and want to learn as much as I can about them so I'll know how to take care of them."

3. Student to teacher: "I used to take a strong stand against abortion, but I've changed my mind recently. One of my closest friends decided on a criminal abortion and died from it. After thinking about it more, I believe a girl should be able to make a decision and get proper medical aid."

4. Teacher to teacher: "We're having a lot of tension at home. I've got lessons to prepare and papers to correct after I fix our meals. My husband wants me to spend all my time with him, though. I don't know how we can work this out!"

5. Teacher to teacher: "My heart attack was a real scare to me, but it woke me up to a lot of the real values of life. I have more appreciation of the little things that students and teachers do for me. I plan to make a few changes in my life now."

6. Student to teacher: "I don't see why kids are doing so much protesting these days. They're cutting off their noses to spite their faces. After all, the older generation brought us this far. They lived through a couple of wars, and fought to get us the prosperity we have. I wish we could get along better than we do."

7. Student to teacher: "There's no way I can get all your work done this week. This is one of my dad's 'off-weeks.' He drinks like a fish and there's no peace in the house when he's like that. He badgers everyone in sight as long as he's awake."

# Awareness of Nonverbal Behaviors in Helping

# 12

Facial expressions, the use of time, hand gestures, position a person takes in a room, eye contact, posture, style of dress, loudness of voice, touching, placement of furniture—each of these is a modality of nonverbal communication. There are many more. All of them are potentially important to a helping relationship because they can communicate underlying feelings and motives.

The study of nonverbal communication is fascinating. The diversity of modalities and range in expression that can be observed is almost endless. But, nonverbal communication can also be frustrating because the process of interpreting the meaning of nonverbal cues is imprecise. There are many things to see, but it is difficult to know the exact meaning of what you have seen.

Frequently, no single bit of nonverbal communication is meaningful. Still, the pieces add up, and for the perceptive helper nonverbal cues add color, richness, and depth to the understanding of the other person. Trends can be detected, intensity of feelings may be more fully experienced, and conflicts and motives may be recognized before the helpee can express them in words.

We shall use a liberal definition of nonverbal communication: *any human behavior that is directly perceived by another person and that is informative about the sender.* This definition of "nonverbal" is liberal because it allows us to include an unlimited variety of behaviors if we find them useful. This definition of "communication" is liberal because it does not require that the sender has intended to communicate.

## CATEGORIES AND EXAMPLES OF NONVERBAL COMMUNICATION BEHAVIORS

Nonverbal behaviors include the attending skills described in Chapter 6 and the behaviors discussed in the preceding chapter on the dimension of warmth.

The list below presents a few specific nonverbal communication behaviors from among the thousands that may be observed in human interactions. It can only suggest the wide range of behaviors that exist.

The purpose of this list is to help you become more aware of the variety and complexity of nonverbal communication. It is believed that with greater awareness you will develop greater understanding of the ways in which the nonverbal signals you send out are interpreted by others. Also, by improving your skills in reading the nonverbal responses other persons make to your communication, you will learn how you yourself are perceived.

The nonverbal behaviors below are categorized to assist the process of observation and awareness. Because meaning is so highly individual and dependent on context, only minimal information on possible interpretations has been included. Consult the recommended readings cited at the end of this chapter for further information about interpretations of nonverbal cues.


## I. NONVERBAL COMMUNICATION BEHAVIORS USING TIME

### Recognition

Promptness or delay in recognizing the presence of another or in responding to his/her communication

### Priorities

Amount of time another is willing to spend communicating with a person
Relative amounts of time spent on various topics


## II. NONVERBAL COMMUNICATION BEHAVIORS USING THE BODY

### Eye contact (important in regulating the relationship)

Looking at a specific object
Looking down
Steady to helper
Defiantly at helper ("hard" eyes), glaring
Shifting eyes from object to object
Looking at helper but looking away when looked at
Covering eyes with hand(s)
Frequency of looking at another

### Eyes

"Sparkling"
Tears
"Wide-eyed"
Position of eyelids

*Skin*
Pallor
Perspiration
Blushing
"Goose bumps"

*Posture (often indicative of physical alertness or tiredness)*
"Eager," as if ready for activity
Slouching, slovenly, tired looking, slumping
Arms crossed in front as if to protect self
Crossing legs
Sits facing the other person rather than sideways or away from
Hanging head, looking at floor, head down
Body positioned to exclude others from joining a group or dyad

*Facial expression (primary site for display of affects; thought by researchers to be subject to involuntary responses)*
No change
Wrinkled forehead (lines of worry), frown
Wrinkled nose
Smiling, laughing
"Sad" mouth
Biting lip

*Hand and arm gestures*
Symbolic hand and arm gestures
Literal hand and arm gestures to indicate size or shape
Demonstration of how something happened or how to do something

*Self-inflicting behaviors*
Nail biting
Scratching
Cracking knuckles
Tugging at hair
Rubbing or stroking

*Repetitive behaviors (often interpreted as signs of nervousness or restlessness but may be organic in origin)*
Tapping foot, drumming or thumping with fingers
Fidgeting, squirming

Trembling
Playing with button, hair, or clothing

*Signals or commands*
Snapping fingers
Holding finger to lips for silence
Pointing
Staring directly to indicate disapproval
Shrugging shoulders
Waving
Nodding in recognition
Winking
Nodding in agreement, shaking head in disagreement

*Touching*
To get attention, such as tapping on shoulder
Affectionate, tender
Sexual
Challenging, such as poking finger into chest
Symbols of camaraderie, such as slapping on back
Belittling, such as a pat on top of head

## III.   NONVERBAL COMMUNICATION BEHAVIORS USING VOCAL MEDIA

*Tone of voice*
Flat, monotone, absence of feeling
Bright, vivid changes of inflection
Strong, confident, firm
Weak, hesitant, shaky
Broken, faltering

*Rate of speech*
Fast
Medium
Slow

*Loudness of voice*
Loud
Medium
Soft

*Diction*

Precise versus careless

Regional (colloquial) differences

Consistency of diction

## IV. NONVERBAL COMMUNICATION BEHAVIORS USING THE ENVIRONMENT

*Distance*

Moves away when the other moves toward

Moves toward when the other moves away

Takes initiative in moving toward or away from

Distance widens gradually

Distance narrows gradually

*Arrangement of the physical setting*

Neat, well-ordered, organized

Untidy, haphazard, careless

Casual versus formal

Warm versus cold colors

Soft versus hard materials

Slick versus varied textures

Cheerful and lively versus dull and drab

"Discriminating" taste versus tawdry

Expensive or luxurious versus shabby or spartan

*Clothing (often used to tell others what a person wants them to believe about him/her)*

Bold versus unobtrusive

Stylish versus nondescript

*Position in the room*

Protects or fortifies self in position by having objects such as desk or table between self and other person.

Takes an open or vulnerable position, such as in the center of the room, side by side on a sofa, or in simple chair. Nothing between self and other person.

Takes an attacking or dominating position. May block exit from area or may maneuver other person into boxed-in position.

Moves about the room.

Moves in and out of the other person's territory.

Stands when other person sits, or gets in higher position than other person.

# SOME CHARACTERISTICS OF NONVERBAL COMMUNICATION BEHAVIORS

This section describes some general characteristics of nonverbal communication behaviors. Later sections will deal with behaviors related more specifically to the helper or the helpee.

## Nonverbal Behaviors Are Habits

As is true of other habits, they are automatic and you generally are not aware of them. Try this experiment to demonstrate the strength of habits: Place your hands in front of you, palms together, and clasp your hands with your fingers intertwined. Note how natural it feels. Notice which thumb is on top. Place the other thumb on top and reposition the fingers so they are again intertwined. This will probably feel quite awkward. The way you did it the first time is the way you always do it. You have a habit of clasping your hands together in a certain way. If you did it with equal frequency the two ways, they would feel equally natural. You may wish to repeat this experiment by folding your arms over your chest, then reversing the position.

Changing habituated nonverbal patterns is a long and difficult process. Even so, if you find yourself using nonverbal behaviors that reduce your ability to be helpful to others, it may be worth the effort required to change them.

## Deception Leaks Out Nonverbally

Since nonverbal behaviors are habits, it is difficult to deceive another person with words—your nonverbal gestures reveal your true feelings even though you seek to disguise those feelings with your words. Freud (1905) pointed out the complexity of deception and the interplay between verbal and nonverbal modes when he wrote: "He that has eyes to see and ears to hear may convince himself that no mortal can keep a secret. If his lips are silent, he chatters with his fingertips; betrayal oozes out of him at every pore."

Recently, Mehrabian (1971) and Ekman and Friesen (1969, 1972) have shown experimentally that persons cannot mask all signs of feeling from view. This certainly is a practical argument in favor of congruence on the part of the helper!

Nonverbal communication is given greater validity than verbal communication. When verbal and nonverbal messages are in contradiction, the helpee will usually believe the nonverbal message. For example, if a helper says he/she is interested in talking, but is frequently glancing at his/her watch, the helpee will probably conclude that the helper would rather not talk at this time.

## Nonverbal Channels Are the Primary Means of Expressing Emotion

There seems to be little doubt that the nonverbal component of communication is essential to full and adequate understanding of the person speaking. A research study by Haase and Tepper (1972) concluded that "to rely solely on the verbal content of the message reduces the accuracy of the judgment by 66 percent." Statistical analysis of communication in both verbal and nonverbal channels by Mehrabian and Ferris (1967) resulted in the following coefficients for each of the main effects: .07 for verbal components, .38 for vocal components, and .55 for facial components.

These data suggest that the impact of nonverbal behaviors is very great indeed. Unless the helper can receive the information conveyed through nonverbal behavior, whether it is intentional communication or not, he/she will miss essential information about the helpee.

## Nonverbal Behaviors Vary Culturally

Nonverbal messages may have different or even opposite meanings from one culture to another. There are no truly universal meanings. For example, in our society a simple up-and-down head nod means "yes" and a side-to-side shake means "no," but in Bulgaria and among some Eskimos these signals mean the opposite. Helpers should be aware of the nonverbal language used by the persons with whom they interact.

## Nonverbal Behaviors Vary with the Individual

Take, for example, the behavior of arms folded across the chest. This is often interpreted as a sign of defensiveness or rigidity. That's true *part of the time*. But, it may also occur because: (1) it is comfortable, (2) the person is cold, (3) the person is covertly scratching, (4) the person is hiding a blemish or tattoo on the arm, (5) the person is hiding dirty hands, or (6) any of a number of other reasons. Similarly, tears may come from joy, relief, anguish, guilt, or self-pity. Silence may be generated out of spite, embarrassment, confusion, feelings of being at an impasse, or overwhelming gratitude. Making and acting on snap interpretations is likely to get you into trouble, so always set nonverbal behavior in context.

## THE HELPER'S NONVERBAL BEHAVIORS

Even though you do not consciously control many of your nonverbal behaviors you can become consciously aware of them and control some of them. Table 12.1 summarizes some of the behaviors that are frequently associated with high or low levels of the core conditions. (Several clusters of behavior are described by a common stereotype in place of a lengthy behavioral description.) Only those that are of unique inportance to a particular condition are listed. These behaviors, along with good eye contact and the other behaviors described as

### Table 12.1. NONVERBAL COMMUNICATION OF THE CORE CONDITIONS

| | HELPER NONVERBAL BEHAVIORS LIKELY TO BE ASSOCIATED WITH LOW LEVELS | HELPER NONVERBAL BEHAVIORS LIKELY TO BE ASSOCIATED WITH HIGH LEVELS |
|---|---|---|
| Empathy | Frown resulting from lack of understanding | Positive head nods; facial expression congruent with content of conversation |
| Respect | Mumbling; patronizing tone of voice; engages in doodling or autistic behavior to the point that he/she appears more involved in that than with the helpee | Spends time with helpee; fully attentive |
| Warmth (see also Chapter 11) | Apathy; delay in responding to approach of helpee; insincere effusiveness; fidgeting; signs of wanting to leave | Smile; physical contact; close proximity |
| Genuineness | Low or evasive eye contact; lack of congruence between verbal and nonverbal; less frequent movement; excessive smiling | Congruence between verbal and nonverbal behavior |
| Concreteness | Shrugs shoulders when helpee is vague instead of asking for clarification; vague gestures used as a substitute for gestures or words that carry specific meaning | Drawing diagram to clarify an abstract point; clear enunciation |
| Self-disclosure | Bragging gestures; points to self; covers eyes or mouth while talking | Gestures that keep references to self low-key, e.g., a shrug accompanying the words, "It was no big deal" when talking about a personal incident |
| Immediacy | Turning away or moving back when immediacy enters the conversation | Enthusiasm |
| Confrontation | Pointing finger or shaking fist at helpee; tone of voice that communicates blame or condemnation; loudness of voice may intimidate some helpees so that opportunity to help is lost; wavering quality of voice; unsure of self | Natural tone of voice; confident |

attending skills, must usually be present to attain high levels of a given condition.

As noted in the previous chapter, the dimension of warmth includes nonverbal media more than any other core condition. Concreteness includes the use of nonverbal media the least.

Some helper behaviors may be ambiguous. For example, the helper may show signs commonly associated with anxiety (excessive perspiration, wavering voice, trembling) when verbally communicating at high levels of the transition or action conditions. If the helpee notices these behaviors he/she may interpret them as (1) inexperience or fear of failure or (2) complete emotional involvement with a complex and difficult job at hand. Where there is no change in amount of eye contact, proximity, or degree of congruence during transition or action phases, this may be interpreted as (1) competence and comfort (which may or may not be true) or (2) lack of involvement. The interpretation made by the helpee influences his/her perception of the helper's self-confidence or of the quality of the helper's involvement.

Rate of speech is another variable. A slow rate, with a weak, faltering tone, may be perceived as lack of confidence. The same slow rate with a full, steady tone may show that the helper is carefully thinking about what he/she is saying as he/she speaks, something very respectful of the helpee.

Vocal emphasis can change the meaning of the words of a sentence. Thelen (1960) points out that the tiny muscles of our vocal chords are extremely sensitive to the various states of tension in our body and reflect these changes in audible ways. Consider the following sentence and the variations on it, adapted from Ends (1969): "I DID NOT SAY YOU STOLE THE RED PEN!" Notice that by simply changing the emphasis upon one of the principal words, as though the speaker were "pointing" to that word, the message of the sentence can be altered. There will also be considerable change in the listener's perception of the speaker's attitude toward him/her.

"*I* did not say you stole the red pen!'
  *Message:* "Somebody else said so and I think they're right."
  *Attitude:* "Your stealing makes me angry and you should be punished!"

"I did *not* say you stole the red pen!"
  *Message:* "I deny having said such a thing."
  *Attitude:* "It annoys me to be misquoted!"

"I did not *say* you stole the red pen!"
  *Message:* "But we both know you did."
  *Attitude:* "It bothers me that you won't openly confess to it!"

"I did not say you stole the *red* pen!"
  *Message:* "But let's face it, this wouldn't be the first time we caught you stealing somebody else's pen."
  *Attitude:* "Your stealing disgusts me!"

Helpers should be aware of nonverbal behaviors they use and seek to understand their basis. Exaggerated effusiveness may be motivated by a need to buy the friendship of the helpees. Other behaviors may result from a desire to dominate the helpees or to communicate to them the helper's power, strength, or knowledge. Passive-aggressive helpers may use nonverbal means such as pouting to send messages that would be considered inappropriate or rude if put into words. Any of these circumstances would reduce the quality of the helping relationship.

Learn and use the most effective nonverbal behaviors, but remember that the essence of good communication lies in the quality of the message and not in the style of delivery. It is not necessary to be a silver-tongued orator to be effective as a helper. Tyler (1969) says, "One of the rewards of continuing counseling experience is the realization that what one says need not be fluent or elegantly phrased in order to be effective." If you give a person a nice present, they don't care how it's wrapped!

## USING THE HELPEE'S NONVERBAL CUES

As a helper you will observe the nonverbal behaviors of the helpee. These observations can assist you in understanding the helpee—they add to your perceptions of the helpee and his/her situation. If you always respond at the minimally helpful or higher levels of empathy and respect, and formulate interpretations in a tentative frame, perceptions of helpee nonverbal communication can be constructive to both helper and helpee.

Remember that nonverbal communication is highly idiosyncratic, or personalized; an act or gesture may have opposite meanings for two persons or for the same person on two different occasions. For example, a frown might mean concentration in one instance, annoyance in another. *Nonverbal behaviors must always be judged in context and their meaning considered tentative.* Use perceptions of the helpee's nonverbal behaviors as *clues* to possible underlying feelings or motives rather than as proof that such exist.

Johnson and Pancrazio (1973) propose "that overt indicators of pupil desire to communicate can easily be learned by observant teachers." They suggest that the way to learn these idiosyncratic indicators is by trial and error—to call on the student whenever you think he/she wants to communicate. Even if he/she does not, to offer the opportunity shows respect, they contend.

The helpee's behavior is also a form of feedback that can help you better assess the relationship. The helpee's behavior is, in part, a product of the nature of your behavior. Table 12.2 outlines some clusters of helpee behavior that may allow the helper to confirm or reject a hunch about the helpee's attitude. Use this with caution—as part of a total approach toward understanding the helpee.

When checking out your hunches, make it easy for the helpee to accept your observations and ideas. A simple remark, delivered with warmth, often results in helpee disclosure, e.g., "You have been very quiet today," or "You seem to be pretty excited about something." If you are making an interpretation, phrase it tentatively, for example, "I notice you are staring at your desk instead of working. It makes me wonder if you might be worried about something."

**Table 12.2  HELPEE NONVERBAL BEHAVIORS FREQUENTLY ASSOCIATED WITH ATTITUDE TOWARD HELPER**

| | RELATIONSHIP OF MUTUAL ACCEPTANCE | DEPENDENT QUASI-COURTSHIP | CAUTIOUS, CONSIDERING, EVALUATING | REJECTING, HOSTILE |
|---|---|---|---|---|
| Head | Affirmative nods | | | shakes head |
| Mouth | smile | mirroring | tightness | sneer; tightness |
| Level of arousal | alertness | passive | alertness | disinterest |
| Position | faces helper; moves toward | places self in subordinate position | stationary; uses physical barriers | disinterest; moves or turns away; attacking moves or simulated attack |
| Eye contact | equal to helper's | much; seductive | little; looks down | avoids; defiant |
| Hands | palm open or up | reaching | fidgeting; rubbing face | clenched fists; gripping |
| General | spends time around helper; touches | "puppy dog" behaviors; mirroring of helper's mannerisms | locking up of emotions; uses great care over what is communicated; afraid to be fully open | unresponsive; passive-aggressive behavior; overt disruption of activity; noisy |
| Posture | open | courtship; seductive; helpless | protective | defensive |
| Proximity | normal | very close | | distant |

*How to Use This Table:* Each column lists behaviors that might be seen under certain conditions. If the helper-helpee relationship is characterized by the helpee attitude described in the column heading, you are likely to see at least several of the behaviors listed. But, you should not assume the attitude from the behaviors. The behaviors may be used as clues to the quality of the relationship and explored as appropriate.

There may be occasion to point out nonverbal behaviors used by the helpee that interfere with his/her functioning in society (e.g., poor eye contact, a tendency to intrude on the personal space of another, behaviors that are crude or obnoxious). To point these behaviors out is a didactic confrontation (see Chapter 19) and should be preceded by a strong base relationship.

## EXERCISES IN NONVERBAL COMMUNICATION

Most of the information we get about our own nonverbal communication must come from others. We do not observe our nonverbal behaviors in any ways analogous to the verbal communication feedback we receive by hearing our own voice. In American society, our nonverbal communication is rarely analyzed; we typically receive little feedback and no formal training on the subject. Use the exercises below to gain more awareness of nonverbal signals. Consult the recommended readings to learn more about cross-cultural differences and meanings.

1. Observe nonverbal communication used by others. Note examples of specific behaviors which you particularly like or dislike. List nonverbal behaviors that seem to interfere with and/or terminate conversations between two persons. List other nonverbal behaviors that seem to cause a conversation to move ahead and that might indicate that the helpee is accepting the helper as a person and accepting what is being said.

2. Observe your own nonverbal communication behaviors. Study the list at the beginning of the chapter to become more aware of nonverbal behaviors you use. List nonverbal behaviors that you wish to modify. List any that you think might be misinterpreted by others.

3. Keep a list of ways in which nonverbal behaviors are used and examples of each. The following classification system for nonverbal behaviors was adapted from Ekman and Friesen (1969):
    a. Those that make complete nonverbal statements, e.g., to beckon by curling the index finger, or signals by athletic officials. These nonverbal behaviors have rather definite and widely understood meanings, much as a word has a dictionary definition.
    b. Those that modify verbal communication by accentuating, qualifying, or masking the meaning of the words, e.g., the effect of inflection as demonstrated in the "red pen" exercise, or a clenched fist that belies the accompanying words.

    c. Those that illustrate verbal communication, e.g., to demonstrate size or shape of an object, or the motion of a golf swing.

    d. Those that regulate the interaction, e.g., to frequently look at a watch as a way of saying, "I'm in a hurry" or "I would like to leave," or to remove sunglasses as a way of saying, "I'm willing to be myself and let you see me as I really am."

    e. Those that display emotions, e.g., facial expressions, or to pound the fist or stamp a foot.

4. With a partner, take turns talking about anything of interest to you. Have an observer make notes of nonverbal behaviors and give you feedback at the end. The observer should look closely for behaviors by the listener that might slow down the flow of communication from the speaker.

In the following two chapters, exercises for combining the facilitative conditions of empathy, respect, and warmth are included. The Global Scale for assessing the combined facilitative conditions is also introduced in Chapter 13 and practice exercises for achieving skill in its use are included.

## RECOMMENDED READING FOR FURTHER STUDY

The books below contain interesting and reliable general reviews of the topic of nonverbal communication:

Davis, F. 1971. *Inside Intuition: What We Know about Nonverbal Communication.* New York: Signet, 223 pp.

Harrison, R. P. 1974. *Beyond Words: An Introduction to Nonverbal Communication.* Englewood Cliffs, N.J.: Prentice-Hall, 210 pp.

Knapp, M. L. 1972. *Nonverbal Communication in Human Interaction.* New York: Holt, Rinehart & Winston, 213 pp.

Ruesch, J. and W. Kees. 1966. *Nonverbal Communication: Notes on the Visual Perception of Human Relations.* Berkeley: University of California Press, 205 pp.

These books deal more specifically with nonverbal communication in the classroom:

Galloway, C. M. 1970. *Teaching Is Communicating: Nonverbal Language in the Classroom.* (Bulletin No. 29) Washington: National Educational Association, 24 pp.

Grant, B. M. and D. G. Hennings. 1971. *The Teacher Moves: An Analysis of Non-Verbal Activity.* New York: Teachers College Press, 133 pp.

For application to counseling, see:

Walters, R. P. In press. "Nonverbal communication in group counseling." In G. M. Gazda, *Group Counseling: A Developmental Approach.* (2nd Ed.) Boston: Allyn and Bacon.

# REFERENCES

Ekman, P., and W. F. Friesen. 1969. "The repertoire of nonverbal behavior: Categories, origins, usage, and coding." *Semiotica* 1, 49–98.

Ekman, P., and W. V. Friesen. 1969. "Nonverbal leakage and clues to deception." *Psychiatry* 32, 88–105.

Ekman, P., and W. V. Friesen. 1972. "Hand movements." *The Journal of Communication* 22, 353–374.

Ends, A. W. 1969. "Proficient teaching: Communication in process." *Educational Media: Theory into Practice.* Edited by R. V. Winman and W. C. Meierhenry. Columbus, Ohio: Merrill, p. 184.

Freud, S. 1963. "Fragment of an analysis of a case of hysteria (1905)." *Dora: An Analysis of a Case of Hysteria.* New York: Collier Books, p. 96.

Haase, R. F., and D. T. Tepper. 1972. "Nonverbal components of empathic communication. *Journal of Counseling Psychology* 19, 417–424.

Johnson, W. D., and S. B. Pancrazio. 1973. "Promoting effective pupil thinking through nonverbal communication." *College Student Journal* 7, 92–96.

Mehrabian, A. 1971. "Nonverbal betrayal of feeling." *Journal of Experimental Research in Personality* 5, 64–73.

Thelen, H. A. 1960. *Education and the Human Quest.* New York: Harper.

Tyler, L. E. 1969. *The Work of the Counselor.* (3rd Ed.). New York: Appleton-Century-Crofts, p. 41.

# Scale for Global Ratings of Responding

# 13

The Global Scale has been developed in order to allow an overall assessment of communication. At level 3.0, the type of responding is called facilitative responding. This mode is a combination, at level 3.0, of empathy, respect, and warmth. Communication at the global level 3.0 is basically a nonjudgmental listening style. It is not necessarily intended to solve the helpees' problems, but rather to allow them to tell us more about themselves and their concerns in relation to themselves. Some helpees find that facilitation is necessary and sufficient for problem resolution, while others require a more intense, more personal interaction.

When more involvement is indicated, helpers have at their disposal five transition and action dimensions (to be introduced later in this manual) that allow more helper involvement in problem resolution. The prerequisite to moving into the transition and action dimensions is adequate facilitation. Entering these dimensions prematurely or inappropriately will likely be ineffective at best and hurtful at worst. It is true that from time to time a helper will "hit on" a solution that is acceptable to the helpee very early in the helping relationship, but this occurs too infrequently to be justifiable.

Table 13.1 summarizes the characteristics of communication at each level of the Global Scale. Study this summary before reading further in order to get an idea of the process of helping developed in this model. Communication at levels 1.0 and 2.0 includes the Ineffective Communication Styles given in Chapter 5 as examples of damaging and ineffective communication. Level 3.0 involves facilitative responding. Level 4.0 will be introduced in this chapter, and studied and used in the following chapters.

## GLOBAL SCALE FOR RATING HELPER RESPONSES

Level 1.0  NOT HELPFUL: HURTFUL

A response in which the helper:
   ignores what the helpee is saying,

### Table 13.1.  GLOBAL SCALE (Short Form)

| LEVEL | KEY WORD | RESULTS | HELPER ACTIONS CHARACTERIZED BY | HELPER'S GOAL |
|-------|----------|---------|--------------------------------|---------------|
| 1.0 | Harmful | Not helpful | Criticism | Inappropriate; to gratify self by dominating the helpee |
| 2.0 | Ineffective | Not helpful | Unsuitable advice | Inappropriate; stated goal to help; real goal is to be a hero |
| 3.0 | Facilitative | Helpful | Relationship building | To earn the right to help |
| 4.0 | Additive | Helpful | Problem solving | To help |

ridicules the helpee's feelings,

seeks to impose his/her beliefs and values on the helpee,

dominates the conversation,

challenges the accuracy of the helpee's perception,

or uses problem-solving dimensions in a way that damages the relationship.

### Level 2.0  NOT HELPFUL: INEFFECTIVE

A response in which the helper:

communicates a partial awareness of the helpee's surface feelings,

gives premature or superficial advice,

responds in a casual or mechanical way,

reflects total content but ignores the feelings of the helpee,

uses problem-solving dimensions in a way that impedes the relationship,

or offers rational excuses for withholding involvement.

### Level 3.0  HELPFUL: FACILITATIVE

A response in which the helper:

reflects accurately and completely the helpee's surface feelings, and communicates acceptance of the helpee as a person of worth.

### Level 4.0  HELPFUL: ADDITIVE

A response in which the helper:

demonstrates his/her willingness to be a helper, and accurately perceives and responds to the helpee's underlying feelings (empathy)

appropriately uses one or more of the problem-solving dimensions to:

assist the helpee to move from vagueness to clarity (concreteness),

reveal perceptions of the helpee in their entirety (genuineness),

share similar experiences (self-disclosure),

suggest things the helpee might do (expertise),

point out discrepancies in the helpee's words and/or actions (confrontation),

or talk about present feelings between the helpee and helper (immediacy).

The following examples will serve to illustrate the four levels of the Global Scale. Each of the four examples is an illustration of a different level of responding. Even though *all* of the responses in a particular example are not the same level, most are, and the interaction taken as a whole represents a particular level. The same problem situation is used in order to facilitate comparison of the different levels.

The following description will help you to know the student whose problem is dealt with in the illustration:

Arnold Desney is a fourteen-year-old junior high school student who is an only child and comes from a low socioeconomic home. He lives with both parents. Arnold's verbalized problem seems to be under-socialization. He is comfortable around adults and children younger than himself. His parents are away from home a lot, and when they are home there is a great deal of arguing in the household. When they are out of town, Arnold stays with his grandmother. Arnold's parents think he is old enough to take care of himself; thus, he is reluctant to discuss school problems with them. At school, Arnold seems to have a severe problem with children his own age. His peers make fun of him, tease him, and ridicule him. No one in his class seems particularly close to him. At home, Arnold plays with two ten-year-old boys. Arnold's teacher notices the rejection by other students in the class and sees Arnold being bullied by his peers.

## LEVEL 1.0

*"Arnold, please wait. I need to talk to you for a few minutes." The teacher waits until the room is empty and says, "The reason I wanted you to stay is because I would like to talk to you about that incident outside the building this morning."*

| ARNOLD | TEACHER | DISCUSSION |
|--------|---------|------------|
| Oh, you saw that, huh? | Did I ever! You know I thought to myself, Arnold is out there getting into trouble again. I'll bet he's starting a fight. Then I thought about how my children used to fight when they were your age and then I thought that maybe there was nothing to it. But somehow I get the idea that in your case it's different. After all, my children were always big for their ages and could protect themselves pretty well against all the kids in school. I was worried that maybe you would hurt one of them. | This response is Level 1 because it is dominating the inter-action. Arnold did not request the meeting, much less a review of the teacher's family history. This kind of interaction is confus-ing to the helpee. He is thinking, "Why is she sticking her nose in?" |

| ARNOLD | TEACHER | DISCUSSION |
|---|---|---|
| Those guys are really bullies. They pick on everybody. | Bullies pick on people who let themselves get picked on. | This response is ridiculing and thus hurtful. The helpee is thinking, "You just don't understand." |
| Yea, but they were ganging up on me. One of them gets behind me, the other one gets in front of me and they play jokes on me; they kick me. There's two of them and one of me. | Are you sure you aren't making it worse than it really is? | This response challenges the accuracy of the helpee's perception of his own situation and the teacher thinks maybe it is not so bad. This is analogous to your saying to your friend, "I have a stomachache," and the friend replies, "No, you don't." |
| You just saw them this one day. It's happened lots of times. Today was nothing compared to sometimes. | There was a rumor that your family was going to move next year. Is that true? | This response ignores what the helpee has said. Many times, ignoring takes the form of changing the subject. Usually not done intentionally, the negative effect is almost always felt by the helpee. |
| No, we're not moving. I'll have to put up with them again next year. | If I were you, I would stay away from them, even if I had to change my route going home. | This response seeks to impose the helper's beliefs and values onto the helpee. It is irrational to expect that what is right for one person is necessarily right for another person; yet this response has that flavor. It fails to allow for individuality by exploring what is possible for the helpee. |
| They would think that I was afraid of them if I did that. | What you need is to be a little more afraid, Arnold. Your attitude provokes others to bully you. | This response uses the dimension of confrontation inappropriately. It is pointing out a deficit in a way that will surely be perceived as punishing by the helpee. |
| O.K. Can I go now? | | |

## LEVEL 2.0

*"Arnold, please wait. I need to talk to you for a few minutes." The teacher waits until the room is empty and says, "The reason I wanted you to stay is because I would like to talk to you about that incident outside the building this morning."*

## LEVEL 2.0 (Con't)    LEVEL 2.0 (C

| ARNOLD | TEACHER | DISCUSSION |
|--------|---------|------------|
| Oh, you saw that, huh? | Were you scared? | This response picks up partially on the helpee's surface feelings. There is much more that could have been communicated. Also the question gives the response a tentative flavor. There is enough information from the observation of the incident to make an affirmative statement of surface feelings. |
| I was scared okay, but what really bothers me is that all the other kids just laughed. | Many children are insensitive to others. You'll just have to grin and bear it. | The first response is a casual, general response that has virtually no personal meaning. Instead of tuning in to where the helpee is, this helper is generalizing. The second sentence, of course, is a cliche that is very mechanical and impersonal. Statistics do not matter at this point in the helping relationship. The key is to establish a personal relationship, not to relate the helpee's concerns to others in a general way. |
| Yea, but it really makes me feel bad. I wish somebody would help me out. | You wish someone would help you out? | This response picks up on a part of the content and ignores the feelings. This type of response tends to direct the interaction by choosing only part of the content to reflect instead of communicating completely, thus leaving the direction open to the helpee. |
| Yea, well I think I need some help. I don't know if you know it or not but those boys have been picking on me all year. They slip up behind me, play jokes on me. . . . | If all that is true, I think what you should do is report them to the principal. | This response represents premature use of the action dimensions. The helper is giving advice that the helpee has probably already considered. After all, advice off the top of your head is probably something that the helpee has already considered. For some reason, this is not an option for him. It is more important to explore with the helpee what he considers to be his options before offering such advice. |

## LEVEL 2.0 (*Con't.*)

| ARNOLD | TEACHER | DISCUSSION |
|---|---|---|
| I would never do that. They would really get me then! I could never go around them any more. | Well, Arnold, I can remember when I was your age that's the way I handled tough situations at school. The principal seemed to appreciate the information. | This response is considered inappropriate use of the self-disclosure dimension. The helpee has already rejected this strategy for problem solving, yet the helper seems to be trying, through self-disclosure, to convince the helpee that he is wrong. |
| I still don't think that I want to tell the principal. | I'm sorry, Arnold, but that's about all I can offer. I don't want to get involved personally in this matter since the other boys are also in my class and I have to try to get along with as many of the students as possible. | This response is level 2.0 since the helper has given a rational excuse for declining to enter the helping relationship. |
| O.K., can I go now? | | |

## LEVEL 3.0

*"Arnold, please wait. I need to talk with you for a few minutes." The teacher waits until the room is empty before continuing.*

| ARNOLD | TEACHER | DISCUSSION |
|---|---|---|
| | I overheard some conversation between you and a couple of other guys outside the building this morning and I wondered if that was anything that would be worthwhile to talk about? | This is level 3.0 response, openness to involvement, and it leaves further interaction as a helpee decision. The teacher simply communicated concern for the helpee and leaves it there. |
| Well, I really don't know what you could do about it. Those guys have been picking on me all year—since school started this year—and I haven't been able to do anything about it. | That must be a pretty frustrating thing to put up with. I don't know for sure if there is anything I can do about it, but I certainly hope that things could change, and maybe the way to begin would be just talking about it. I would be glad to. | This response is rated level 3.0 because the helper communicates the surface feelings and is open to involvement. |

## LEVEL 3.0 (Con't.)

| ARNOLD | TEACHER | DISCUSSION |
|---|---|---|
| Yeah, I don't mind talking about it, because it's gotten to the point that if things don't change, then something's just gotta give because, like I say, it's been going on all year, and it seems like the last couple of weeks it's gotten worse. | It's something that has just kind of been building up and right now it's to the point where you're not sure if you are going to be able to put up with it any longer. You're at the end of your rope. | Level 3.0. This response encourages further helpee self-exploration. |
| Yeah, that's right. You see, they always pick the time to pull a practical joke on me when there are other kids around. The other kids always laugh. | So, that makes it embarrassing on top of just being pretty hard to take. | Level 3.0. The helper is doing neither more nor less than listening and communicating that he/she heard and is trying to understand. |
| Oh, it's really, really embarrassing. I want to just—you know—I just want to run and hide somewhere. | Just disappear and not be seen. | Level 3.0. The helper is staying with the helpee in his exploration. |
| I get up in the morning and I don't want to come to school. I just hate walking down the hall because those guys—you know—they usually just slip up behind me when I'm not looking. | So that is spoiling the whole thing. They're interferring with more than just your time here at school, but it's something you kind of live with all during the day, even when you're not around here. That's a real bummer. | Level 3.0. Facilitative. |
| That's right and—you know—the kids at school don't want to associate with me and I guess they figure if they associate with me then those guys will probably pull tricks on them, too. So most kids really just don't want to be friends with me. | So, they deal with it by leaving—by not having anything to do with you and that leaves you pretty lonely, I guess. | Level 3.0. Facilitative. |
| Yeah, it is lonely. It *is* lonely at school. Now, I have friends at home who don't go to my school because they're younger than I am, but boy, at school it really does get lonely. I usually wind up having lunch by myself. I usually go home by myself after school. | So, around here you're just pretty much isolated from all the other kids. You do, though, have friends that you see around home. | Level 3.0. Facilitative. Notice that through good listening the helpee feels comfortable self-exploring and becoming more and more personally relevant. |

## LEVEL 3 (Con't)

| ARNOLD | TEACHER | DISCUSSION |
|---|---|---|
| Yes. They are both ten years old, but they're the best friends I have. | That gives you someone to play with when you're home. It's really nice to have other people in your life whom you get along with, that you can do things with. | Level 3.0. Facilitative. |
| Well, it's all I have right now. You know, I really don't have any friends at school and these people, these kids at home are neighbors and they're always around and we usually get together most every day after school. | And that is a pretty good thing, at least as far as it goes. That kind of takes care of after school for having things to do. | Level 3.0. Facilitative. |
| But I would really like to have some friends at school. It's a matter of just kind of being embarrassed, you know, when you're kind of made fun of you want to just go hide rather than try to be friends with the kids. That's why I just kind of stay to myself. | You'd rather just stay out of everyone's way rather than be given more attention and just end up being embarrassed because of it. | Level 3.0. Facilitative. |
| That's right. You know, the less attention I attract the better because it seems like it never works out. | At least it hasn't been working out right now. | Level 3.0. Facilitative. |
| Uh huh. | You'd like for things to be different now. | Level 3.0. Facilitative. |
| Well yeah, if I could start over again. | If you could start over, then you could do things differently and they might work out better for you. | Level 3.0. Facilitative. |
| Before the kids got the bad impression of me I think I could have made some friends. | But the way it looks now, they've kind of got an idea about what you're like and as you see it, there's no way to change their bad impression. | Level 3.0. Facilitative. |

## LEVEL 3 (Con't)

| ARNOLD | TEACHER | DISCUSSION |
|--------|---------|------------|
| Let's just put it this way, I haven't been able to. . . . I don't know what to *do*. I just know that something's got to give. | It can't go on like this very much longer. | The helper has at this point helped the student move to a point of discussing some of the action strategies that are available to him. By listening, the helper has established rapport with the helpee and also has a better idea of the helpee's life situation. |
| That's right. | | |

## LEVEL 4.0

*The bell has rung and the students are leaving the class. The teacher moves toward Arnold and says, "Arnold, I need to see you for a minute if you have time." They wait until the other students leave.*

| ARNOLD | TEACHER | DISCUSSION |
|--------|---------|------------|
| | I saw what happened outside the building this morning. It looked like it must have been pretty unpleasant for you. I wondered if it really was. | This response is a global Level 3.0 and is an openness to involvement with the helpee. The helpee has the decision of whether or not to talk with the teacher. |
| Yes, it was bad, but I don't know what I can do about it. I tried to ignore them but the last couple of weeks it's been worse and I can't ignore it any more. | This is something that has been going on for awhile and it looks like it's not going away by itself. It must be pretty unpleasant for you at school. | Level 3.0. Facilitative. |
| It's gotten to be a terrible problem for me. It's more than just what happened this morning. | Sounds like it is pretty important to you and if you want to talk about it I'd be glad to listen. If there's any way I can help you with it, I'll be glad to. | This is a global level 4.0 response that involves a commitment on the part of the helper. This goes beyond an openness for involvement and actually makes a commitment for involvement with the helpee. |
| Well, I appreciate the offer to help. One of the worst things is that they always pick a time when other kids are around. Then everybody always laughs. I want to just run and hide. | That must be terribly embarrassing for you. It sounds like you're pretty helpless to do anything about this. | Level 4.0. This response accurately hits on the underlying feelings of helplessness. |

## LEVEL 4 (Con't)

| ARNOLD | TEACHER | DISCUSSION |
|--------|---------|------------|
| I'm really at the end of my rope. I don't have any friends here and the future doesn't look any brighter. | You've tried some things to solve the problem but so far nothing has worked. | This is a global level 4 concreteness response. The helper is attempting to elicit specificity from the helpee. This kind of response will usually elicit information concerning what the helpee has tried to this point. |
| I tried to ignore them, but that hasn't worked. Also, I've tried to be friendly to some of the kids, but they don't seem to want to associate with me. I'll try anything to solve this problem. | I've noticed some things that might be affecting the way people react to you, Arnold. I think maybe you are sending some messages to the other kids that you don't really mean to send. | This is the beginning of helper genuineness. It is continued in the next helper response. |
| I'm not following you. | Well, sometimes at lunch I notice that you go out of your way to sit by yourself. The other kids *may* think that you're really a snob and don't want to associate with them. I think you have a lot going for you and a lot you can offer to the other kids. | This is a global level 4.0 genuineness response. The helper is communicating his/her feelings about the helpee, both positive and negative. |
| The reason I try to stay away from the other kids is because I'm embarrassed to be around them. | I can remember moving to a new town when I was in school. Since it was to a different part of the country the kids used to make fun of the way I talked. I can remember the embarrassment I felt every time I opened my mouth. My teacher helped me get over that. | This is a global level 4.0 self-disclosure response. The helper shares personal information that relates to the helpee's problem. |
| Really! Well I guess you know how it feels, then. Do you have any ideas about what I could do? | I think a start might be to look at some of the little things that you are doing which may be turning the other kids off. Maybe we could start with lunch and just try doing some things differently at lunchtime. | This is a global level 4.0 expertise response. The helper has made a suggestion after hearing the things that Arnold has tried for himself. If this course of action is followed, there will be considerable discussion concerning *how* the changes will be implemented, keeping in mind what is possible for the helpee. |

## LEVEL 4 (Con't)

| ARNOLD | TEACHER | DISCUSSION |
|--------|---------|------------|
| Well, I don't know if I could. | You said a few minutes ago you would try anything; now you're about to back off from taking a risk. We won't push you into anything that's going to be too threatening for you. | This is a global level 4.0 confrontation response. The helper points out the discrepancy here in order to encourage the helpee to follow through on an action strategy. |
| I guess at this point I don't have much to lose since I don't have any friends here now. | I'm really happy you're going to work on this problem. Knowing you as I do, I don't have any doubt that things are going to to be better. The changes might be slow at first, but the important thing is that you stick with the plan. | This is a global level 4.0 genuineness response. The helper again has taken a stand concerning his/her faith in Arnold. Genuineness takes form in the expression of the helper's own feelings about the helpee. |
| I really appreciate what you're doing for me. My parents don't understand and since I don't have many friends, I was really desperate. | Thank you for the compliment. I *am* interested in helping you, and it makes it worthwhile to know that you really appreciate it. | This response is a global level 4.0 immediacy response. The helpee has brought up the subject of the relationship between the two of them and the helper responded accordingly. |

At this point in the helping relationship, the helper and helpee can begin an action plan. There are many ways to do this, and aspects of many different theories of helping can be incorporated into the plan. Some of these strategies, and references to others, will be discussed in Chapter 21, Strategies for Change.

## PRACTICE IN RATING HELPER RESPONSES ON THE GLOBAL SCALE

When you are certain you understand the identifying concepts for each level, rate the helper responses in situation 1. Write the rating number in the blank to the left of the response number. If you rate any response at 3.5 or 4.0, underline the portion that is additive, i.e., goes beyond reflective responding.

> Behavioral Objective: The trainee should be able to rate
> 75 percent of the responses correctly (within 0.5 of the
> rating shown in the Answer Key is considered accurate).

## Helpee Situation 1

Teacher to teacher: "Our principal is really living in the Dark Ages. He won't let me follow through on any of the new teaching techniques I learned in college."

HELPER RESPONSES

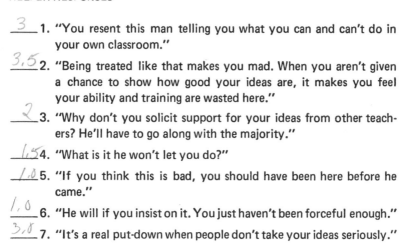

<u>3</u> 1. "You resent this man telling you what you can and can't do in your own classroom."

<u>3.5</u> 2. "Being treated like that makes you mad. When you aren't given a chance to show how good your ideas are, it makes you feel your ability and training are wasted here."

<u>2</u> 3. "Why don't you solicit support for your ideas from other teachers? He'll have to go along with the majority."

<u>1.5</u> 4. "What is it he won't let you do?"

<u>1.0</u> 5. "If you think this is bad, you should have been here before he came."

<u>1.0</u> 6. "He will if you insist on it. You just haven't been forceful enough."

<u>3.8</u> 7. "It's a real put-down when people don't take your ideas seriously."

Look at the responses you did not rate correctly and refer to the Global Scale to determine why each was rated as it was. When you are confident you understand the use of the rating system for situation 1, rate the helper responses to situations, 2, 3, and 4 (responses 8 through 22). Study those on which you were not accurate by referring to the Global Scale.

## Helpee Situation 2

Student to teacher: "I could get good grades too, if I did what she does during the test!"

HELPER RESPONSES

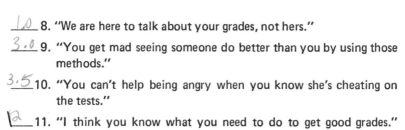

<u>1.0</u> 8. "We are here to talk about your grades, not hers."

<u>3.0</u> 9. "You get mad seeing someone do better than you by using those methods."

<u>3.5</u> 10. "You can't help being angry when you know she's cheating on the tests."

<u>2</u> 11. "I think you know what you need to do to get good grades."

## Helpee Situation 3

Teacher to teacher: "We'd be better off without those stupid psychologists! I sent one of my problem students up there for discipline last week, and she's been worse since she got back. Now I have reason to think the psychologist told her I'm just a poor teacher."

HELPER RESPONSES

_3_ 12. "You're angry and a little suspicious about the psychologists. As far as you can tell, they aren't doing much of a job."

_1_ 13. "You're paranoid."

_2.5_ 14. "You feel that all they do is sit up there in the office while we put up with the kids all day."

_2_ 15. "Why don't you go talk to her about it?"

_2_ 16. "You think we should just get rid of the psychologists."

_3.5_ 17. "You felt a little unsure about how to handle the situation yourself, so you sent her upstairs. That didn't help either, and now you're stuck with a bigger problem. You're asking yourself, 'What do I do now?' "

## Helpee Situation 4

College student to college student: "I'm falling way behind in my course work this quarter, and I just don't know how I'm going to catch up."

HELPER RESPONSES

_1.0_ 18. "What courses are you taking?"

_1.5_ 19. "I know just what you mean. The same thing happened to me last year."

_3_ 20. "It's discouraging when you get in such a bind and can't see any way out."

_2_ 21. "Whenever I get behind I make it a point to study in the library. That way I get more done."

_3_ 22. "You feel frustrated because you can't seem to get caught up."

# GLOBAL RESPONDING

*Behavioral Objective: The trainee should be able to write helper responses at level 3.0 on the Global Scale.*

Read each helpee situation and try to understand where the helpee is in terms of affect and content. Formulate your response and write it down as quickly as possible in order to retain the conversational style. Check your response against the criteria of a level 3.0 response on the Global Scale. If your response is not at least a level 3.0, rework it to meet level 3.0 criteria.

## Helpee Situations

1. Teacher to teacher: "Mrs. Rogers uses my classroom fourth period for her art class. I like Mrs. Rogers, but you should see the way she leaves my room. I don't know how to approach her about it."

2. Teacher to teacher: "Every afternoon after school Mrs. Byrnes stops by my room on her way out. Most every day she stays ten or fifteen minutes talking about everything under the sun. I'm at a loss as to what to do."

3. Tenth grade female student to teacher: "Mom doesn't want me to go anywhere without telling her exactly where I'm going, who I'm with, and what time I'll get home. Don't you think that's kind of extreme?"

4. Teacher to teacher: "My husband's father is going to spend the next month with us. I wouldn't mind so much except that he drinks a lot and I think it is a bad influence on our children."

5. Student to teacher: "You know I had a baby boy last year. Well, my mother is spoiling the child like you wouldn't believe. She corrects me every time I try to discipline the baby."

6. Counselor to principal: The teachers are throwing kids out of their classrooms and sending them to me. Then they expect that the very next day the kids will be little angels. I can't work miracles!"

7. Student to teacher: John told me that he cares for me, but then he hardly ever pays any attention to me. I'm beginning to wonder if he really meant it."

8. Teacher to teacher: "My husband has been coming home in a really lousy mood lately. He won't talk about it much so I don't know if it's me, or his job, or what."

9. Student to history teacher: "I keep thinking that we will do something in this class, but we don't. It's a big waste of time."

10. Student to teacher: "I'm beginning to think that I can make a better living illegally than legally. Going to college just isn't worth it when I can make more money another way."

11. Student to teacher: "Mrs. Rose, I've been getting these headaches before every test in here and I think it's the stress I'm under trying to pass this course and still work every afternoon after school."

## Answer Key

| Helpee Situation 1 | Helpee Situation 3 |
|---|---|
| 1. 3.0 | 12. 3.0 |
| 2. 3.5 | 13. 1.0 |
| 3. 2.0 | 14. 2.5 |
| 4. 1.5 | 15. 2.0 |
| 5. 1.0 | 16. 2.0 |
| 6. 1.0 | 17. 3.5 |
| 7. 3.0 | |

| Helpee Situation 2 | Helpee Situation 4 |
|---|---|
| 8. 1.0 | 18. 1.0 |
| 9. 3.0 | 19. 1.5 |
| 10. 3.5 | 20. 3.0 |
| 11. 2.0 | 21. 2.0 |
| | 22. 3.0 |

# Facilitative Responding

# 14

Facilitative responding is preferred during the early stages of a helping relationship because it allows helpees to be comfortable being themselves and revealing that self to the helper. The discussion that follows reviews what facilitative responding is and does and summarizes the major reasons why it is effective.

1. A facilitative response is one in which helpers verbally and nonverbally communicate that they have heard what helpees have said and are attempting to understand how they feel.

2. The necessary components of a facilitative response are the following: (1) empathy—reflecting accurately and fully the helpee's surface feelings; (2) respect—communicating acceptance of the helpee as a person; and (3) warmth—showing attentiveness and caring through nonverbal behaviors.

3. A facilitative response is similar enough to the helpee's statement that the two could be interchanged. The helper's response communicates the content and affect of the helpee's statement with accuracy and equal intensity. The helper does not add anything to what the helpee has said, but neither does he/she leave anything out.

4. Facilitative responding begins with thorough listening, but listening and repeating by rote is not sufficient. As equally essential as listening are the acts of reading the helpee's nonverbal messages, sending appropriate nonverbal messages while listening, synthesizing the communication received from the helpee, and making mental notes of important items or hunches for possible future use. The complexity of these tasks demands the most intense, conscious involvement and participation of which the helper is capable.

5. Facilitative responding provides a nonthreatening atmosphere in which helpees feel accepted and feel free to express themselves in any manner they choose. In this atmosphere a relationship of

mutual trust and caring can develop between helper and helpee. This relationship is referred to as a "base relationship" because it provides a foundation upon which meaningful dialogue on significant personal matters can build.

6. Facilitative responding puts a boundary around the helper's role. The process of facilitative responding defines what helpers can do to be effective and, thereby, defines what is ineffective. Helpers, then, know that they should avoid inappropriate or premature behaviors such as judging, advising, imposing, criticizing, confronting, dominating, ridiculing, or belittling.

7. Facilitative responses assist helpees in getting a complete and accurate picture of themselves. In a mirror you can see things about your physical body that you cannot see otherwise. In a similar way, facilitative responses serve as a mirror of the helpee's psychic self.

When helpee's statements are reflected to them, as an empathic response does, they may "see" their views more clearly. They may be able to see their views in their own mind. When they do, they test the validity of their perception, their memory, and their judgment. Helpees say to themselves, "Is that really true? Really how I feel? Really what I believe?" They may discover contradictions within their statements or omissions in what they have said or believe. They may decide that some of their assumptions or expectations are unrealistic. Facilitative responding gives helpees an opportunity to correct misstatements and to clarify matters not sufficiently explained to the helper. The experience of self-exploration leads to better and more complete understanding of the situation and of self, both of which are necessary prerequisites to growth and problem solving.

8. Most persons rarely have the experience of being understood by another. How often do you know, without doubt, that a person you are talking with is giving you his/her full attention? Facilitative responding is a way of demonstrating to another person that you are listening with your full attention. This is one of the greatest compliments you can give a person.

## NONFACILITATIVE VERSUS FACILITATIVE RESPONDING

*Behavioral Objective: The trainee should recognize specific hazards in responding without the facilitative conditions or with premature use of the action dimensions, and he/she should understand the advantages of responding facilitatively.*

The two dialogues below illustrate different ways of responding to the same helpee situation. The first dialogue exemplifies the helper responding in nonfacilitative ways; the second shows the helper responding in the manner of the model.

Read both dialogues carefully and study the discussion of them. In both dialogues, which concern the same helpee and problem, the helper is a graduate student serving as a college dormitory counselor. The helpee is a resident on the same floor and knows the helper by name but has never talked with him about anything of a serious nature.

## Dialogue 1.  NONFACILITATIVE HELPER

| DON (Helpee) | RUSS (Helper) | DISCUSSION |
|---|---|---|
| Hi Russ! | Hi Don! How ya doin'? | Standard greeting. So far, so good. |
| Well, I don't know. I've been just thinkin' the last couple of days about going to graduate school, I checked with them today, they said I should take the GRE and I don't know anything about it. | I can tell you about it. That will be the most boring day of your life! | The helper flippantly responds to this request for information. |
| Well, I don't know a thing about it. I had to take the SAT; is it like the SAT? | Ah, it's just another test. It's a pushover though. | Another low-level response that does not tune in at all to the helpee's concern over the test. |
| Well, I don't know, I've been thinkin' about graduate school, I know that I'd have more job offers with a Master's Degree, but. . . . it's just a hard decision to make. It means either moving away or staying here and that's just a hard decision. | Well you might as well take the test. Like I say, there's nothing to it. You just have to sit there for a long time, but it's not hard. | This request for understanding/involvement is responded to by the helper suggesting premature and inappropriate action. Instead of picking up on the concern over the decision, the helper told the helpee what he *should* do in this situation. How could the helper possibly have enough information about the helpee to tell him what he should do? Should this be the helper's role? |
| I have a chance to take a job this summer as soon as I graduate, and it probably won't pay as much as if I had my Master's, but at least it would be an opportunity to make a little money. | Yeah, salaries are really bad. I think the establishment's trying to rip us off. | Again, personal opinions are given by the helper as a response to the helpee's request for understanding/involvement. The message to the helpee is, "I would rather talk about what *I* want to talk about instead of listening to you." |

119

## Dialogue 1. (Continued)

| DON (Helpee) | RUSS (Helper) | DISCUSSION |
|---|---|---|
| You know you go to school for four years and then you figure you can make a decent salary. When they offer you five or six hundred dollars a month you just want to laugh in their faces. | Yeah, well if you feel like laughing in their faces. . . . | Another low-level, flippant response. The helpee continues to get the message that the helper is not going to be much help. |
| I don't know—is graduate school as hard as they say? | No. . . no, it's easier. | Instead of responding to the helpee's concern over the difficulty of graduate school, the helper prefers to answer the helpee's surface questions. Is this what the helpee wanted? |
| Easier than undergraduate? | Oh, I think so. . . as long as you do what pleases the professor, and you ought to know how to. . . you should have learned how to do that by now. | At this point the helpee gives up on discussing any personally relevant information and thus succumbs to the ineffective helper. |
| Well, maybe I'll just stay here another year and go to graduate school. | Well, you might as well. You're gonna miss a lot of good parties if you don't. . . . | This response is similar to all of the others of this ineffective helper. He is more comfortable responding to superficial issues. |
| Well, thanks for the information, Russ. | Sure thing. We'll see ya around. | The helpee *thinks,* "I know this guy doesn't understand what I was trying to tell him. I'll just end the conversation nicely by thanking him for his information." This is a very common technique that many times misleads ineffective helpers into thinking that they have been very helpful. |

## Dialogue 2. FACILITATIVE HELPER

| DON (Helpee) | RUSS (Helper) | DISCUSSION |
|---|---|---|
| Hi Russ! | Hi Don! How's it goin'? | Standard greeting. |

## Dialogue 2. (*Continued*)

| DON (Helpee) | RUSS (Helper) | DISCUSSION |
|---|---|---|
| Well, I don't know, I've been thinking the last few days about going to graduate school and I went over to the graduate school today and they said I had to take the GRE before I apply and I don't know anything about it. | Well, you know it's a test that's designed to predict whether or not a person will have success in graduate school. | Helper appropriately responds to the implied request for information. |
| Yeah, I've never done especially well on those. I took the SAT... did well enough to get in here, undergraduate. But, I don't even know if I could do well enough to get in, or even if I want to go, at this point. | So, you're really uncertain about several things, in addition to being curious about the GRE test itself. | Facilitative response. This kind of response will almost always elicit more information from the helpee (self-exploration). |
| Yeah, I'm wondering if I get into graduate school, if I really want to do that next year. | I suppose there are several things that you've thought about that you could do and right now you haven't narrowed it down to one thing. | Facilitative response—helps helpee clarify his options. |
| That's right. I do have a job possibility for next year if I want to go to work right after I get my bachelor's degree. But that's gonna mean moving away from here to a town where I don't know anybody. | It would be like... starting all over again and getting acquainted and getting used to a new location. | Facilitative response communicates the essence of the message from the helpee. |
| That's right and I've done that before. Boy, I know what that's like. | Pretty hard at first. | Facilitative response—empathy is apparent. |
| Yeah, we moved to five towns when I was in high school. My dad was transferred from one town to another and it seemed like every time I met some people and felt good about my friends, we had to move. | That must have been pretty upsetting. | Facilitative response—the helper perceives and communicates a surface feeling. |
| It was upsetting. In fact, I never really felt like I fitted in because when I moved into a town the groups were already established in the schools. It seemed like I was always an outsider. | But now you feel quite at home here and you hate to give that up. | Facilitative response. |

## Dialogue 2. (*Continued*)

| DON (Helpee) | RUSS (Helper) | DISCUSSION |
|---|---|---|
| Right, this is my fourth year. . . . | You'd like to make it last as long as you can. | Facilitative response. |
| Yeah, well I have friends here and I know the town and that makes a difference and that means something to me. | It's especially meaningful to you because it's something you've never had before. | Facilitative response. The helper is summarizing—using information that the helpee had given earlier in the interaction. Helper and helpee are beginning to put the pieces together without going beyond responding to the surface affect and content. |
| That's right, and I just wonder if I really want to go to graduate school next year or whether it's just the fact that I'm comfortable here and I have friends and for the first time I feel like I fit in somewhere. | So, it sounds like you are saying that it wouldn't be a sufficient reason for going to graduate school just so you could stay here in town. | Facilitative response— clarifies helpee's verbalization. |
| Not really, because it would mean another year when I'm not being very productive, not making any money. And I'm not sure if that's the right thing to do. I think if I had a *job* in this town next year, I think I'd be very happy. | As you see it, living here and working here next year would be the ideal situation. | Even though, as outlined below, the helper does not feel that this is the best option, he is willing to reflect the idea so that the helpee can see more clearly what he is saying. |
| Yeah, I think so. After four years I'm kind of tired of studying and taking tests and sitting in classes. It'd be nice to have a little break and work if I could stay here. Going away is really scary right now and I'm not sure if I'm willing to do it. | It just seems like you're saying that it would be impossible to ever duplicate the good things that you have here. | Facilitative response— the helper is attempting to capture the helpee's contentment with his present situation. |
| Well, I'll put it this way. It took almost four years to get where I am now, and to start all over is almost not an option for me right now. | It just seems impossible to start over again, and yet going to graduate school isn't what you want to do either. If you went to graduate school it would be because you were afraid to do something else, not because you really wanted to. | The helper used several pieces of information communicated earlier to make this response. The message is clear when the interaction is scrutinized that the decision to stay in school is considered for the wrong reasons. The helpee said this, but it took someone who was concerned enough to listen in order to clarify his real motives. |

### Dialogue 2. (*Continued*)

| DON (Helpee) | RUSS (Helper) | DISCUSSION |
|---|---|---|
| I think that's right. I was afraid that what you said was true, and now I'm pretty sure it is. | I think there are other options and one of them would be to develop your skills in meeting new situations so that it wouldn't have to take you as long to establish yourself in a new place as it took you here. | This response comes from the helper's expertise and/or life experiences. Since he is not able to follow through on the graduate school question because it is a cop-out, he makes a suggestion that has the potential of preparing Don for handling new situations more effectively. |
| You mean it's possible to learn something like that? | Yes, I think it is. | Appropriate helper response to helpee request for information. |
| In the long run that might be the best thing to do; at least it's worth a try. You know who I could see for that kind of thing? | Yes, there are groups in the student counseling center sponsored by the student affairs division which are helpful in that regard. I attended one of those when I was a sophomore. | Again, an appropriate response to a request for information. Since Don seems very interested in the idea, Russ self-discloses the fact that he had been involved in a similar group. |
| Did you? | Yeah. | The helpee is sort of in disbelief. When a presently well-functioning helper discloses that "he has been there too," it tends to give the helpee renewed hope. The helpee might think, "This person made it, so maybe I can make it." Self-disclosure can be a very potent dimension if used properly. |
| Did it help you? | I think it was probably one of the absolutely best things that happened to me here. | Appropriate response to helpee request for information. |
| Well, I didn't know that. I think I'll sure look into it. Do you have to have an appointment? | Oh, why don't you just give them a phone call and ask for information. They'll probably set up an appointment for you to talk to somebody. | Appropriate response to helpee request for information. |
| Okay, gee thanks for the information! | Sure! | Standard closing. |

# RESPONDING WITH FACILITATION

Behavioral Objective: The trainee should be able to write facilitative helper responses in a natural style at level 3.0 or above on the Global Scale.

Write facilitative responses for the following stimulus situations. Remember that not only the content but also the affect must be included in the response in order to be rated interchangeable.

## Helpee Situation 1

Student to student: "Why do they make us take biology for our degree when that has nothing at all to do with our area? I get the feeling they're just trying to torture us with these unrelated courses."

HELPER RESPONSE _____

_____

## Helpee Situation 2

Student to student: "I can't believe Dr. Watson waited until the week before classes end to assign this paper. Why don't we just refuse to do it and report him to the head of the department?"

HELPER RESPONSE _____

_____

## Helpee Situation 3

Teacher to teacher: "Our problems would be over if they would just give us some way to enforce discipline. That's why my class is so disorderly."

HELPER RESPONSE _____

_____

## Helpee Situation 4

Student to student: "I guess I just don't feel like a student any more after staying out of school for two years."

HELPER RESPONSE _____

_____

## Helpee Situation 5

Student to student: "I would like to stay here on weekends and date Mary, but my parents make me feel guilty if I don't go home. I hate to hurt their feelings, but I want to stay here."

HELPER RESPONSE _____

_____

## Helpee Situation 6

Student to student: "I don't really want to be a teacher. Mother is a teacher and I was expected to be one. I never had a choice. Should I change my major to something that I'm interested in?"

HELPER RESPONSE _____

_____

## Helpee Situation 7

Tenth grader to teacher: "Well, I guess John and I will get married this summer. He wants to so that he can move out of his house. I guess I won't be here next year."

HELPER RESPONSE _____

_____

## Helpee Situation 8

Student to student: "That Mary Smith is such a fake. She's the biggest put-on I've ever seen. What really makes me mad is that the guys fall for that!"

HELPER RESPONSE _____

_____

# IDIOSYNCRATIC CREDITS

One of the fundamental precepts of this communication model is the establishment of a base relationship through facilitative communication before action dimensions are used. An exception to this rule involves helpers who have what we call "idiosyncratic credit" with the helpee. Idiosyncratic credit means that the helpee grants privileges to a helper because of who or what the helper is.

There are four major reasons why idiosyncratic credit may be given to a particular helper

1. *Degrees, title, vocation.* Consider "labels" such as: doctor, president, judge, minister, attorney, coach, man-of-the-year, champion, palm reader. These all mean different things to different persons, but each of them commands respect from many persons. Because of respect, they have the opportunity to become "active" with the person who feels the respect.

2. *Common experience.* The phenomenon of giving credibility to and acting upon the suggestions of persons whose background is similar to one's own is well established and partially accounts for success of self-help groups such as A. A. and Synanon.

3. *Association.* Being part of a team or organization that is respected enhances the respect given its members. As a member of the education profession you are given credit for extensive expertise—you are granted privileges that a person outside the team does not have.

4. *Reputation.* Some persons, because of their perceptual skills and good sense, become known as persons whose advice is worth taking and discover, perhaps to their own surprise, that persons seek them out for their opinion. Some popular newspaper columnists, because of their acceptance by a wide readership, are often successful in giving advice abruptly and pointedly. If you were to say the same thing in a similar situation, you might find yourself in a lot of trouble! Thus, a response which would be level 2 from one person can have level 4 impact on a helpee when given by a person whose advice is deemed reputable. Idiosyncratic credits often make the difference in whether a response is level 2 or level 4.

Even though the base may initially be acknowledged, ultimately it must be *earned.* For example, you might go to a dentist unknown to you, on the strength of his/her credentials. You will grant him/her the authority *once* to apply his/her professional expertise—to drill or extract at his/her judgment—as a result of his/her idiosyncratic credits. But you will not return to him/her unless satisfied with his/her professional services. He/she must *earn* future opportunity to help you.

## THE EFFECTS OF THE USE OF QUESTIONS
## IN THE HELPING RELATIONSHIP

One of the most prevalent forms of communication employs the use of questions. This section is included in the manual so that educators can evaluate themselves on their use of questions and can learn more appropriate ways to communicate when indicated. First, let us consider when the use of questions is indicated in interpersonal communication.

# APPROPRIATE USE OF QUESTIONS

### To Obtain Identification Data or Objective Information

Data about the helpee may involve information required by the board of education or the school. General information forms are frequently completed on all helpees who seek agency assistance. Even though the information appears to be rather straightforward, some of it could be embarrassing to the helpee. For this reason the preferred method is to have the helpee complete the form to the extent that he/she is able before the helper checks it for completeness and accuracy. In many instances, open-ended questions that elicit spontaneous helpee self-disclosure may be preferred over direct questions that allow the helpee to weigh how he/she wants to answer the question—regardless of accuracy or authenticity—to please the helper most.

### To Clarify

When the helpee is being vague or evasive, a well-placed question may be useful for clarification. For instance, if a helpee is having difficulty describing the feeling, the educator may be able to offer a word in order to test an hypothesis. Specificity is especially important in defining a problem and in describing a plan of action or steps to be taken in problem solving. (This is discussed under the concreteness dimension in the following chapter.)

### To Pinpoint

There are occasions when educators must be very specific about the information they receive from the helpee. For example, when teachers are faced with a first aid situation they need to be very specific in the interaction. Direct questions are usually the best means for obtaining specificity of feedback in this case.

# INAPPROPRIATE USE OF QUESTIONS

Perhaps the greatest misuse of direct questions is the tendency to rely on them to carry on a conversation. The use of direct questions may have the following deleterious effects on the relationship between a helper and a helpee.

1. *Creates a dependency relationship.* The use of direct questions by helpers places helpees in a dependent relationship, and they are likely to become more dependent on the helper and less dependent upon themselves.

2. *Places responsibility for problem solving on the helper.* The use of direct questions places the responsibility for problem solving on helpers rather than on helpees where it ultimately must be if helpees are to solve their problems. (Exceptions to this general condition may exist when the helper must intervene on behalf of the helpee without the helpee's cooperation.)

3. *Reduces active involvement of the helpee in the solution of his/her problems.* When helpees depend on direct questioning of the helpers, helpees become "lazy" and do not actively engage in uncovering solutions to their own problems.

4. *Reduces the helpee's acceptance of responsibility for his/her behavior.* When helpees are not actively involved in the solution of their problems, they also do not assume responsibility for their behavior, but rather place blame on the "expert" who placed them in a dependent, uninvolved position.

5. *Creates a dependent/weak personality.* When helpers are able to give good advice to helpees without the helpees' active involvement in developing the plan, they may become very dependent on the expert helper and seek other experts rather than think for themselves. The other side of this problem is discussed in (4) above in which helpees may refuse to accept personal responsibility for their behavior.

6. *Reduces helpee self-exploration.* Overuse of direct questions tends to interfere with depth self-exploration by helpees since helpers have accepted that role. When asking questions, helpers control the direction in which the conversation moves. Particularly during self-exploration helpees know better than helpers what should be discussed. If helpees are given understanding and support, they will take the conversation where it needs to go at the fastest rate at which they can progress. This is more efficient than hit-or-miss probing by helpers.

7. *Produces invalid information.* The use of direct questions allows helpees to anticipate what helpers might prefer as an answer and, thus, they often produce what helpers seem to want to hear rather than what is, in fact, true.

8. *Produces unrealistic helpee expectations.* The overuse of direct questions places helpers in positions of experts where helpees expect solutions to their problems because they have patiently provided answers to the helpers. In counseling or psychotherapy interventions, developing these expectancies often leads to disappointment and disillusionment on the part of helpees.

9. *Produces helpee resentment.* Many questions asked by "helpers" are asked out of curiosity rather than because they have direct bearing on the situation. These probes generally create resentment within helpees. It is difficult to build an interaction around questions, because it is rare when helpers can ask more than a dozen relevant questions. Therefore the longer the interaction, the more likely that the questions will become progressively more irrelevant. (Facilitative responses *give* something—empathy, respect, and warmth—to helpees. They provide an atmosphere in which helpees are comfortable being themselves. In contrast, questions *demand* something from helpees and therefore may be threatening to them. Helpees may fear that they will be pushed into areas they are not ready to deal with and so respond only superficially or seek to shift the conversation to another topic.)

10. *Creates a "lazy," inattentive helper.* When helpers feel that they can always ask the helpee for clarification of a helpee statement or feeling, they often pay less attention to the helpee and thus miss many cues. In other words, they do not attend fully to the helpee and rely on the helpee to "help them out," thus placing themselves in the role of the helpee whom they are supposed to be helping. The extent to which the helper has to ask questions of the helpee is a benchmark of the degree to which the helper is in tune with the helpee or is, in fact, capable of helping the helpee. The greater the number of questions, the less likelihood that the helper can assist the helpee.

These ten conditions relate to the use of *direct* questions by a helper. Open-ended questions usually do not have the same effect because they encourage helpee involvement and self-exploration. Therefore, the potential helper should develop expertise in the use of open-ended questions and statements.

# Perceiving and Responding with Concreteness

Read 130-154

# 15

In this chapter you will learn how to use the scale for rating helper statements on the dimension of concreteness described in Chapter 2. As with previous scales, levels 1.0 and 2.0 are not helpful, level 3.0 is minimally helpful, and the appropriate use of level 4.0 is the most helpful method of communication that you will learn to use in this model (see Table 15.1.)

During the early stages of helping, helpers respond to concrete data by reinforcing high levels of concreteness in helpee statements. By responding with clear, concise, detailed statements regarding helpees' problems, helpees are reinforced in their attempts to clarify their own problems. They know the helpers are willing to discuss the problems in detail. This initial step—to reinforce self-exploration and problem exploration—is part of the general plan.

After a problem has been explored concretely, helpers begin to reinforce helpees for generalizing about their situation (lower levels of concreteness). This encourages helpees to explore more freely and broadly their "self" and their problem. To understand more fully, helpees must relate their specific concerns to other conscious and unconscious aspects of their lives. For example, suppose that Mary Jones, an administrator, knows she has a tendency to be racially prejudiced. It might be helpful for her to understand the origin of her prejudice, the types of situations where she is likely to act with bias, how her prejudices have made life simpler for her as well as how they have complicated it by interferring with her relating more fairly and fully. As she explores her problem she begins to gain a better perspective. She may come to realize that her parents have subtly passed on their prejudices to her and that she has not extended herself openly to blacks because of her deep-seated fears of being socially ostracized by her prejudiced friends.

During later stages of helping (action), helpers move back to high levels of concreteness. Helpees are now trying to choose specific alternatives so that they can take action. Helpers assist them in formulating specific goals and the means to achieve these goals. As helpers respond with specific alternatives,

## Table 15.1. CONCRETENESS SCALE

| 1.0 | 1.5 | 2.0 | 2.5 | 3.0 | 3.5 | 4.0 |
|---|---|---|---|---|---|---|
| The helper responds to the helpee's personally relevant feelings and experiences in abstract or vague terms, in a specific but inaccurate manner, or in a premature and hurtful fashion. | | The helper responds to the helpee's personally relevant emotions and situations in general or intellectual terms that do not incorporate the helpee's frame of reference. The helper does not focus on specific manifestations of helpee concerns. He/she may ask the helpee to be more specific without modeling specificity himself/herself. | | The helper responds to the helpee's personally relevant material in clear, specific, and concrete terms. He/she mostly centers his/her attention around most things that are personally important to the helpee. The helper accepts abstractions on the part of the helpee but models specificity. | | The helper responds fluently, directly, and quite thoroughly to specific concerns of the helpee and actively solicits specificity from the helpee. During the earlier stages this may involve asking for clarification of vague or abstract helpee statements. During later stages it may entail assisting the helpee to enumerate clear and definite alternatives that derive from the interaction, summarizing his/her newly acquired self-understanding, or outlining plans for future action. |

---

KEY WORDS—Concreteness Scale

Level 4.0—models and actively solicits specificity
Level 3.0—specific
Level 2.0—general
Level 1.0—vague, inaccurate, premature, hurtful

they also reinforce concrete suggestions of helpees. For example, on closer examination Mary Jones may find that her fears have been exaggerated. She may then practice constructively asserting herself with her prejudiced friends to reduce her own unwanted prejudices. She may plan to make more contacts with blacks in her school, expecting that, as she increases her knowledge of unique individuals, the less she will be inclined to overgeneralize.

## HELPEE CONCRETENESS

It is also important for the helper to be aware of concreteness of helpee statements. Communicating with helpees who are vague, abstract, or unusually intellectual is difficult. When the helpee shows low levels of concreteness, it is especially important for the helper to display high levels of concreteness in order to get the helpee to focus on specifics.

## ILLUSTRATION OF CONCRETENESS SCALE

### Helpee Situation

Chico Rodriguez is a nineteen-year-old high school senior. He and his parents moved to the United States from Puerto Rico three years ago. Quick-tempered and overly sensitive, Chico's position is one of "takin' nothin' from nobody." His teachers have made reasonable efforts towards accepting him but tire quickly of his hostile outbursts. School has been open for only three months and this is the fourth time Chico has been sent to speak with Dr. Beverly Brown, the principal. Chico says:

> "I just don't know what to do. Everybody says stay in school and get a good education. But these teachers don't give a damn whether you learn anything or not. They just come here to get their paychecks."

HELPER RESPONSES

Level 1.0: "You know as well as I do that there are a lot of dedicated teachers on my staff."

*Discussion:* This response is quite specific but inaccurate; it completely ignores the student's experiences. The principal appears to be more interested in defending her staff than she is in helping the student resolve his problem. It is highly unlikely that a helpee will use this type of response to self-explore a problem.

Level 1.0: "Well, as you know, each person is guaranteed the right to an education by our constitution. Our forefathers foresaw the importance of a good education too."

*Discussion:* This response is highly abstract, intellectual, and impersonal. It ignores the student's personal feelings and perceptions entirely. The helpee will feel misunderstood when the helper makes such a reply.

Level 1.0: "With such a hostile attitude I can clearly see why you are having trouble getting along with your teachers."

*Discussion:* The principal's response is specific, but such a blunt, insensitive, and punitive evaluation is almost sure to bring about an argument (in which case the helpee will try to defend his self-respect) or an abrupt termination of the discussion if not the relationship.

Level 2.0: "Things cannot always be to our liking. Why do you think your teachers feel the way they do?"

*Discussion:* This response relates to some of what the student has said, but in a general way. It rather communicates a lack of interest in hearing more about the particular personal concerns of the student regarding his educational situation. This type of response generally inhibits direct and personal communications; it does not facilitate self-exploration but tends gradually to bring the helpee's self-explorations to a halt.

Level 3.0: "You're in an awkward spot. You're fed up with your teachers' lack of concern but you're not sure how wise it would be to quit school."

*Discussion:* The principal describes clearly and concretely what she perceives as the student's most important areas of conflict and concern. When the helper models specificity of expression she minimally facilitates helpee self-exploration and self-understanding. As is evident in this reply, high levels of concreteness serve to sharpen empathic communications.

Level 4.0: "As you see it, the education you're receiving stinks; the teachers are more concerned about money than they are about you. What changes do you think could be made that would make school worth your while." (See discussion following the next 4.0 response.)

Level 4.0: "Sounds as if you're so disgusted with your teachers that you're thinking of quitting school. Do you see the situation as entirely hopeless? After all, what price might *you* have to pay if you don't finish high school?"

*Discussion:* In the 4.0 responses the principal directly and specifically deals with the emotions and intellectual material of the student. She invites the student to offer corrective suggestions (first 4.0 response) and to examine his attitudes more closely and consider future ramifications of his actions (second 4.0 response). When the helper is functioning at level 4.0 of concreteness, she accelerates the rate of helpee self-exploration and self-understanding.

# PERCEIVING CONCRETENESS

*Behavioral Objective: The trainee should be able to rate responses on the Concreteness Scale with an average discrepancy score of 0.5 or less.*

Rate each of the helper responses on the Concreteness Scale, putting the number (1.0, 1.5, 2.0, 2.5, 3.0, 3.5, or 4.0) in the blank to the left of the helper response.

## Helpee Situation 1

A college freshman at a state university is speaking with her roommate of two quarters. The girls have disclosed quite a few intimacies and get along fairly well.

"Well, on the one hand, I promised my folks that I wouldn't mess around with any drugs. On the other hand, I made that promise before I had been here and seen how popular grass is. It seems like a lot of fun, and from what I've heard it's really pretty safe."

HELPER RESPONSES

_____ 1. "When was the last time you spoke with your parents about this?"

_____ 2. "Aren't you a little old to be so hung up on what your parents think?"

_____ 3. "You're in a real jam. You want to be straight with your parents but you also want to get turned on."

_____ 4. "Conflicts between parents and their offspring are inevitable."

_____ 5. "If you had known then what you do now about drugs, you might not have made such a promise. How do you think your parents would respond to your change in attitude?"

Check the Answer Key at the end of the chapter for the correct ratings, and calculate your average discrepancy score by dividing the sum of the individual discrepancy scores by five. Review the ones you missed to learn why they are rated as they are, then proceed to Helpee Situation 2.

## Helpee Situation 2

Barbara is a twenty-two-year-old beginning teacher at an elementary school situated in a middle class neighborhood. A large number of black children from a nearby ghetto are bussed into the school. In her contact with the parents of these children Barbara has found many of them to be rather standoffish—if not hostile—towards her. As a child and adolescent, Barbara was frequently rejected by adult figures around her. Unfortunately, she still maintains a rather catastrophic attitude towards being rejected and is prone to overreact. Her self-image seems to depend more on what others think of her than on what she thinks of herself. Subsequently, Barbara tries to get people to like her by always being sweet, tender, overconforming, or playing fragile. Barbara is speaking with a close friend, Dan:

> "Don't get me wrong, I mean if the school board thinks it's a good idea for us to make home visits, then who am I to question it? But not everyone makes you feel at home. Some of the young black parents seem to be so unfriendly. I'm only interested in making things better for their kids" (voice cracks slightly and eyes get teary). "Why can't they be nice to me?"

HELPER RESPONSES

_____ 6. "New ways of doing things always seem to meet with resistance. I've never really fully understood this."

_____ 7. "You figure your intentions are to be helpful, but the young black parents don't seem to like you. Not being liked seems to hit you hard. Could this have anything to do with your growing up, Barbara?"

_____ 8. "You're so sensitive to not being liked that you'd fall over if a stranger said, 'Boo.' "

_____ 9. "There are any number of reasons why people are hostile to strangers. What specific reasons have you thought of?"

_____ 10. "You're doing what's expected of you by your superiors. But it sure hurts to be treated so coldly when you're only trying to help the students."

_____ 11. "Blacks today are searching for a clearer identity. They demand to be held in respect, and they're trying to respect themselves more. Black people are sick and tired of being led around on the white man's leash. Some of them are naturally going to distrust you just because of your color."

Calculate your average discrepancy score by dividing the sum of the individual discrepancy scores by six. Check your answers with the Answer Key at the end of the chapter.

## Helpee Situation 3

Alfred is a twenty-year-old college sophomore who lives in a residence hall for men. He is awkward and unskilled in most social settings. His style of dress and grooming are noticeably different from that of his peers; Alfred's appearance is about ten years behind the times. He is speaking with Stan, his undergraduate resident advisor. Stan is very popular with both the men and the women on campus. He is a drama major and is often cast in the leading role for local productions. Stan is sitting with a book in his lap; the door to his room is open.

"Well. . . you probably wanna know why I'm here. I mean. . . well, I guess you would. Why. . . uhm. . . well I have this problem. Yeah. . . uhm. . . it's not a . . . and this has been going on since I was. . . since I was a little boy. My parents, they. . . uh. . . they always told me I'd, well, you know, grow out of it but. . . I haven't. Well, it's. . . it's just always been hard for me. I mean, other guys could. . . uh. . . well, they could always do it, but. . . but not me. I can't even look at them, look them straight in the face. . . it's just so hard. I never could. . . uh. . . start a. . . a what you might call a . . . a conversation with a. . . well, with girls."

HELPER RESPONSES

_____ 12. "Alfred, can we talk about it tomorrow? I've got to go pick up my date now."

_____ 13. "All your life you've felt really up-tight around girls. It's rough to feel so different."

_____ 14. "This is a hard campus to meet girls on. A lot of guys in the dorm are having trouble getting weekend dates."

_____ 15. "I guess you really feel like an oddball. It looks easy for other guys to get to first base, but you doubt yourself so much you don't even get up to bat. I'd like to be your friend. How can I help?"

_____ 16. "Your bashfulness has cost you a lot. You'd like to learn how to rap with girls as other guys do. I've found some things that have worked well for me. Maybe I can share them with you. First, though, won't you tell me more about yourself?"

Calculate your average discrepancy score by dividing the sum of the individual discrepancy scores by five. Check your answers with the Answer Key at the end of the chapter.

# RESPONDING WITH CONCRETENESS

*Behavioral Objective: The trainee should be able to write helper responses in a natural style at level 3.0 on the Concreteness Scale.*

Read each helpee situation and try to pinpoint specific and personal concerns in the statements. Formulate your response and write it down as quickly as possible to retain the conversational style. Check your response against the criteria of a level 3.0 response on the Concreteness Scale. If your response is not a level 3.0, rework it to meet level 3.0 criteria.

## *Helpee Situation 1*

Bright and high-achieving high school sophomore to his counselor:

> "I really like my mechanical drawing classes, and I think I'd probably turn out to be a pretty good engineer. Then again, I really enjoy my volunteer work at the hospital. I do well in biology and chemistry, so I'd probably do quite well in nursing. Maybe I'll find some other. . . but, well, my father keeps telling me that I've got to hurry up and choose a career. I just don't know."

HELPER RESPONSE: _____

_____

## *Helpee Situation 2*

Your forty-four-year-old bachelor neighbor has invited you in for a cup of coffee. He is seated across the kitchen table from you, staring blankly into the coffee cup which he has been stirring silently for fifteen or twenty seconds. Finally, he says:

> "I went to see her last week. It's been about three years since my last visit, but mom was the same as always. The moment I went into her house I felt unwelcome as hell. They say 'time heals,' but it's not always true."

HELPER RESPONSE: _____

_____

137

## Helpee Situation 3

Susan is a polite, cooperative, sensitive, and relatively nonassertive nine-teen-year-old college sophomore majoring in elementary education. She is speaking with her faculty advisor, having just arranged an emergency meeting with him.

"We just got our assignments for student teaching and, well, I'm just so upset (eyes are red and appear watery). They've paired me up with the meanest and most insensitive teacher in the school. I had to work with her for field experience and it was just terrible. She embarrasses the kids, ridicules them; well, I've even seen her drag them across the room by their hair."

HELPER RESPONSE: _____

_____

### Answer Key

| Helpee Situation 1 | Helpee Situation 2 | Helpee Situation 3 |
|---|---|---|
| 1. 2.0 | 6. 1.0 | 12. 1.0 |
| 2. 1.0 | 7. 4.0 | 13. 3.0 |
| 3. 3.0 | 8. 1.0 | 14. 2.0 |
| 4. 2.0 | 9. 2.0 | 15. 4.0 |
| 5. 3.5 | 10. 3.0 | 16. 4.0 |
|  | 11. 2.5 |  |

# Perceiving and Responding with Genuineness

# 16

In this chapter you will learn how to use a scale for rating helper statements on the dimension of genuineness, described in Chapter 2. As with previous scales, levels 1.0 and 2.0 are not helpful, level 3.0 is minimally helpful, and the appropriate use of level 4.0 is the most helpful method of communication you will learn to use in this model (see Table 16.1).

## HELPER GENUINENESS

When you "have it all together," you are unified, integrated, or congruent, i.e., *genuine*. When you are genuine you are *being* the person you *are* from moment to moment. More specifically, genuineness refers to the extent to which you are consciously aware of and acceptant of your visceral feelings and accurately match appropriate verbal and nonverbal communications to them. The "appropriate" in the preceding sentence refers to the fact that in this model we are concerned with what might be more accurately labeled as *facilitative* genuineness. Thus, people who are integrated mean what they say and, at the deepest levels, say exactly what they feel, keeping in mind that they are trying to be helpful to the helpee.

Although genuineness is a complicated concept, we all tend to recognize it in an intuitive or commonsense manner. For example, each of us can quickly sense from the tone of voice, gestures, or mannerisms of some of the "actors" used in TV commercials that they are "playing a role." They are "putting on a facade" in saying things they don't feel. You do not experience the person; you experience his/her role.

Whenever we communicate from a state of incongruence between our feelings and our awareness of these feelings, we tend to send discrepant or contradictory messages. When the discrepancy is between awareness and communication we may think in terms of falseness and deceit. When the incongruence

## Table 16.1. GENUINENESS SCALE

| 1.0 | 1.5 | 2.0 | 2.5 | 3.0 | 3.5 | 4.0 |
|---|---|---|---|---|---|---|
| A response in which the helper uses his/her feelings to punish the helpee, or a response in which the helper's communications are clearly unrelated to what other cues indicate he/she is feeling. There is considerable incongruence between his/her feelings and his/her verbal and/or nonverbal expressions. The helper may be defensive (unaware of his/her feelings), or quite false and deceitful (communicating feelings that he/she is plainly not experiencing). | | A response in which the helper's communications are slightly unrelated to what other cues indicate he/she is feeling. There is incongruence between his/her feelings and his/her verbal and/or nonverbal expressions. He/she responds according to some preconceived role. | | The helper demonstrates no incongruence between his/her expressions and his/her feelings. He/she gives a controlled expression of feelings which facilitate the relationship, refraining from expressing feelings which could impede the relationship. | | The helper is spontaneous and dependably real. His/her verbal and nonverbal messages, whether they be positive or negative, are congruent with how he/she feels. In the event of hurtful responses, he/she communicates these constructively, in his/her effort to open up new areas of inquiry. |

---

KEY WORDS—GENUINENESS SCALE

Level 4.0—spontaneous; fully congruent
Level 3.0—controlled expression
Level 2.0—role played
Level 1.0—punitive; defensive; deceitful

is between visceral experience and awareness we may think in terms of defensiveness or denial of awareness. In either case, it will be harder for others to "know where they stand" with us. Eventually, we may be perceived as being untrustworthy. When you are genuine, you use no facade to disguise how you feel, and there is no question as to whether or not you are aware of how you truly feel. You are dependably real.

## ASSESSING THE GENUINENESS LEVEL

It is important for the helper to assess the level of genuineness of the helpee. Helpees who are protecting themselves with facades and elaborate roles are difficult to assist. However, the helper who, over a period of time, consistently offers high levels of the conditions of human nourishment, is likely to increase the genuineness of the helpee. But, when the helper and helpee retreat to the safety and deadness of their roles, very little of value can occur.

## ILLUSTRATION OF GENUINENESS SCALE

The helpee situation below illustrates the four levels of the Genuineness Scale. Ratings are based on the Genuineness Scale alone. The responses might be rated differently on other dimensions.

### Helpee Situation

Jeremie is a husky ninth grader, the oldest of six children. He and his family are trying to make a living from a small farm located on the outskirts of a metropolitan area. His parents have always been poor, proud, and ruggedly independent. Jeremie attends school in a middle-class neighborhood quite a distance from his home. A small group of male students at his school regularly taunt him because of his background. Jeremie tries hard to ignore them but does not always succeed. School has been in session for four months and Jeremie has been in five fistfights. He has been victorious in each of these battles and has received his parents' support in each instance. His teacher is basically a rather shy and nonassertive person. Uncomfortable with the open expression of hostility, she has written a number of letters to Jeremie's parents requesting that they, in essence, teach him how to keep his hands to himself. Jeremie's father finally decides he's had enough and phones the principal, Mr. Scott. Unfortunately, Mr. Scott has only been in his position for two weeks and is totally ignorant in regard to the problem.

"This is Luther McCain and I'm the father of Jeremie McCain. I wanna get one thing straight with you, mister. I'm sick and tired of you do-gooders tryin' to tell me how to raise my boy! I want him to grow up and respect hisself and make others respect him. I ain't takin kindly to you tryin' to make him a sissy."

HELPER RESPONSES

Level 1.0: "Well, I'm certainly most interested in hearing more about it" (as the principal holds the telephone receiver away from his ear, positions it so his assistant can hear, smiles sarcastically, and begins to open his daily mail).

*Discussion:* Clearly the principal has little real concern for Mr. McCain; he is treating his problem by condescendingly making light of it and withdrawing from it. Mr. McCain is deprived of vital nonverbal cues relating to the principal's true feelings, subsequently, he may be duped. If Mr. Scott continues to perpetuate the fraud, Mr. McCain will probably not be fooled for long.

Level 1.0: "Now just a minute sir! I've been on this job for just two weeks. I'm not responsible for anything that happened before my arrival."

*Discussion:* The principal begins by refusing to accept the parent's manner of presentation; he tries to "put him in his place." Then he defensively tries to absolve himself from any *present* responsibilities to Mr. McCain and his son by pointing out that he is a new arrival and has no obligations to them for the past. Mr. McCain is quite embittered to begin with. But after hearing responses like these from the principal, his frustration is likely to increase. How might he then feel and what might he then be inclined to do?

Level 2.0: "As the principal of this school I assure you that I'll do all I can to help you."

*Discussion:* The principal cannot be faulted too much. After all, he is reading from the right script, isn't he? What he is saying is surely quite socially acceptable. Notice, however, that Mr. Scott, by omission, is not involving himself with the emotional experiences that Mr. McCain is sharing. By retreating to the safety of a fixed role, Mr. Scott may further alienate Mr. McCain over a period of time.

Level 3.0: "You're obviously fed up with people interfering with your family affairs. I find myself in an awkward spot, though; I've only been in this school for two weeks and I'm not familiar with your son's situation."

*Discussion:* The principal is congruent in his expression. He is, however, hesitant to directly express how he is feeling in response to Mr. McCain. In addition, although Mr. Scott may be favorably disposed towards helping children, he makes no reference to his future intentions towards Jeremie. Helpers who respond to helpees at this level are usually seen as real and trustworthy. Though the helpee may sense that you are withholding some of your deeper feelings, he knows that he can trust what you have communicated. Helpees are inclined to gradually lay aside their defenses as the helper continues to show that his intentions are constructive and that he himself is not afraid to relate openly.

Level 4.0: "You very much resent anyone trying to tell you how to bring up your son, but frankly I'm a little uncomfortable. I want to help Jeremie grow strong too, but I'm new here and I don't even know who Jeremie is" (as Mr. Scott's verbalizations change in unison with his emotions, his voice inflections are appropriate).

*Discussion:* Mr. Scott withholds nothing from Mr. McCain. He is genuinely himself as he responds without hesitation and says exactly what he is thinking and feeling. As Mr. McCain does not appear to like "beating around the bush," he will no doubt appreciate Mr. Scott's directness and authenticity. Both men will probably waste little time in getting to the root of Jeremie's school adjustment problems. Helpers who strive to be deeply and constructively genuine work toward a fully sharing relationship. They fully understand the self-destructive behaviors of themselves and others and work toward the reduction or elimination of such patterns. Such helpers are maximally effective in their efforts to promote helpee growth and/or problem resolution. Their credibility simply makes their impact more potent.

## PERCEIVING GENUINENESS

*Behavioral Objective: The trainee should be able to rate helper responses with an average discrepancy score of 0.5 or less.*

Rate each of the helper responses on the Genuineness Scale, putting the number (1.0, 1.5, 2.0, 2.5, 3.0, 3.5, or 4.0) in the blank to the left of the helper response.

### Helpee Situation 1

Laura Hill is a twenty-four-year-old fifth grade teacher. Although she knows her subject matter well, she knows little about good classroom management. The assistant principal and several faculty members have been working with her, but progress is slow. At present, she is in her classroom awaiting the arrival of the state inspection team. She alternates between biting her nails, straightening her suit, glancing at the doorway, aligning desks, and reminding the students to be well behaved. A student says to her: "Mrs. Hill, aren't you nervous with the state inspection team coming to watch our class this morning?"

HELPER RESPONSES

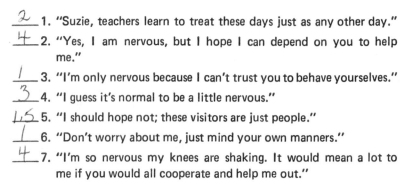

___2___ 1. "Suzie, teachers learn to treat these days just as any other day."

___4___ 2. "Yes, I am nervous, but I hope I can depend on you to help me."

___1___ 3. "I'm only nervous because I can't trust you to behave yourselves."

___3___ 4. "I guess it's normal to be a little nervous."

___4.5___ 5. "I should hope not; these visitors are just people."

___1___ 6. "Don't worry about me, just mind your own manners."

___4___ 7. "I'm so nervous my knees are shaking. It would mean a lot to me if you would all cooperate and help me out."

Calculate your average discrepancy score by dividing the sum of the individual discrepancy scores by seven. Check your answers with the Answer Key at the end of the chapter.

## Helpee Situation 2

There has been a considerable amount of name calling, quarreling, and physical violence among the students at Springs Elementary. Much of this appears to be based on socioeconomic class differences. Deeply concerned with student and community welfare, the principal recently got together with her faculty and several volunteer members from the community. They made plans for a school/community supper to be held on a Thursday evening. Students were asked to tell their parents, friends, and neighbors, invitations were sent home, posters were placed around town, and announcements were made on the radio.

It is the night of the dinner and most of the professional and paraprofessional staff are in attendance. Although there are over 350 students in the school, only twelve interested citizens from the community have come. The principal is sitting with a small group of faculty and parents. Usually quite talkative and gregarious, she has been rather quiet and serious. She glances regularly around the room noticing the numerous empty chairs. Midway through the meal a parent says to the principal, "How do you feel about the small turnout tonight?"

HELPER RESPONSES

| 8. (Speaking briskly) "Well, I'm sure the people who didn't show up here tonight had a good reason for not coming. You've got to remember that they have other obligations."

_2_ 9. (Changing her facial expression to now appear undaunted) "In my line of work you learn to take such things in stride."

_4_ 10. "I'm happy you're here (smiles warmly) but, frankly (face becomes serious), I'm deeply disappointed. Everyone worked so hard to make this a big success."

_+ ?._ 11. (Smiling and speaking jovially) "Well, the food is good and the service has been excellent. Eat up everyone, there's plenty more where this came from."

_4_ 12. (Speaking slowly and with appropriate intonation) "I'm sad— I was really looking forward to a big turnout. I keep looking around and wondering what went wrong."

_3_ 13. "Pretty bad."

Calculate your average discrepancy score by dividing the sum of the individual discrepancy scores by six. Check your answers using the Answer Key at the end of the chapter.

## Helpee Situation 3

On Monday, Miss Carter gave her fourth graders a brief homework assignment to be handed in on Tuesday. John has failed to bring in the work on three consecutive days. Each day he has verbalized the same apology and good intentions: "I'm sorry, I forgot my homework. I won't do it again. I'll bring it tomorrow."

HELPER RESPONSES

_1_ 14. "You've said that day after day. You're just trying to see how far you can push me before I lose my cool. Well, this is it! You're going to the principal now."

hiding behind role _2_ 15. "Teachers can't allow students just to keep putting off their work. It's time you brought your assignment in."

_4_ 16. "You're finding it difficult to remember to bring in your work, and I'm finding it difficult to be patient."

_1_ 17. "You'd better stop lying to me and bring it in tomorrow if you know what's good for you!"

_3_ 18. "John, you've told me that for three days. I want to believe you, but it gets harder each day."

_2_ 19. "If you don't bring in your homework tomorrow, you will do it before you leave school."

Calculate your average discrepancy score by dividing the sum of the individual discrepancy scores by six. Check your answers using the Answer Key at the end of the chapter.

# RESPONDING WITH GENUINENESS

*Behavioral Objective: The trainee should be able to write helper responses at level 3.0 on the Genuineness Scale, in a natural style.*

Read the helpee situation and formulate your response as though you were speaking to the helpee. Write it down as quickly as possible to retain the conversational style. Check your responses against the criteria of a level 3.0 response on the Genuineness Scale. If your response is not a level 3.0 or better, rework it to meet level 3.0 criteria.

## Helpee Situation 1

Marvin, an eighth-grade student, stops to talk to you (his teacher) after class. Marvin is not a popular student with his peers or other teachers. He is unfriendly, distrustful, and apparently convinced that others are "out to get him." You understand and accept Marvin's way of interacting with his world but realize that he will not be able to satisfy his own needs adequately unless he changes his style. You have always tried to show a sincere and constructive interest in him. You are trying hard to show yourself to be worthy of his trust and friendship. John says to you: "I don't think you like me. I've been doing my best, and you've been giving me low grades anyhow. It wouldn't be so bad if you didn't embarrass me in class. You call on me when you know I don't have the answers."

HELPER RESPONSE _____

_____

## Helpee Situation 2

Sam, an eleventh grader, has been in two of your classes during his high school career. You know him well and he respects you a great deal. For the past year he has talked a lot about going to an Ivy League college. Sam is an average high school student, and you don't think he would stand a chance of being accepted by an Ivy League school. Finally, he asks you the big question: "I'd like to go to Princeton. Do you think that would be a good school for me?"

HELPER RESPONSE _____

_____

## Helpee Situation 3

Mrs. Jenson is a forty-five-year-old teacher on your staff (you are a high school principal), and her work has always been quite satisfactory. She maintains good discipline in the classroom, is competent in her subject matter, and has a good delivery of the material to the students. However, when it comes to knowing her personally, you're at a loss. Mrs. Jenson has always presented herself to you in a most professional manner. After receiving an emergency phone call, she rushes up to you sobbing, "Oh my God, I just can't believe it! I just can't believe it! When I left him this morning he told me he was feeling so much better. The doctor said he looked good. Oh Lord, how can he be dead?"

HELPER RESPONSE _____

_____

## Answer Key

| *Helpee Situation 1* | *Helpee Situation 2* | *Helpee Situation 3* |
|---|---|---|
| 1.  2.0 | 8.   1.0 | 14.  1.0 |
| 2.  4.0 | 9.   2.0 | 15.  2.0 |
| 3.  1.0 | 10.  4.0 | 16.  4.0 |
| 4.  3.0 | 11.  4.0 | 17.  1.0 |
| 5.  1.5 | 12.  4.0 | 18.  3.0 |
| 6.  1.0 | 13.  3.0 | 19.  2.0 |
| 7.  4.0 | | |

# Perceiving and Responding with Self-Disclosure

# 17

In this chapter you will learn how to use a scale for rating helper statements on the dimension of self-disclosure as described in Chapter 2. Self-disclosure at level 1.0 is not helpful. Level 2.0 is not helpful. Level 3.0 is minimally helpful, and the appropriate use of level 4.0 is the most helpful method of self-disclosure that you will learn to use in this model (see Table 17.1). (In the following chapter, a case study is presented to illustrate the combined use of the transition dimensions of concreteness, genuineness, and self-disclosure.)

## HELPER SELF-DISCLOSURE

In order for helpees to get the most out of a helping relationship eventually, they need to know who the helpers really are so that they can relate to them fully. Once the helpers have established a good basic relationship with helpees, it is appropriate for helpers to reveal themselves—and their uniqueness as persons—to helpees. High-level helpers will genuinely and concretely reveal themselves through a past or present or future frame of reference. For example, they may share where they have been, what they have been through, and how they got through it; why they behaved as they did and why they behave as they do; what attitudes they used to hold and those they hold now; what they used to value and what they value now; what goals they used to have for themselves and what goals they have for themselves now. Effective helpers do not meet their helpees with a mask; they are willing to be known as unique human beings and are easy to get to know.

## ILLUSTRATION OF THE
## SELF-DISCLOSURE SCALE

The helpee situation on page 150 illustrates the four levels of the Self-Disclosure Scale. Ratings are based on the Self-Disclosure Scale alone. They might be rated differently on other dimensions or on the Global Scale.

## Table 17.1. SELF-DISCLOSURE SCALE

| 1.0 | 1.5 | 2.0 | 2.5 | 3.0 | 3.5 | 4.0 |
|---|---|---|---|---|---|---|
| The helper actively remains detached from the helpee and reveals nothing about himself/herself or discloses something about himself/herself to meet his/her own needs exclusively. The helper changes the focus of the interaction to himself/herself, resulting in the helpee feeling overwhelmed and thinking that the helper is not interested in him/her, or becoming disillusioned with the helper's ability to help. | | The helper does not volunteer personal information about himself/herself. He/she may answer direct questions, but only hesitantly and briefly. The helpee, then, only gets to know exactly what he/she asks about the helper. | | The helper reveals his/her ideas, attitudes, and experiences relevant to the helpee's concerns, in a general fashion; he/she reveals his/her uniqueness as a surface level. Therefore his/her uniqueness as a person is not communicated. The helpee, then, knows only a little about the helper's ideas or experiences that may be useful in dealing with his/her own problem. | | The helper freely and spontaneously volunteers information about his/her own personal ideas, experiences, and feelings when they are relevant to the helpee's interests and concerns. These may involve a degree of risk taking on the part of the helper. The helper reveals his/her uniqueness as a person. |

KEY WORDS—Self-Disclosure Scale

Level 4.0—volunteers specific material
Level 3.0—volunteers general material
Level 2.0—does not volunteer
Level 1.0—withholds, overwhelms

149

## Helpee Situation

Benny is one of the brightest, friendliest, and most verbal eighth graders in the school. Unfortunately, he is also one of the most awkward. He regularly knocks over trays in the lunchroom, bumps into people anywhere near him, and drops his books in the hallways and classrooms. Benny does his best work in English, and he has learned to like and admire his English teacher, Mr. Goldman. Mr. Goldman is tall, slim, and athletic looking. Benny has stayed after class to talk with him.

> "Gee, Mr. Goldman, you know, whenever they pick sides on the playground, I'm always about the last one to be chosen. All the kids know I'm clumsy and can't help their team out much, if any. It's really a bummer. I like to play, but they're just too good for me. Around my neighborhood I'm the biggest guy and they all want me to play, even though I'm clumsy. But here I don't have a chance. What do you think I should do?"

HELPER RESPONSES

Level 1.0: "I don't really have any idea. Lots of people get left out of things."

*Discussion:* The helper avoids giving any personal information.

Level 1.0: "I've been a loner most of my life too. People usually don't like me and that's just fine with me. Who wants friends anyhow?"

*Discussion:* This self-disclosure can be overwhelming to the helpee.

Level 2.0: "You may need to get some coaching so you can play better. Maybe your dad could help you improve."

*Discussion:* The helper has answered the helpee's question but volunteers no personal information. The helpee doesn't know if the helper has experienced a similar situation, nor does he have any idea of the helper's personal reaction to the problem.

Level 2.0: "You feel it's not fair for them to choose you last."

*Discussion:* This is a response to the helpee's feeling. It gives no clues as to the helper's reactions or ideas.

Level 3.0: "At one time I felt left out at school too. I'm not sure that the way I solved the problem will work for you. Would you like to tell me some more about the whole thing?"

*Discussion:* The helper volunteers personal information in general terms. The information offered is relevant to the helpee's problem and keeps the focus of the interaction on the helpee.

Level 4.0: "You know, when I was in the eighth grade, no one wanted me on their softball team. It took me a long time to get over that. It sounds like you're experiencing some of the same kind of disappointment I did at your age. Maybe we can work this out together."

*Discussion:* The helper is freely himself. The helpee can see him as a unique individual because the helper has disclosed himself in concrete terms. The helper has acknowledged that he shared the same kind of experience as the helpee and also expressed the uniqueness of his experience without distracting the helpee from his own personal concerns.

## PERCEIVING SELF-DISCLOSURE

Behavioral Objective: The trainee should be able to rate helper responses on the Self-Disclosure Scale with an average discrepancy score of 0.5 or less.

Rate each of the helper responses on the Self-Disclosure Scale, putting the number (1.0, 1.5, 2.0, 2.5, 3.0, 3.5, or 4.0) in the blank to the left of the helper response.

### Helpee Situation 1

Janie and Cheryl are doing their student teaching in the same high school. They have had three courses together in the College of Education and have therefore become acquainted. Cheryl says to Janie:

"What was the idea of butting in on my class today? I can handle Jerry by myself. I knew he was fooling around, and I was just waiting until he was in so deep he couldn't lie his way out again."

HELPER RESPONSES

_____ 1. "I knew what I was doing. If you let that little runt get too far ahead of you, you'll never be able to keep him in line. I've got an understanding with that boy, and I know he won't give you trouble again."

_____ 2. "My meddling with your class has really made you angry, especially since you know what you are going to do with Jerry."

_____ 3. "I know you're angry. I've had people interfere in my classes, too, and it really gets me mad."

_____ 4. "I acted very foolishly. Sometimes I'm just so eager to help, I run out of patience. I'm really sorry."

_____ 5. "I'm awfully sorry I stuck my nose into your affairs. I've got a bad habit of doing things like that. I hope you'll forgive my intrusion."

_____ 6. "How can you be so sure you were going to be so effective with Jerry?"

_____ 7. "I realized I was out of line as soon as I corrected Jerry, but it was too late. I appreciated your not saying anything in class. If that had been me I would have blown up on the spot."

Calculate your average discrepancy score by dividing the sum of the individual discrepancy scores by seven. Check your answers using the Answer Key at the end of the chapter.

## Helpee Situation 2

Bobby, age seven, did not have a very happy year as a first grader. His teacher was dull, strict, and unfriendly. He left school in June, never wanting to return again. However, over the summer vacation, his play-mates have been telling him what a great teacher they had for the second grade. She was friendly, warm, enthusiastic, and made school fun. Bobby decided to give school one last chance. On the first day of school he walked into the classroom and found his teacher to be the friendly lady the kids had been telling him about. With a big smile on his face, he exclaimed: "Boy, am I happy to be in your class!"

HELPER RESPONSES

_____ 8. "Oh?"

_____ 9. (Smiling warmly and touching Bobby's shoulder gently) "Gee, I'm so happy to hear you say that."

_____ 10. "You're really glad I'm your teacher instead of someone else."

_____ 11. "It really makes me feel great to hear you say that."

_____ 12. "You're lucky to have me. I'm one of the few teachers in this school who knows how to keeps kids in line."

_____ 13. (Hugging Bobby) "Gee, I feel so good that you seem to like me."

Calculate your average discrepancy score by dividing the sum of the individual discrepancy scores by six. Check your answers using the Answer Key at the end of the chapter.

## RESPONDING WITH SELF-DISCLOSURE

Behavioral Objective: The trainee should be able to write helper responses in a natural style at level 3.0 on the Self-Disclosure Scale.

Read the helpee situation and formulate your response as though you were speaking to the helpee. Write it down as quickly as possible to retain the conversational style. Check your response against the criteria of a level 3.0 response on the Self-Disclosure Scale. If it is not level 3.0 or better, rework it to meet level 3.0 criteria.

## Helpee Situation 1

A teacher and principal are having a cup of coffee together in the teacher's lounge. There are just four days left in the school year. The teacher says, smiling:

> "Relief is in sight, but (more seriously) I don't know what I'm going to do this summer. Part of me wants to do nothing but relax and recuperate, and part of me wants to take some course work at the college."

HELPER RESPONSE _____

_____

## Helpee Situation 2

Art is a sophomore at a state university. He lives in a residence hall on campus but has come home for the weekend. He is speaking with his father.

> "You know, Dad, I got an F in chemistry last week, but I just can't make myself study. I piddle the time away in my dorm room, or wax the car, or just read magazines, even though I've got another test coming up. I want to do well, but I just can't seem to get down to work."

HELPER RESPONSE _____

_____

## Helpee Situation 3

A college junior who is a newlywed relates her feelings to a female friend.

> I'd really like to quit school and have more time with my husband. He's in his last year of law school and says he can study better when I'm around. I could always finish up school later. My folks, on the

other hand, keep bugging me. They've sacrificed a lot to put me through school. I'd hate to disappoint them after all they've done for me."

HELPER RESPONSE _____

_____

## Helpee Situation 4

A young divorcee with two children is speaking with one of her closest personal friends.

"I met this guy in a lounge a couple of weeks ago. We've seen a lot of each other, but every time we go out together—well—he's got his hands all over me. I like him a lot, but he's—well—I just can't tell if he's sincere, he's just so smooth. I really want to please him, but I don't want to play the part of a fool."

HELPER RESPONSE: _____

_____

### Answer Key

| Helpee Situation 1 | | Helpee Situation 2 | |
|---|---|---|---|
| 1. | 1.0 | 8. | 1.0 |
| 2. | 2.0 | 9. | 4.0 |
| 3. | 3.0 | 10. | 2.0 |
| 4. | 4.0 | 11. | 3.5 |
| 5. | 4.0 | 12. | 1.0 |
| 6. | 2.0 | 13. | 4.0 |
| 7. | 4.0 | | |

# A Case Study Illustrating the Use of Concreteness, Genuineness, and Self-Disclosure

# 18

During the spring, Mrs. Benedetto and her seventeen-year-old son Tony moved from Philadelphia to a small town in southern Florida. Shortly after Tony entered the local high school as a sophomore, he tried out for the varsity baseball team. At first, the coach thought it was sheer luck. But as Tony showed that he could consistently hit the home run ball, the coach realized what perfect timing and awesome power Tony had. Even without a Tony Benedetto, the coach had managed to put together a team who, for four years in a row, had brought home the state championship. With Tony's help, a fifth was virtually assured. Since the townspeople had come to identify closely with the success of "our boys," Tony had the potential of becoming a local hero.

However, after several weeks in school, it became quite obvious that Tony was somewhat of a misfit. While most of the students were rather conservative in their dress, Tony's usual outfit consisted of a pair of engineer boots with horseshoe cleats, dirty jeans, and an old denim jacket with the sleeves cut off at the shoulders. His muscular arms were covered with a variety of tattoos, most of which appeared to have been amateurishly inked in. Tony appeared to trust no one with his personal possessions. He refused to loan pens, pencils, or paper to others, and always seemed to be keeping an eye on his books whenever he was out of his seat. The obscenities he frequently used were "eye openers" for most of his peers—and for some of the staff. Of more immediate concern, however, was Tony's quick temper and tendency to physically intimidate others if they asked him personal questions about himself or his family.

The coach could not attribute all of Tony's adjustment problems to the fact that he was possibly feeling somewhat insecure in his new environment. But before he explored his intuitions, the coach thought it best that he first gather more data about Tony. He spoke with a number of Tony's teammates, and they agreed that Tony seemed to be a basically nice guy with a few quirks. His classroom instructors reported that he did his schoolwork and was earning B's and C's; they also noted his maladaptive patterns of dress, speech, and aggression.

Based on his personal experience of Tony and on the information he had gathered from others, the coach judged that Tony really did want to be accepted by his peers and to achieve well in school. He guessed that Tony was simply using certain social adjustment mechanisms which may have been useful in a former setting but which now prevented him from meeting his own needs and desires satisfactorily. The coach assumed that he had developed a good rapport with Tony and that Tony trusted and respected him. He also estimated that Tony was bright enough to appreciate that different environments call for somewhat different patterns of behavior in the satisfaction of one's needs.

One afternoon, following a practice game, the coach asked Tony to stop by his office. They talked for a short while about how the team was shaping up. Then the dialogue continued in the following manner.

Coach: "Tony, I'm interested in how you're doing, coming to a new school and all. Your ball playing is tops, and when I spoke with your teachers they told me you're doing well in your classwork. What part of Philadelphia are you from?"

Tony: "South Philly."

Coach: "How were things in school there?"

Tony: "Oh, I did all right."

Coach: "Your grades were pretty good there too?"

Tony: "Yeah, about the same as here."

Coach: "You got along pretty well with the other students?"

Tony: "Yeah, with the ones who went to *my* school."

Coach: "I guess there were a lot of gangs in your area, huh?"

Tony: "Sure were."

Coach: "A lot of fights?"

Tony: "Yeah, especially between the gangs from different schools."

Coach: "You had to be tough just to get by, huh?"

Tony: "Well, you had to be tough if you wanted to get ahead."

Coach: "Tony, I'd like to see you be happy here at school and in the community. Yet, I've got a feeling that maybe you don't quite understand how the kids are down here. In the school you used to go to you hit it off pretty well with the other students because you thought and behaved like they did. You knew you fitted in."

Tony: "Okay, coach, what's your point?"

Coach: "Well, some of your old ways probably will make it harder for you to get along and find friends here."

Tony: "You mean like the way I dress?"

Coach: "That's one example. But Tony, I'm most concerned about your temper. I had a bad temper when I was your age, and it got me into a lot of trouble."

Tony: "Yeah, coach, but what do you really know about living in the streets?"

Coach: "Well, in Baltimore where I grew up, life wasn't a piece of cake. I don't know if you do, Tony, but when I went to school most of us carried knives or dog chains. I've heard that you've threatened to carve up a few students you've tangled with. Such threats are a part of life where you and I came from, but not here. The kids in this town get upset at that kind of talk. They really don't understand it. If you keep it up, they'll probably be afraid to be your friends."

Tony: "Maybe they're just prejudiced against Northerners or Italians."

Coach: "There might be a few that are, but most of them aren't. Prejudices like that just aren't as popular among kids today. They're a lot easier on each other than your parents were on one another."

Tony: "I don't know what to say right now."

Coach: "Well, do your parents like it here?"

Tony: (Drops head and hesitates) "I never knew my father, but my mom likes it here a lot. She says we're gonna stay here for a long time."

Coach: "I'm sorry you had to make it without a father. That can be a bummer. Has your mother found a good job yet?"

Tony: "Yeah, she's gonna be a disc jockey for a radio station here in town."

Coach: "How do you feel about that?"

Tony: "Mom's worked crummy jobs all her life. She went to night school for two years to learn this new job."

Coach: "Then I guess you're pretty proud of her."

Tony: "Sure am. She's quite a lady!"

Coach: "Well, it looks as though this will be your school for the next couple of years then."

Tony: "Yeah, I know, but why do you keep trying to change me?"

Coach: "Seems to me that you have two choices. You can change some things about yourself, become a big baseball champion, and have lots of people wanting to be your friends. Or you can make no adjustments to your new environment, refuse to fit into the way young people are around here, and have few or no friends."

Tony: (Tony stares at the coach for a moment. Then he gazes out the office window at the kids playing on the ballfield. He appears to be in deep thought.)

Coach: "Tony, if I didn't think you had a lot going for you, I wouldn't speak to you like I'm doing. But you're a likeable young man with a good mind and a strong and agile body. You seem to be a pretty sensitive person, so I think you've gone a little overboard."

Tony: (Dumbly) "What do you mean?"

Coach: "Oh, come on Tony! I'm leveling with you, how about you doing the same?"

Tony: "Okay, maybe you're right, maybe I don't have to be so touchy."

Coach: "That's the way I see it, Tony. Most of the kids here are not going to try and steal your things. Neither are they going to try to hurt you or embarrass you. The kids say they like you but that you're sort of prickly."

Tony: "Well, I'll think about it."

Coach: "Fair enough, Tony. I hope I didn't sound like I was preaching (smiles warmly); I get a little carried away when I really like somebody."

Tony: (After about an hour, Tony returns to the coach's office, takes a large folded knife out of his pocket and hands it to the coach) "Here coach, I won't be needing this anymore."

Coach: (Refusing to take it) "I'll tell you what, Tony. Most of the men around here go fishing on the weekends. How about you and me taking a little trip to my favorite bass lake tomorrow? (Tony smiles). You can bring your fishing knife with you, okay?"

Tony: (Tony puts it back in his pocket and firmly extends a handshake to the coach) "It's a deal, Coach!"

## Epilogue

Before going home that day the coach met with three of the more popular players on the team. He pointed out that Tony had come from a tough school up north and that he had formed a thick shell around himself for protection. The coach explained that Tony did not know exactly how young men were expected to act in such a small town setting. He asked the players to have patience with Tony and to do what they could to help him learn new ways of getting along with others. The coach then thanked them for their time, saying that he believed that they could be of significant help and that their efforts would be appreciated. As the weeks went by, Tony continued to progress in his social adjustment. He gradually changed his manner of dress, began sharing his personal possessions, cut down on his lewd language (especially around the girls and his teachers), and no longer lost his temper when people asked him personal questions. Although he remained somewhat hesitant to talk about his past, he was not offended when someone made inquiries in this area. By the end of the summer, the team had won another state championship and Tony was elected captain for the following year. Just prior to this announcement, Tony had had his last tattoo removed; it had read, "Born to lose."

# Perceiving and Responding with Confrontation

# 19

In earlier chapters you were introduced to transition dimensions of concreteness, genuineness, and self-disclosure. You learned that when you moved to additive levels on these dimensions, i.e., included elements in your response that had not been part of the helpee's statement, you had to draw upon your own experiences. In doing this you did not remain entirely nonevaluative or unconditional with the helpee. You can risk being evaluative (judgmental or conditional), but only when you have built a strong relationship with the helpee through repeated use of the facilitative dimensions of empathy, respect, and warmth.

Now you are going to incorporate into your repertoire of skills two additional dimensions that involve being evaluative: confrontation and immediacy of relationship. These dimensions are referred to as *action dimensions* because it is through their implementation that the helpee's action toward problem resolutions frequently is generated. Figure 2.1 in Chapter 2 illustrates this process.

In studying this chapter you will learn to use this action dimension of *confrontation.* In the next chapter you will study the dimension of immediacy of relationship.

We have previously (see Chapter 2) defined confrontation as helpers informing the helpees of a discrepancy between things that they have been saying about themselves and things they have been doing. The value of confrontation is that it provides the helpee with another point of view to consider in the process of self-evaluation. If the helper is competent, his/her perception of the helpee's problem areas should be more accurate than the helpee's perception (see Table 19.1).

Again, there is a scale to use in rating helper statements on the dimension of confrontation. Level 1.0 is not helpful. Level 2.0 is appropriate before a base relationship is built. Level 3.0 is a minimally helpful confrontation, and level 4.0 is the most helpful level of confrontation that you will learn to use in this

## Table 19.1. CONFRONTATION SCALE

| 1.0 | 1.5 | 2.0 | 2.5 | 3.0 | 3.5 | 4.0 |
|---|---|---|---|---|---|---|

**1.0 – 1.5:**

A response which does not allow any consideration of discrepancies existing for the helpee. The helper may accept the discrepancies expressed by the helpee, may contradict the expressed or felt conflict of the helpee, ignore the discrepancies or give direction prematurely. In any of these instances the helper is closing off possible fruitful avenues of investigation.

**2.0 – 2.5:**

The helper does not explicitly draw attention to discrepancies in the helpee's behavior. He/she does not overtly accept or deny these discrepancies but does not point them out to the helpee, either. He/she may simply remain silent about the discrepancies or reflect the helpee's feeling about them. The helpee, therefore, is not explicitly aware of possibly useful areas of inquiry.

**3.0:**

The helper indicates discrepancies without pointing out the specific directions in which these lead. He/she is tentative in comparing diverging communications expressed by the helpee. This allows the helpee to explore different areas in which he/she may become aware of diverging trends in his/her behavior.

**3.5 – 4.0:**

A response which clearly points out discrepancies which the helper has noticed and the specific directions in which the discrepancies lead. This focuses the helpee's attention on specific discontinuities in his/her behavior. It facilitates his/her dealing with areas of which he/she had been unaware or brings out more clearly a discrepancy of which he/she had been vaguely aware.

---

Key Words—Confrontation Scale

Level 4.0—firm directional statement of discrepancy
Level 3.0—tentative expression or exploration of discrepancy
Level 2.0—does not refer to discrepancy
Level 1.0—accepting, contradicting, ignoring, premature advice

model. Facilitative confrontation presupposes high levels of the other dimensions described in the manual. Confrontation without a base relationship created through the communication of empathy, respect, warmth, and genuineness, is rarely helpful. The helper must also possess accurate understanding of the helpee. The existence of a base relationship gives the helper permission to confront. The understanding increases the probability that the confrontation will be accurate and helpful.

Confrontation is wasted unless the helpee can use what is said. Confrontation can be very damaging and is often threatening to the helpee, but a certain amount of anxiety will increase the chances of confrontation's being useful. Some general guidelines about the conditions that regulate the intensity of confrontation appear below.

## REGULATING THE INTENSITY OF CONFRONTATION

*These Things Make Confrontation Less Intense and Less Threatening:*

1. Establish a good base relationship of mutual trust and caring.
2. Precede the confrontation with responses rated at level 3 on the Global Scale.
3. Generalize. Talk about people in general instead of specifically the helpee. This gives the helpee a chance to make it personal. For example, "Many people find that when they quit treating other persons with respect, problems start cropping up in their own lives."
4. Build in some loopholes for the helpee by using such words as: sometimes, maybe, once in a while, often, you think you'd like to. For example, "It sounds like now and then you almost get the urge to cheat a little on a test." This makes it easier for the helpee because your manner is not accusing him.
5. Use humor. This will probably fit in better when the other person is taking information for better self-understanding than it will when confrontation is used in a disciplinary or enforcing situation.
6. Consider the spirit in which confrontation is given. There is no justification for being punitive, vengeful, or hurtful.
7. Improve the attractiveness of your own life. If you are living your own life in a way that other people would like to imitate, it is easier for them to accept help from you.

*These Things Make Confrontation More Intense and Threatening:*

1. Personalize. Make it clear to the helpee that you are talking about him.

2. Specify events. A high level of concreteness forces the helpee to either accept or to reject the accuracy of what you say.

3. Deal with issues close in time. There is more threat involved in dealing with behavior that is close in time than with something that happened a long time ago.

4. Deal with actions instead of just words. If you are talking about something the other person *said,* it is easy for him/her to say, "That is not what I meant." It is more difficult to rationalize behavior than it is to explain away words.

5. Use what the helpee has said or done earlier to contradict what he/she is saying or doing *now.*

The intensity of confrontation must be strong enough for the confrontation to have an effect but not so strong that it causes the helpee to feel inadequate or unable to act constructively. Regulating the intensity requires the helper's best judgment. It is desirable to begin with gentle confrontation and raise the intensity gradually, as indicated by the helpee's reaction to the confrontation.

*If Confrontation Is Too Strong, Several Undesirable Outcomes Are Possible:*

1. The helpee uses defense mechanisms to build a wall between the two of you, thus reducing constructive communication.

2. The helpee is driven away.

3. The helpee is angry and goes on the attack, which is likely to ruin your chance to help.

4. The helpee pretends to accept the confrontation but actually ignores it.

5. The helpee feels helpless and seeks to become inappropriately dependent on the helper.

*If the Confrontation Is Too Weak, The Outcome Can Also Be Quite Undesirable:*

1. The helpee loses respect for you. He/she may assume that you don't really believe in what you are talking about or that you do not have the courage to speak up on behalf of your beliefs.

2. There is no effect. The helpee does not notice the purpose of your confrontation or it "goes in one ear and out the other."

3. Your confrontation is so feeble that it actually reinforces the discrepant behavior. The confrontation is interpreted as if you had said, "I think that this discrepancy is really okay but I was obligated to say something to you about it as a mere formality."

If any of the effects listed under "too strong" or "too weak" confrontation occur, the confrontation has probably not been useful. Above all, the helpee must sense that the helper is being real, not "playing games" or being phony in his/her confrontation. As a general rule, it is wise not to confront unless you have established a base relationship with a person and plan to stay involved with him/her. On the other hand, confrontation is an essential element in enforcement and disciplinary situations. In such cases, the establishment of a helping relationship may be secondary to the need for regulation and control.

## TWO TYPES OF CONFRONTATION

### Experiential

An experiential confrontation points out discrepancies the helper has noticed in his/her own personal experiencing of the helpee: (1) The helpee may be contradicting something he/she has previously stated, (2) The helpee's behavior may contradict his/her verbal expression, or (3) The helpee's experiencing of himself/herself may be different from the helper's experiencing of the helpee.

An experiential confrontation may refer to limitations (confrontation of weakness) or to resources (confrontation of strength).

### Didactic

In didactic confrontation the helper provides the helpee with additional information concerning problems. The helper may point out helpee behaviors that are socially undesirable or fill in gaps in the helpee's information about social reality. Another type of didactic confrontation is when the helper enforces a regulation, or exercises some kind of social control over the helpee. Some didactic confrontations deal with inappropriate helpee behavior, and that particular situation is discussed in Chapter 22. An example of a confrontation about social reality would be to say to the helpee, "Perhaps you are not aware of this, but when you are in a small group you talk rather loud—louder than most other persons. I think this is having an adverse effect for you. Many persons will get somewhat annoyed by the loudness even though they are interested in what you have to say."

## EXAMPLES OF DIFFERENT LEVELS OF CONFRONTATION

### Helpee Situation 1

Male student to teacher: "I'm about ready to give it all up. I just can't see how I can make a success of it. I've tried as hard as I know how, yet I'm not doing as well as I'd like to in class. It's not enough for me to get

A's; I also want to feel I'm learning something that will be useful when I get out of school."

Level 1.0: "I'm really happy that you're making good grades."

*Discussion:* The helpee's conflict of feelings is completely ignored in this response, and the helper appears to accept the discrepancy.

Level 1.0: "You're getting good grades; so that means you are already successful."

*Discussion:* This response contradicts the discrepancies felt by the helpee. The helper tries to sell the helpee on viewing himself as a success when the helpee is in fact dissatisfied with accomplishments to the extent of considering himself a failure.

Level 1.0: "You don't seem to know when you're well off. If you can't be happy with A grades then maybe you should just quit school."

*Discussion:* This response points out the discrepancy prematurely, as well as being punitive in the way in which the advice is given.

Level 2.0: "You feel dissatisfied because you are not getting enough from your classes even though your grades indicate you are."

*Discussion:* This response does not fully and accurately express the helpee's conflict or discrepancy. The helpee does not view grades as a good indicator of learning, but the helper chooses to use them in that way.

Level 3.0: "While you are succeeding by someone else's standards, your own feelings tell you that you are failing."

*Discussion:* This response offers a tentative statement of the discrepancies felt by the student but without an indication of the direction in which he could move.

Level 3.0: "You want to do more than achieve A's, but I haven't heard you describe what you are doing to make your learning more meaningful."

*Discussion:* This response leaves the student free to consider what things he could do to improve his situation.

Level 4.0: "You are defeating yourself right now. You are rejecting grades as a sign of success, and yet you have not made it clear to yourself just what *will* make learning meaningful to you. It's up to you to define goals for yourself now."

*Discussion:* The helper offers the helpee another view of his problem. In this confrontation the helper is giving direction to the student by describing the action he should take to move toward a resolution of his conflict. The helper is taking a calculated risk here, and the helpee may reject this confrontation. However, the helper has acted on his/her best judgment, i.e., the helpee is prepared for the confrontation. The helper has heard the helpee's plea for an undistorted, external evaluation of his conflict and has answered that plea. The helper still places the responsibility for appropriate action on the helpee.

# PERCEIVING CONFRONTATION

*Behavioral Objective: The trainee should be able to rate helper responses on the Confrontation Scale with an average discrepancy score of 0.5 or less.*

Rate each helper response on the Confrontation Scale, putting the number (1.0, 1.5, 2.0, 2.5, 3.0, 3.5, or 4.0) in the blank to the left of the helper response.

You may assume that the helper and helpee have developed a friendship. It is difficult to rate high levels of confrontation without further samples of the interaction. You may, therefore, wish to discuss your ratings with the trainer and other members of your class.

## *Helpee Situation 1*

Student to teacher: "I've lived here all my life but I don't know anybody. Even here at school I just can't seem to make friends. I try to be nice to other kids, but I feel all uncomfortable inside and things just don't go right. Then I tell myself I don't care, people aren't any good, everyone's out for himself, I don't want any friends. Sometimes I think I really mean it."

HELPER RESPONSES

_____ 1. "You're in a real bind. You want to make friends but you find yourself excusing yourself when you don't succeed as you'd like to."

_____ 2. "There's nothing wrong with that. Many people learn to live secluded lives."

_____ 3. "You're concerned because you haven't been able to make friends."

_____ 4. "You're excusing yourself when you find it's difficult to go out to others. You know that you need and want others in your life. As long as you make excuses, you will feel this emptiness."

_____ 5. "Can you tell me what are some of the things you've done to make friends?"

_____ 6. "You can join this club I belong to. We have a small group and need members. You'll make lots of friends and have lots of fun."

_____ 7. "When you tell yourself you don't care, that people aren't any good, you wind up feeling crummy inside."

Calculate your average discrepancy score by dividing the sum of the individual discrepancy scores by seven. Check your answers using the Answer Key at the end of the chapter.

## Helpee Situation 2

Student to teacher: "I can't see why you gave me a C on my paper. I worked on it six weeks. It was twice as long as Joe's and you gave him an A. That doesn't seem fair to me."

HELPER RESPONSES

_____ 8. "You don't think C is a fair grade for your paper."

_____ 9. "You're angry I gave you a C when your paper was twice as long as Joe's. Do you have any ideas about why I have given you a lower grade?"

_____ 10. "You've put a lot of effort into this paper, and it really burns you up to get a lower grade than Joe. Let's go over the objectives I set up and see if I need to change your grade."

_____ 11. "There's no reason for you to be angry. C is a good grade for you."

_____ 12. "You feel I wasn't fair in grading your paper."

_____ 13. "I'm sure your final grade will be very good. You're doing well in my class except for this one paper."

_____ 14. "The idea of Joe doing a paper half as long as yours and getting an A really burns you up."

Calculate your average discrepancy score by dividing the sum of individual discrepancy scores by seven. Check your answers using the Answer Key.

## RESPONDING WITH CONFRONTATION

*Behavioral Objective: The trainee should be able to write helper responses at level 3.0 on the Confrontation Scale, in a natural style.*

Read the helpee situation and formulate your response as though you were speaking to the helpee. Write it down as quickly as possible to retain the conversational style. Check your response against the criteria of a level 3.0 response on the Confrontation Scale. If it is not a level 3.0 or better, rework it to meet level 3.0 criteria.

## Helpee Situation 1

Student to teacher: "I don't see why we can't wear short shorts. I want to be an individual and express my own feelings and values. This is just a scheme you teachers thought up to keep us in place."

HELPER RESPONSE _____

_____

## Helpee Situation 2

Supervisor to teacher: "Why, oh yes, I'd be happy to, ah, come in and observe your, ah, class. I'm, ah, happy you want, ah, help to improve your teaching. Of course, I'm a little busy right now, and, I mean, I might not be able to get to your class for a few weeks. But, ah, I'll see what I can do."

HELPER RESPONSE _____

_____

## Helpee Situation 3

Student to teacher: "I'm not such a bad kid, really, you know. I don't really mean to bug you so much. It's just that you get in the air so easy. All I've got to do is look around and you're on my neck. If I do a little talking in class, you'd think I'd committed a major crime or something."

HELPER RESPONSE _____

_____

## Helpee Situation 4

Female student to male teacher: "I know why you want me to stay after school. And it isn't to help me with math." (Nonverbal cues:

Student looks teacher up and down with a smirk on her face.)

HELPER RESPONSE _____

_____

## Helpee Situation 5

This teacher had talked to you a little bit about some of the things she wished to bring up at the faculty meeting. You felt you had listened to her without committing yourself as for or against her views. She says: "You really let me down this time. I thought you would back me up, and you just sat there like a bump on a log. Couldn't you catch my hints to come in and support me?"

HELPER RESPONSE _____

_____

## Helpee Situation 6

This student often makes comments to needle his teachers and other students. You have seen him bother others as long as they were embarrassed by his comments. You have also seen him beg off, saying, "I didn't really mean it," when confronted. He makes the following statement to you: "I guess if you could have made something of yourself, you wouldn't have become a teacher."

HELPER RESPONSE _____

_____

## Helpee Situation 7

This student is bothered. You have seen other students picking on him until he got into a fight during lunch with three of his classmates. One of the coaches punished the four students for the remainder of the lunch and play period. They will be punished on the following day also. All of this happened right before the start of your class. (Nonverbal activity: The student is shuffling his feet and moving around in his desk. He can't keep his arms still and is clenching and unclenching his fists.)

HELPER RESPONSE _____

_____

## Answer Key

| Helpee Situation 1 | Helpee Situation 2 |
|---|---|
| 1. 3.0 | 8. 2.0 |
| 2. 1.0 | 9. 3.0 |
| 3. 2.0 | 10. 3.5 |
| 4. 4.0 | 11. 1.0 |
| 5. 3.0 | 12. 2.0 |
| 6. 1.5 | 13. 1.0 |
| 7. 3.0 | 14. 2.0 |

# Perceiving and Responding with Immediacy of Relationship

# 20

The dimension of *immediacy of relationship* can be defined as communication between the helper and the helpee about their relationship as it exists at that moment in time. Such interaction may heighten the level of anxiety of either the helper or helpee because of the possibility of negative components in the discussion. It is easier to talk about persons who are not present than it is to talk about persons who are; it is easier to talk about things that have happened in the past than it is to talk about things that are happening in the present. High level communication of immediacy of relationship involves talking about persons who are present and feelings that exist at that particular moment. Thus, it is desirable that a strong base relationship exist before using the dimension of immediacy of relationship.

In order to be comfortable dealing with this dimension, the helper needs to be comfortable with his/her own self-image. If the helper is threatened by what might be said by the helpee about the value of the relationship, it may be an indication that the helper is in the relationship primarily to meet his/her own needs and not primarily for the benefit of the helpee.

The helper should, on an ongoing basis, evaluate the strength and nature of the relationship. The scales for rating the helpee that appear in Appendix C are useful in obtaining a somewhat objective appraisal of the relationship. The helper should evaluate for both positive and negative aspects, since most relationships will have both strengths and deficiencies.

Many times, clues to the helpee's attitude toward the helper are hidden within other messages. The helper may recognize that there are barriers which are making it difficult for help to take place. He/she should then seek to deal with and resolve these rather than trying to push ahead in a task-oriented way toward some predefined goal, since the helpee may not be working toward the goal because of obstacles in the relationship. If the relationship between the helper and helpee is strained or is not meaningful to the helpee, help is unlikely to take place.

# EXAMPLES OF DIFFERENT LEVELS
# OF IMMEDIACY

As with the other dimensions, there is a scale for rating the levels of the dimension of immediacy of relationship (see Table 20.1). Level 3.0 is obtained when the helper simply reflects the helpee's references to what might be the helper-helpee relationship; the helper does not make the association explicit, nor does he/she deny it.

Additive responses (level 4.0) occur when the helper accurately and appropriately relates helpee references to their relationship. Although the response may be perceived accurately with a minimum interaction of helpee-helper-helpee, more interactions are often necessary.

Low level immediacy of relationship responses occur when the helper disregards most of the helpee messages that refer to the helper (level 2.0), or he/she totally disregards all helpee communications that relate to the helper (level 1.0). Some level 1.0 immediacy responses can be rated from simply a helpee-helper interaction; however, level 1.0 and level 2.0 immediacy of relationship responses usually require a minimum of helpee-helper-helpee interactions for accurate ratings.

# ILLUSTRATION OF THE IMMEDIACY
# OF RELATIONSHIP SCALE

The helpee situation below illustrates the four levels of the Immediacy of Relationship Scale. The situation assumes that the helper and helpee have a strong relationship. Ratings are based on the criteria of the Immediacy of Relationship Scale alone.

## Helpee Situation

Male high school student to counselor during tenth counseling session: "We've been talking about my future for weeks now, and it just doesn't seem to be doing any good. I might as well quit coming. In fact, I didn't even want to come in today."

HELPER RESPONSES

Level 1.0: "I think I have something here that will interest you. It's that book on forestry that I told you about last week."

*Discussion:* This response is rated level 1.0 because the helper does not respond to the statement by the helpee that the relationship is not leading toward his making necessary plans or decisions. The book seems to be held out as bait to entice the helpee to stay for another session.

## Table 20.1. IMMEDIACY OF RELATIONSHIP SCALE

| 1.0 | 1.5 | 2.0 | 2.5 | 3.0 | 3.5 | 4.0 |
|---|---|---|---|---|---|---|
| Helper ignores all cues from helpee which deal with their interpersonal relationship. | | Helper consciously gives token recognition to helpee statements about their interpersonal relationship but postpones discussing it or dismisses it after having commented on it superficially. | | Helper discusses the interpersonal relationship between himself/herself and the helpee, but in a general rather than a personal way, which obscures the uniqueness of their relationship. Helper is open to sharing responsibility for any defects which may exist in the relationship. | | Helper and helpee explicitly discuss their interpersonal relationship as it exists at that moment. |

KEY WORDS—Immediacy of Relationship Scale

Level 4.0—explicit, current
Level 3.0—open, general
Level 2.0—postpones, dismisses
Level 1.0—ignores

173

Level 2.0: "You think we're not getting anything done. Maybe we can talk about it sometime."

*Discussion:* Although the problem is acknowledged by the helper, the response is rated level 2.0 because he/she postpones discussing it.

Level 2.0: "Don't give up. This is a natural occurrence in long-term counseling."

*Discussion:* This response is rated level 2.0 because it treats the helpee's criticisms superficially, as though they were not important, and then drops the subject.

Level 3.0: "You're not satisfied with the way things are going. It's not unusual to feel that way. Most counseling relationships bog down from time to time."

*Discussion:* This response is rated level 3.0 because, while it recognizes and is open to discussing the issue the helpee has raised, it generalizes it. The helper talks about something that sometimes happens to people, not about the frustration and discouragement the helpee is having at that moment about that interview. It is easier for the helper to talk in generalities, but it is less helpful than talking about immediate feelings and events.

Level 4.0: "You're feeling a lot of frustration because nothing seems to be happening. It sounds like you think I'm not able to help you with this. Maybe we ought to talk about *that.*"

*Discussion:* This response is rated level 4.0 because the helper has responded to the most current feeling that the helpee has expressed—criticism of their relationship—and is willing to deal with it.

## PERCEIVING IMMEDIACY OF RELATIONSHIP

*Behavioral Objective: The trainee should be able to rate helper responses on the Immediacy of Relationship Scale with an average discrepancy score of 0.5 or less.*

In the exercises below, assume that a strong base exists. Rate the helper responses on the Immediacy of Relationship Scale by putting the number (1.0, 1.5, 2.0, 2.5, 3.0, 3.5, or 4.0) in the blank to the left of the helper response.

*Helpee Situation 1*

Student to teacher on last day of class: "You're the best teacher I ever had. I'll never have another teacher I like as much. We got along together so well."

HELPER RESPONSES

___1. "I'm glad you liked class this year. We had a very congenial group."

___2. "Thank you. That's nice to hear."

___3. "What are you going to do this summer?"

___4. "We did get along well. It pleases me to hear you say that because I think a lot of you and will always remember having you in my class."

___5. "I suppose you're glad this is the last day of school. You'll probably be doing a lot of interesting things this summer."

___6. "That's so nice to hear! This year was fun for both of us; I'm glad we can share these feelings together now."

___7. "That's a nice thing to say. I hope you will have a good summer."

___8. "Come by and see me sometime in the fall and we can sit down and reminisce."

Check your ratings against the Answer Key at the end of the chapter and calculate your average discrepancy score by dividing the sum of individual discrepancy scores by eight. Review those you missed to determine why they are rated as they are.

## Helpee Situation 2

Student to teacher: "Sure, you're always nice to me, but you have to be; you're paid for it. It's part of your job."

HELPER RESPONSES

___1. "You know what the assignment is. I think the thing for you to do is continue with your work."

___2. "You feel that I'm not really being myself—sort of phony."

___3. "I really do care about you. Sometimes I have a hard time getting across how I really feel. Maybe that's why you wonder if I'm leveling with you."

___4. "It really must be pretty important for you to be sure of the feelings I have about you. I guess right now it's kind of difficult for you to believe that I care about you just because you're *you*, apart from the fact that having you in my class is part of my job."

___5. (Assume base relationship) "It sounds like you may have been hurt sometime in the past after showing your real feelings to someone. I wonder if you now have trouble accepting kindness because you're afraid of the price you may have to pay for it. Maybe I've tried harder to be nice to you because I've realized you haven't been comfortable with me. I believe that I do genuinely care about you, and I hope we can continue to be honest about our relationship."

_____ 6. "I guess you find it hard to believe that someone could like you when they're getting paid to do a job that involves helping you. I do what I do because I enjoy doing it more than other things I could have chosen. I really think the reason I'm nice to you is because I just plain like you and so I want to be nice to you. I hope you'll find out I'm not phony about that."

_____ 7. "It's hard to accept kindness from others, isn't it?"

_____ 8. "Bernie, I don't have time to discuss our relationship just now."

## RESPONDING WITH IMMEDIACY OF RELATIONSHIP

*Behavioral Objective: The trainee should be able to write helper responses in a natural style at level 3.0 on the Immediacy of Relationship Scale.*

Read the helpee situation, carefully determining whether or not a base is to be assumed. Decide what you would say if you were speaking with the helpee and write it down as quickly as possible to retain the conversational style.

If a base with the helpee is assumed, your response should meet the criteria for level 3.0 on the Immediacy of Relationship Scale and level 3.0 on the scales of the facilitative dimensions.

If no base is assumed, your response should be level 2.0 on the Immediacy of Relationship Scale and level 3.0 or higher on the facilitative dimensions.

Evaluate your response and rework as necessary to meet the appropriate criteria.

### Helpee Situation 1

This girl has been in your class for five months. She likes the subject you teach—English—and has also begun to like you more and more. It is becoming embarrassing for you because she is in last period class and often stays after school to talk with you about the class. The student says to you, "Mr. Clark, I can't tell you how much I've enjoyed your class. I've become a much more creative writer this year. I hope we can keep on having these talks after school."

HELPER RESPONSE _____

_____

## Helpee Situation 2

You have seen this student in the halls quite often but have never talked with him. He has a reputation for manipulating teachers by offering to do errands for them or help them out. You suspect that he is sliding through by using ingratiating behaviors and being treated favorably in return. He has just walked into your room during your free period and says to you, "Hi! I saw you working here and wondered if there was anything I could do to help." Write a response that will communicate your suspicion that he is trying to manipulate you.

HELPER RESPONSE _____

_____

## Helpee Situation 3

This student, new in your class, has recently transferred from an out-of-state school: "Man, teachers are the same everywhere. They won't give you break number one. Just take one little step out of line and they're on your neck. I don't expect you'll be any different from any of the other teachers I've had."

HELPER RESPONSE _____

_____

## Helpee Situation 4

Two team teachers are discussing their experience with the new team-teaching program. One says to the other, "I entered this program thinking the intellectual stimulation I'd receive from working with another teacher would be worth the change from a traditional classroom. So far, though, this has been one of the worst years ever for me."

HELPER RESPONSE _____

_____

**Answer Key**

| Helpee Situation 1 | Helpee Situation 2 |
|---|---|
| 1.  1.0 | 1.  1.0 |
| 2.  2.0 | 2.  2.5 |
| 3.  1.0 | 3.  3.0 |
| 4.  4.0 | 4.  3.5 |
| 5.  1.0 | 5.  4.0 |
| 6.  4.0 | 6.  4.0 |
| 7.  2.0 | 7.  2.0 |
| 8.  2.0 | 8.  1.0 |

# Strategies for Change

*Problem solving*

# 21

Many trainees ask, "What follows facilitation?" There are several ways to respond to the question. Sometimes the appropriate use of the transition and action dimensions are sufficient for change to take place; at other times there is a need for the implementation of additional strategies. We could say that facilitation is necessary but not necessarily sufficient for change to take place. Some of the factors that help determine this are the severity of the problem, insight of the helpee, motivation of the helpee, and skill of the helper. It has been found that many other strategies that are currently popular can be implemented in the action phase of helping and are complimentary to the model presented in this manual. The text, *Strategies for Helping Students,* by Catterall and Gazda (in press) has been developed especially to provide a variety of interventions for use in the action/program-planning and problem-solving phase. The remainder of this chapter is concerned with the application of the action phase to a specific case. When the helpee in question is viewed along his five basic developmental modalities (see Figure 21.1), a more complete understanding of the helpee's strengths and deficits can be obtained.

The helpee in this situation is a fourteen-year-old eighth grader with above average intellectual ability. Academically, he does poorly, and often disrupts classroom activity by misbehavior which usually leads to his losing his temper after being reprimanded.

In this real case study, the helpee sees himself as an under-achiever, intellectually, emotionally, and physically. In order to counteract his low self-image, he allows himself to be coerced and manipulated by others which usually ends with the helpee receiving most of the blame for disruption, much to the satisfaction of his "friends." Attempts at denial and excuse generally lead to an explosive temper outbreak and a heated verbal battle with the teacher. The protocol that follows (a portion of a longer series of sessions) was one of several held with the helpee during the school year. The helper (interviewer) was one of the student's classroom teachers who knows the helpee very well and has established a good base with him, as the protocol segment illustrates.

The problem area to be illustrated in the protocol and the program that

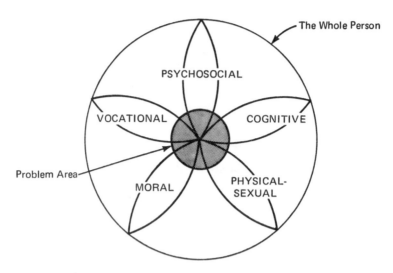

Figure 21.1. Five Basic Developmental Modalities

follows deal with the helpee's maladaptive behavior in the classroom. Since the helpee and helper are both prepared to move toward the action phase of problem solving, we shall pick up that segment of the interaction focusing on the action phase.

Helpee: "You know, it seems that every time there's trouble in the classroom you always look at me as if I'm the one who starts it all the time."

Helper: "David, you get pretty upset at me when there's a disturbance in the classroom and I automatically look in your direction, or even accuse you of causing it."

Helpee: "Mm-mm. Sometimes it makes me so I want to get back at you, especially when I wasn't even doing something."

Helper: "You feel it's really unfair when I do this to you, so much so, that sometimes you just want to get even with me."

Helpee: "Yeah... (pause), I know a lot of the times I do deserve it since I goof around so much. I guess you think it's me all the time because everyone says that I'm the worst kid in the class."

Helper: "You get mad when I always think you're the cause of the trouble, yet you seem to realize that a lot of times you are, and maybe this is why I do it. You may also be wondering if being labeled 'the worst kid in the class' doesn't have something to do with all of this."

Helpee: "Yeah, I don't know why it is, I mean, even last year in the seventh grade the teacher gave me an award at the end of the year for the one who caused her to get the most gray hairs. I didn't know whether to bring it home or throw it away."

Helper: "You don't know why people think of you this way, but you feel by goofing off in class, this is maybe what they expect of you anyway—so why not do it?!"

Helpee: "That's kind of the way it is. Even the kids who never get in trouble and always make real good grades try to get me to do things that *I'll* get in trouble for, but they're the ones who told me to do it."

Helper: "A lot of the times you find yourself doing things that you don't really want to do, and which usually get you in trouble, but you feel afraid of disappointing the fellows. And then when you get in trouble, you get angry and lose your temper with me. And David, it just seems like you and I can never get it together."

Helpee: (Pause) ". . . Yeah, you're right about losing my temper at you. I do that a lot."

Helper: "And that just makes matters worse because you feel so angry with yourself that maybe you take it out on me, which. . ."

Helpee: "Which just gets me in more hot water, right? I guess I kinda' see what's been happening. I really need to do something about it."

Helper: "You seem to feel that this type of behavior doesn't really get you anywhere, and perhaps there's something you can do about it. Would you be willing to look at some possibilities and maybe try some things that might work better for you?"

Helpee: "Yeah, I think I'd do almost anything if it would keep me from getting in trouble so much."

At this point the teacher met with the school counselor, school psychologist, and David's other teachers to initiate a potential program for David. During this case conference it was decided that the school counselor would meet with David and assist David in developing a profile of his strengths and deficits.

## A DEVELOPMENTAL MODEL FOR USE IN PROBLEM SOLVING

In order to develop a thorough profile of the helpee's strengths and deficits it becomes necessary to develop a scheme into which will fit diverse problem

181

areas. One such scheme takes into account five separate modalities. These modalities are psychosocial, physical-sexual, cognitive, vocational, and moral (see Gazda, G. M. *Group Counseling: A Developmental Approach* [2nd ed.], in press).

Including a helpee's strengths as well as deficits in the profile and considering combinations of the modalities allows us to develop a total program for problem resolution. This profile allows the helper and helpee to set priorities and to begin dealing with the most urgent concern first. Of course, improvement in one modality might very well have an effect on other modalities, so the scheme is constantly subject to revision.

The following interaction will serve to illustrate the Developmental approach. Keep in mind that helper (school counselor) and helpee are in the Action Phase of helping; thus, the helper has earned the right to be more directive.

> Helper: "Okay, David, when we finished up last week I heard you say you were going to be thinking of things to put in your profile."

> Helpee: "Yeah. I've been thinking about it. I understand it better now, especially after I looked at the sample you gave me."

> Helper: "David, I guess you've been pretty busy thinking of things in the different areas that you would like to see change, that is, specific things that you want to *stop* doing and others that you want to *start* doing."

> Helpee: "Yeah, I have been. You know, like in the first area, the psychosocial one, well, I was thinking that I should stop giving Mrs. Harris such a hard time in class. I mean, you know, act right and not lose my temper when I get caught doing something."

> Helper: "Okay, good, David. I get the feeling that you would really like to see some changes in this area."

> Helpee: "Yeah, I would. We also talked a few weeks back about me doing something about... I think you called it self-image. Would that come under this area?"

> Helper: "I think it might. Could you be a little more specific, David?"

> Helpee: "Well, you know, like we were talking about last week. I wish I wasn't afraid to try new things, like sports. I would really like to be able just to play and forget about thinking that I won't be good at it, or feel embarrassed because people are looking at me. I know I run like I have two left feet, but I still want to play."

Helper: "Trying something new is hard for you, especially in sports. You realize that you have some limitations, but you'd like to participate anyway and just enjoy the sport and maybe even get good at it."

Helpee: "Yeah. If I played enough I probably could get good, or a lot better, anyway."

Helper: "Let's record it this way. Write down "losing temper," and "classroom misbehavior" in the psychosocial column, and under the physical-sexual column put "feels clumsy and awkward in sports." David, you seem to be saying that to be good at something it takes practice and work."

Helpee: "Yeah. Like Mrs. Harris says, I could do much better in schoolwork if I tried harder. You know, do my homework and study, and things like that.

Helper: "I sense from the way you said that that you sort of agree with Mrs. Harris."

Helpee: "Yeah, I don't do much in school anyway. Goof around, mostly."

Helper: "The problem with schoolwork would seem to fit the cognitive area, David. It's not an easy thing—to talk about our own faults—even among friends."

Helpee: "Well, I was thinking about the vocational area and how it maybe ties in with my paper route job."

Helper: "Mm-mm."

Helpee: "Well, Mr. Mead, he's my paper route manager, he told me that unless I become more responsible, he'll have to take my route away from me. I suppose that could fit into this area."

Helper: "David, sounds like there's more to the story."

Helpee: "Well, a couple of times I didn't get my papers delivered, or I was late delivering them, and my customers called Mr. Mead on the phone. Boy, was he mad!"

Helper: "Something must have come up to take priority those times you didn't get your papers delivered."

Helpee: "Not really. Actually, one time I forgot, and the other times I just didn't feel like it."

Helper: "It sounds like irresponsibility is a problem area where you would also like to see some change."

Helpee: "Yeah. And another thing, Mrs. Harris always saves last period on Fridays to talk about careers and jobs and all that stuff. She always wants us to talk about what we want to do some day. I think it's stupid. I can never think of anything anyway."

Helper: "You feel this weekly activity is of no real importance, and it's frustrating too, because you never know what to say."

Helpee: "Exactly."

Helper: "Okay, why don't we write down, 'shows little interest in thinking about future vocational choices,' and put that under, 'lacks responsibility,' in the vocational column. David, you look a little puzzled."

Helpee: "Well, I think we've covered all the areas except the moral area, and I'm not sure what to put for this one."

Helper: "Okay, let's take a minute to go over the moral area. I think this will help you understand what we mean by moral. Moral principles are principles of choice for resolving conflicts of obligation. 'Moral' is not simply a tag to be attached to actions we approve of, but a means for deciding what one should or should not do in situations involving competing moral values. Does that clear some things up at all?"

Helpee: "I'm still not sure what to put down on my profile under this area."

Helper: "It might help if we go over the handout I gave you on Kohlberg's stages of moral development. At one of these stages we learn to conform to the personal expectations of others and to social rules."

Helpee: "Lots of times in class I don't do what Mrs. Harris expects me to do. It really gets me in trouble sometimes."

Helper: "Sounds good. Seems like you're getting pretty good at doing this. Well, we've gone over our time, let's stop for today."

As the counseling sessions with David continued, David and the counselor constructed David's Developmental Profile (Table 21.1). The Developmental Profile illustrates that David's problems (like most other persons) are not the result of a single developmental deficit but rather are intertwined, and to change David will involve a program that attacke his deficits (supported also by focusing on his strengths) from many directions (developmental areas).

When the Developmental Profile was completed, it became necessary for David to establish priorities in his program, i.e., just where in the program

## Table 21.1. DEVELOPMENTAL PROFILE

### PSYCHOSOCIAL DEVELOPMENT

| Strengths | Problems (Deficits) | Proposed Treatment |
| --- | --- | --- |
| Able to achieve an appropriate dependence-independence pattern, e.g., saves money from paper route to help pay for summer camp. | Rebellious attitude; frequently causes disruption in classroom and loses temper when reprimanded. | Group counseling; behavior contract regarding disruptive and aggressive acting-out. |
| Strong identification with one's sex mates, also with male hero identity figures, e.g., athletes, movie actors. | Low image of parents; mother seen as nagging and punishing, father as cowardly and uncaring. | Counselor appointment with family to discuss family counseling possibilities. |

### PHYSICAL-SEXUAL DEVELOPMENT

| | | |
| --- | --- | --- |
| Good physical health, onset of puberty and normal development of prominent secondary sexual characteristics; large in size and strong. | Feels clumsy and uncoordinated in physical activities; afraid to participate in organized sports fearing embarrassment or failure. | "Time Projective Technique"[1] — learning to enjoy activities especially athletics for their own sake, by imagining realistically the good things that could happen in the future as a result of athletic participation. Physical fitness remediation program. |
| Able to understand his future role in heterosexual relationships; normal interest in, and search for understanding of, his sexual ability. | Feels uneasy around girls his own age; wishes he didn't have to "show off" to get their attention. | "People Happenings Technique"[2] — presentation of events without the pressures of reality; goal is to explore alternative responses as well as own thoughts, feelings, and behaviors; facilitates counselee's becoming better prepared for dealing with real situations which involve other people. |

### COGNITIVE DEVELOPMENT

| | | |
| --- | --- | --- |
| Above average intellectual ability (full scale IQ of 115 on WISC). | Skill deficiency: particular weakness in general information and vocabulary development. | Tutoring, remediation, proper educational placement by grade and class. |
| Particular strength in motor and simple assembly skills. | Visual perception and spatial conceptualization. | Wood Shop Program; individualized work using geometric forms, Cuisenaire rods, jigsaw puzzles, maps, and graphs. |

### VOCATIONAL DEVELOPMENT

| | | |
| --- | --- | --- |
| Likes to undertake cooperative enterprises, e.g., supplements allowance with a paper route. | Often lacks responsibility; negligent, e.g., plays with friends and may forget to deliver newspapers. | "Life Careers Game"[3] —small group interaction using role-playing techniques simulating decision making and work situations. |

## Table 21.1. DEVELOPMENTAL PROFILE (continued)

| Strengths | Problems (Deficits) | Proposed Treatment |
| --- | --- | --- |
| Ability to concentrate over long periods of time, especially on tasks of special interest. | Has no interest in cognitively developing ideas about occupations and possible career aspirations. | "Life Style Assessment"[4] — technique using vocation of family breadwinner to show total effects on family; counselee learns that vocational choice is more than just a way to earn money. "Projected Life Plan Lines"[5] — technique that brings planning out of the purely thinking realm and puts it into a visual, graphic form; a simple way of "trying on the future" or of seeing more clearly the relationship between decision making, planning, and their resultant consequences. |

### MORAL DEVELOPMENT

| | | |
| --- | --- | --- |
| Able to define right action as that which satisfies his own needs and occasionally the needs of others. | Minimal ability to see the world as made up of social relationships, consequently fails to conform to the personal expectations of others and to social rules (Kohlberg's Conventional Level of Moral Reasoning). | "Moral Dilemmas Discussion Technique"[6] — (a) counselee comes to see certain inadequacies in his reasoning as a result of interacting with more complex arguments made by other people; (b) counselee is placed in the roles of various parties in the dilemma and examines his reasoning from these several perspectives. |

1. George M. Gazda, Richard P. Walters, and William C. Childers, *Human Relations Development:* A Manual for Health Sciences (Boston: Allyn and Bacon, 1975).

2. S. Simon, M. R. Harnell, and L. A. Hawkins, *Values Clarification: Friends and Other People* (PAXCOM—A Division of Modular Communications, Inc., 1973).

3. C. Catterall and G. M. Gazda. *Strategies for Helping Students* (Springfield, III.: Charles C. Thomas, in press).

4. Ibid.

5. N. Gysbers, W. Miller, and E. J. Moore, eds., *Developing Careers in the Elementary School* (Columbus, Ohio: Charles E. Merrill), 1973).

6. "A New Rationale For Guidance," *Focus on Guidance,* January 1974 (Love Publishing Co., Denver, Colo.).

he wished to begin. At this point the helper used the matrix system for selecting a course of action. This system involves a systematic way of choosing the preferred course of action from among several alternatives. The helpee's value system is considered concurrently with the proposed courses of action. The helpee is asked to list his values (those that pertain to the problem) and then label them with any unit from 1 to 5, with the value of the greatest importance being given the greatest weight. (These are arbitrary units and some other unit could work equally well.) It is not necessary to use all weights, and some values may be weighted equally.

In addition to the values, the helpee and helper generate reasonable alternatives to pursue in order to solve the problem. These may be labeled "courses of action." These alternatives are also ranked by the helpee from a negative to a plus, i.e., -2, -1, 0, +1, +2 indicate the degree to which that alternative will enhance or decrease movement toward the particular value in that row of the matrix. The numerical weight assigned to the value is then multiplied by the rating assigned to the alternative and the product is recorded in the appropriate cell. The helper and helpee under consideration here worked out the matrix in Table 21.2.

## Interpretation of Matrix

After the helpee placed weights on his values, and he and the helper developed the seven possible courses of action to follow in his problem-solving program, one course of action emerged and related courses of action were not far behind. The helpee and helper agreed that the reason alternative 1—improve self-image— received the highest weight was because of its close interrelationship with several other alternatives. In other words, an improved self-image might affect classroom behavior, which could reduce temper outbreaks and, subsequently, increased academic achievement might result. Thus, of immediate concern was alternative 1 which involved preparing the helpee to work on and improve his self-image. The helper and helpee then decided to develop a self-image enhancement program for the helpee as the first phase of solving his classroom-related problem. Since this area of deficit was most closely related to the psychosocial area of development, David and his counselor were able to initiate David's corrective program with emphasis on this area of human development.

A sample of the self-image enhancement program is outlined in Figure 21.2. Note that David's total program would involve an integration of strategies built around each of the five basic areas of human development.

## SUMMARY

The purpose of this chapter was to illustrate the implementation, within the action phase of the model, of a program for change with a helpee. We hope to show by this illustration that the action phase may consist of a complex program for a helpee that will require the involvement of several individuals and a careful sequencing of interventions that are acceptable to the helpee. Problem solving within the action phase may be much simpler, too. A single intervention within a single developmental area may be all that is needed to produce corrective action for the helpee.

## Table 21.2. MATRIX SYSTEM FOR SELECTING COURSE OF ACTION

| Counselee's (David's) Potential Courses of Action—Practical Alternatives | | 1 Improve Self-Image | 2 Modify classroom behavior | 3 Explore dynamics of group pressure | 4 Improve interpersonal skills | 5 Control temper | 6 Improve academic achievement | 7 Change schools |
|---|---|---|---|---|---|---|---|---|
| 1. Self-image | (5) | (+2) 10 | (+2) 10 | (+1) 5 | (+2) 10 | (+1) 5 | (+1) 5 | (−2) −10 |
| 2. School | (3) | (+2) 6 | (+2) 6 | (+1) 3 | (+1) 3 | (+2) 6 | (+2) 6 | (−1) −3 |
| 3. Family | (4) | (+1) 4 | (+1) 4 | (0) 0 | (+1) 4 | (+1) 4 | (+1) 4 | (0) 0 |
| 4. Other | (3) | (+2) 6 | (+1) 3 | (+1) 3 | (+1) 3 | (+1) 3 | (0) 0 | (0) 0 |
| Total | | 26 | 23 | 11 | 20 | 18 | 15 | −13 |

Counselee's Value Hierarchy

This matrix was adapted from the system developed by Dr. Robert R. Carkhuff and described in *The Art of Problem Solving* (Amherst, Mass.: Human Resource Development Press, 1973).

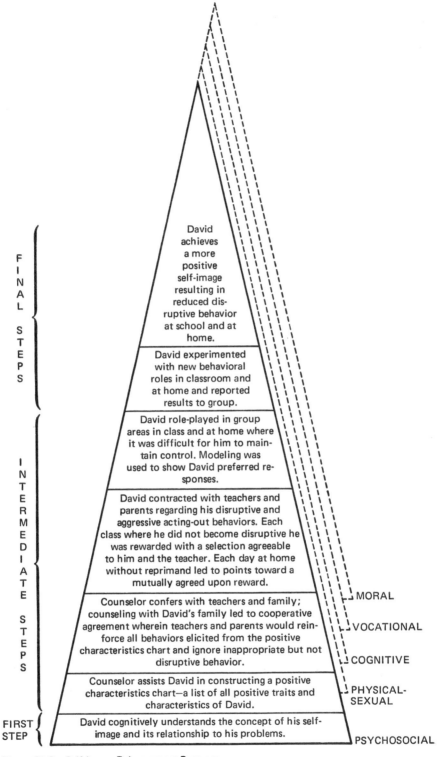

Figure 21.2. Self-Image Enhancement Program

# REFERENCES

Catterall, C. D., and G. M. Gazda, In press. *Strategies for Helping Students.* Springfield, Ill.: Charles C. Thomas.

Gazda, G. M. In Press. *Group Counseling: A Developmental Approach.* (2nd Ed.) Boston: Allyn and Bacon.

# Responding with Information and Action

# 22

Two communication types will be considered in this chapter, appropriately giving information and appropriately providing action. These two categories appear simplistic, and in some ways perhaps they are, but the key to responding appropriately in these two dimensions is to determine whether granting the helpee's request is appropriate. This determination is based on (1) knowledge of the helpee, (2) the timing in the relationship, and (3) understanding the motives of the helpee. So providing action or giving information are not difficult concepts to understand, but proper implementation requires a conscious effort on the part of the helper.

## RESPONDING WITH INFORMATION

As an educator, you are called upon daily to interact in a professional way with students and parents. Though these interactions may seem routine to you, the experience of talking with an educator is not routine to these individuals. Your attention, attitude, and the information you provide are very important to them. In reading the next two paragraphs, try to understand the way in which they may look to you for information.

I am a student. Being in school is, many times, an uncomfortable experience for me because I do not feel that I am a part of what is going on. I do know, however, that I know more about *me* than anyone else in the world. It is rare that another person can tell me something about me that I do not already know or understand. But in school I find myself in a situation in which others attempt to pass off information that is intended to help, but includes things that I either already know or things that are not true about myself. I believe that because of your position, your knowledge, and your years of education, there are many things that I can learn from you.

I just ask that you take enough time to try to understand me and my situation. If that happens, when you speak I will listen to you; and I will probably remember a lot of what you say.

I would like for this experience to be a very positive one, one in which both of us feel comfortable. Not only are your words important to me, but equally important are how you say those words and what you do while you talk to me. If you withhold yourself or your information about me from me, you make me feel like a child; I feel less secure. If you make decisions for me without any input from me or if you take me for granted, I feel powerless.

An essential task of all educators, then, is to help the student feel less dependent and more like a capable, worthwhile human being. The educator has the capacity to do and say those things that will help students feel they have control over their lives, that they are not children, and that they are not powerless. This sounds like a huge assignment, and it is more easily said than done, but it is an achievable task. This section on responding with information will deal with some familiar topics and describe the application of the basic principles of good communication to those situations.

## RESPONDING TO INFORMATION REQUESTS

The following situations are requests for information. Some may have more obvious underlying feelings/concern than others. Read each carefully and attempt to write a minimal and a maximal response.

### Helpee Situations

1. Teacher to teacher: "I'm planning to take the Graduate Record Examination again next month. Since you did so well on it, I thought maybe you could give me some advice."

2. Teacher to teacher: "Have you noticed how I start stuttering when the principal asks me a question in the faculty meeting?"

3. Custodian to assistant principal: "Everybody tells me what I should do here. Nobody ever fills me in on why I have to do it. Could you tell me why the halls need to be swept after every period?"

4. Student to teacher: "Can you tell me if there are scholarships available for nursing schools? I want to go but my parents can't afford to send me."

5. Student to school counselor: "Do you have something I can read on depression?"

6. Principal to teacher: "Do you think I will get the 'most improved' award this year for the reorganization at the school?"

7. Teacher to teacher: "How much personal information about ourselves should we give a student? Sometimes it's hard to avoid it when you get in a conversation."

8. Teacher to teacher: "I'm really unsure of my job performance. I'm afraid to ask anyone but you. I think you can level with me without much threat."

9. Student to teacher: "That was a real interesting talk in class yesterday about the theory of evolution. Do you have some more information that I could borrow to read?"

10. Teacher to school secretary: "Last year we had a form to request new books for the library. Are we still doing that?"

For an alternate exercise, with a partner pick a situation with which you can identify. Role play the same situation more than once using different ways of responding. Discuss and decide which seemed to be most effective for you. After fifteen or twenty minutes come back together as a group and try to reach some consensus concerning requests for information.

## RESPONDING WITH ACTION

Most of what a teacher does in the classroom involves the transfer of information, and students are assisted in learning to become autonomous persons by being allowed to do as many things for themselves as possible. Still, there are occasions when the teacher will take direct action to do something for another person. This is what we mean by responding with action—*doing something* for helpees or intervening in their lives in some tangible, direct way. Facilitative communication is related to these activities and interventions because (1) facilitative communication is necessary in order to find out what the action should be and to establish acceptance of the action by the helpee, and (2) facilitative communication is supportive and restorative in its own right and in that sense is, itself, an "action."

In responding with action it is important to watch for messages within messages. For example, a student says to you, "Would you mind helping me with this assignment for a few minutes? I'm not getting anywhere with it—but then I never do." All of that statement except the last three words is a clear, straightforward request for help. Those last three words, however, give you a huge clue about how the student feels about himself/herself—very unsure. The last three words are a very important message hidden within the more obvious message. The student is probably desperately hoping for some understanding and involvement. In this case, the appropriate response would be to take the action of helping with the assignment but also responding to the need for understanding/involvement when it is possible to do so.

Attending to serious physical needs and protection of the welfare and safety of any person must always come first. In such a case, to communicate with persons before taking action would only waste valuable time. Information, listening, and responding with understanding can follow the necessary action. Each situation or response is evaluated separately.

Do not attempt to do something you are not capable of doing, especially when it involves the physical welfare of another person. It is more respectful to refer the person to someone who is qualified to help than it is to bungle the job of helping. Occasionally a situation may arise that requires your taking the initiative in protecting the best interests of the organization and other persons. In such a situation, action often takes precedence over dialogue. Consider a couple of different kinds of situations:

## Helpee Situation 1

Another teacher, returning from the playground, rushes into your room and says, "The maintenance men left a ladder against the side of the building and there is a small boy climbing it. I'm afraid he'll fall off!"

RESPONSE: Take the action that will most quickly get a responsible person to the scene, at which time the situation is assessed for the best course of action.

## Helpee Situation 2

A man in a gray work uniform says to the school secretary, "I'm from the pest control service. I'm supposed to spray in your storage room."

RESPONSE: The secretary replies, "I would prefer to check with the principal about this first. Excuse me just a moment while I phone."

*Discussion:* No employee should allow entrance to any nonpublic area containing valuable materials, confidential information, or equipment unless he/she has authorization to do so from a supervisor. Posing as a maintenance service person or equipment repair person is a common method of deception used by unlawful persons today. If in doubt, check up.

# WEIGHING THE PROPER RESPONSE

In each of the following situations, write (1) what you would say and (2) what you would do. Would giving the appropriate action probably terminate the interaction, or do you think there is an underlying reason for the request?

## Helpee Situations

1. Teacher to principal: "Yesterday after school the cook's assistant chewed me out for complaining about the food at lunchtime. I want you to report her to the head cook."

2. Teacher to principal: "I really hate to complain about the smoke in the teachers' lounge, but there are several of us who can hardly stand to stay in there. Since smoking in the school is clearly against the rules of the Board of Education, many of us would be very happy if you would enforce them."

3. Teacher to teacher: "Would you mind looking over my lesson plans for next week and giving me your comments?"

4. Teacher aide to teacher aide: "Would you give me a hand in grading these tests? Seems like I always agree to help others with their work and then my own work doesn't get done."

5. Teacher to principal: "Would you please post the regulations for our lunch period? Everybody is operating by a different set of rules and it's confusing."

6. Student teacher to supervising teacher: "I really feel good today—like I could teach the class all by myself. Would you check to see if that would be okay?"

7. Teacher to principal: "I guess I don't feel comfortable telling my teacher aide that she has an offensive odor. Since you're our principal, I thought you should do it."

8. You see a school custodian applying wax to a floor, but the usual "Caution—slippery floor" warning sign has not been posted. You know that classes will be dismissed in five minutes.

9. Teacher to teacher: "My car broke down on the way to school today. Could you give me a ride over to the garage after school?"

10. Teacher to principal: "When second period starts today, would you walk past Mr. Johnson's room? The noise there is about to drive me crazy."

11. Student to teacher: "I worked pretty hard on this homework assignment. Would you look over it before class and tell me if it's okay?"

# Applying the Communication Model to Other Situations

# 23

In the manual we have attempted to help you acquire general skills of communication that can be applied to many different types of situations both in the classroom and in your relationships with colleagues and other persons. This chapter includes a study of additional situations that do not quite fit other sections of the book but that, nonetheless, occur frequently and are very important.

## COMMUNICATION IN EMPLOYMENT RELATIONSHIPS

In the ideal employment situation the needs of all members of the organization are met in ways that are satisfying to each of the persons involved and that contribute to the fulfillment of the goals of the organization. Good communication among the members of the organization is the first step toward creating ideal conditions. A desirable goal is for there to be a relationship each to each among members of the organization, such as we have earlier defined as a base relationship between a helper and helpee. In this relationship administrators understand the goals and needs of their subordinates (empathy), value their opinions, believe in their potential, consider their needs as important (respect), and create a pleasant working environment (warmth). This kind of relationship does not conflict with the attainment of organizational goals or maintenance of discipline within the work group. It does not preclude supervisors' use of authority that has been provided them to help them attain the performance for which they are held responsible.

The relationship between supervisor and employee should be congenial and show mutual caring without undue familiarity: be personal but not show favoritism; be relaxed but purposeful. From this relationship supervisors can be as direct as the situation requires but allow employees all the freedom and flexibility in the performance of their duties as their competence allows. Good communication builds relationships that strengthen supervisors' ability to achieve the best efforts of their team, because the team members are satisfied with the *relationship.*

## RESPONDING TO DISSATISFACTION

One type of interaction that frequently occurs between an administrator and teacher or between a department head and department member results from dissatisfaction with some aspect of the working conditions. The interaction below illustrates several ways of responding to a situation of this type.

### Helpee Situation

Teacher to principal: "This semester I seem to have practically every problem child in the seventh grade. Sometimes my classroom seems like a madhouse. If Billy Watson and his buddy, Ralph, weren't *both* in the class together, maybe things would be okay. I specifically asked that they be assigned to different rooms but, as usual, nobody listened to my recommendation."

HELPER RESPONSE

1. *Hurtful:* "I'm afraid you're imagining things. You know that we listen to what you say."

2. *Hurtful: "My* job is to decide who does what. *Your* job is to do it."

3. *Hurtful:* "You're probably just having a bad day. We all have our bad days. The reason you have those students is because we thought you were the best person for the job."

4. *Ineffective:* "You say some of your students are giving you a hard time today?"

5. *Ineffective:* "Maybe you're not getting enough rest at night."

6. *Minimally helpful:* "Right now you sound mistreated by the way things have been handled and discouraged about how things are going in the classroom. This must be pretty important to you. I'd be glad to talk with you about it and see if there are some other options for us at this time." The principal—in the helper role—must decide whether or not the complaint is legitimate. This judgment determines, in part, the nature of the response. Both of the level 4.0 responses illustrated below assume a base relationship between the teacher and the principal.

7. Additive (Principal believes complaint is unfounded): "The situation in your classroom has made you pretty uncomfortable. You say it seems to you that we did not honor your request to separate the problem boys

this year. Yet, it sounds to me that there may be more to it than that."

*Helpee* (Reply to response number 7): "Well, I don't know, I'm just so confused. I've always thought of you as being fair—a good person to work for—but when I look at what I'm doing, and see what others are doing, it does seem like I get the worst end of things quite often."

8. *Additive* (Helper recognizes complaint as legitimate): "It's been rough for you—it's been getting you down. Now that you point it out to me, I see you're right—I *have* tended to give you more of the difficult students. But it's been because you're skilled in dealing with them, and not for any other reason. Your classroom performance has been excellent. I didn't realize that working with some of these students was such an unpleasant task for you. Maybe there are some other arrangements that will be more satisfactory."

*Helpee* (Reply to response number 8): "Well, it wasn't the work so much but I just couldn't understand why I got all the problem students. It's a compliment in a way, I guess, but it would be nice if you could spread the load around a little more."

## RESPONDING WITH CONSTRUCTIVE CRITICISM

Probably the most difficult situation in supervision occurs when it is necessary to talk with employees about such things as their deficiencies in performance of duties, infractions of rules, or undesirable interpersonal relationships. In terms of this communication model, such interactions often involve conditions and techniques of the action phase of the model. Whether or not this communication is accepted depends upon (1) the quality of the base relationship and (2) the skill with which the helper utilizes the action phase condition of confrontation and other action phase strategies such as problem solving.

The occasion of confrontation does not need to be extremely uncomfortable for either supervisor or subordinate. It can, in fact, be a time of constructive advance in skills and understanding for both parties. Follow the suggestions below to maximize the benefits of these occasions.

1. Don't get overly caught up in the crisis of the moment. Keep the long range relationship in mind.
2. Take care not to accuse prematurely. Listen to the employee's story. Be alert for new data that are relevant to the situation.
3. Give the employee an opportunity to take the initiative in explaining and correcting the situation. Follow the principle of allowing the employees/helpees to do as much for themselves as they are capable.
4. Put the criticism and the problem area in perspective by discussing employees' areas of strength. To let employees mistakenly feel that they are doing nothing right is tragic, but it happens

frequently. Again, stay alert for the effect of the interaction on the employees.

5. The best protection against remedial supervisory work is prevention of problems through clear task assignment and other preparation of the employees to carry out their duties.

6. Avoid "hit and run" confrontation. Things are rarely as simple as they appear on the surface, so allow for explanation of the problem and ample time for interaction.

The following dialogue illustrates an effective administrator implementing the communication model and the resolution of a problem. In this example, a principal is talking to two of her teachers (helpees) about their inappropriate behavior that had been reported to her and that she had subsequently verified. Assume a base relationship between the principal and two teachers in her school.

Helper (principal): "The reason I wanted to see you two together is to discuss a complaint I had a few minutes ago from one of the other teachers."

Helpee (teacher): "Okay, what is it?"

Helper: "It was about the excessively loud talking and laughing in the teachers' lounge this morning. You both know that I rarely get a report like that about either of you from one of the other teachers, but with several classrooms in the area of the teachers' lounge the noise was apparently very disruptive to the surrounding classrooms."

The principal began the conversation by explaining the purpose and tempered the criticism by pointing out, indirectly and briefly, that the behavior of the teachers is generally at the very high professional level.

The teacher may respond to what the principal says in any of the ways a helpee might respond to a confrontation. Several of these are illustrated and discussed below as alternate endings to the dialogues. In each of the alternate endings to the dialogue above, the helper responses are effective and consistent with the high levels of the communication model.

Helpee: "Who said that?"

Helper: "You're hurt to think that one of your colleagues would come to me with this kind of complaint. It sounds like your perception of the situation is different from the one that I heard."

*Discussion:* This response emphasizes the helpee's probable feelings and reactions. It seeks to get the focus of the interaction back on the helpee's behavior. Answering the question that the teacher asked would not facilitate the helpee's exploration of the problem.

Helpee (angrily): "That's a lie! How could we be making noise when we were grading papers in the lounge all morning? You don't know what you're talking about. You *never* do!

Helper: "You have strong feelings about this, so it's something we need to talk about right now. Let's all go in my office so we'll have more privacy."

*Discussion:* The helpee belligerently tries to bluff her way out of this situation. The principal must firmly retain control so she can deal with the original incident in a constructive way, as well as with the helpee's display of animosity for her.

Helpee: "You talk a lot about team work. How can we work as a team if we are not allowed to speak with each other?"

Helper: "You're saying that we need to strike a happy medium between no interaction at all, on the one hand, and disruptive behavior on the other."

*Discussion:* The helpee has overreacted to the helper's response and in effect distorted her message. The helper's response in this situation affords an opportunity for the helpee to disclose more.

Helpees: (Both look at the floor and say nothing. Helper, after about thirty seconds of silence: "There are several things that you might mean by your silence, but I would prefer not to guess about what you're thinking. I would rather hear directly from you, and I hope that you will give me your ideas about this matter."

*Discussion:* When the principal offers to listen to the teachers' perception and feelings related to the situation, the response communicates high level respect.

## RESPONDING TO AN ADMINISTRATIVE DILEMMA

Each of the situations below describes a dilemma for a person who has administrative responsibility for another person. Consider the implications of each alternative action in terms of the communication model.

## *Helpee Situation 1*

A principal overhears two teachers talking about a new teacher who has been hired on a temporary basis to replace another teacher who is on medical leave-of-absence.

"Did you hear that the new teacher just graduated two weeks ago; she's been in college for four years. Let's introduce her to the real world. We'll show her she's not so cool!"

What should the supervisor do? (1) Ignore it. (2) Warn the new teacher so she will be prepared for what may happen. (3) Talk to the two teachers immediately. (4) Talk to the two teachers individually when convenient.

If you choose (1), explain why. If you choose (2), (3), or (4), write a statement consistent with the communication model for the supervisor to use in opening the conversation with the person involved.

## Helpee Situation 2

You are a principal. Miss Bryan, the person speaking to you in this situation, is a teacher's aide in the classroom of Mr. Smith. Miss Bryan says to you, "I really don't know what to do about this, but I think I need to talk to you about it. I think some things need to be done. Mr. Smith has been treating some of the students terribly. Yesterday I saw him shove Bill Richards when he wouldn't cooperate. He thinks no one saw him but I did, and it's not the first time it's happened either. But I'm afraid to talk to him about it."

What should you, as principal, do? (1) Acknowledge hearing the complaint but take no other action. (2) Talk with Mr. Smith and warn him that this kind of behavior is unacceptable. (3) talk with Mr. Smith about whether or not he is getting along well with Miss Bryan. (4) Talk with Bill Richards. (5) Other (describe). Explain your choice and write a statement that would be appropriate to use in introducing whatever course of action you would take.

## Helpee Situation 3

Six weeks ago Mr. Bridges, the principal, hired Mrs. Johnson as the new school secretary. Mrs. Johnson replaced a secretary who had been at the school for many years. She was hired with a clear understanding that it was for a trial period of two months and subject to review at the end of that time. Although Mrs. Johnson's work seemed to be satisfactory in most ways, Mr. Bridges thought he had sensed annoyance from several of his teachers, and he had a general uneasiness about her dependability. He had about decided that he had hired the wrong person.

What should Mr. Bridges do? (1) Wait until the end of the trial period and see if the situation changes. (2) Warn her that her performance to date is not satisfactory. (3) Talk with some of the senior teachers to get their impressions of

Mrs. Johnson's work. (4) Encourage her to begin looking around. Explain your choice and write a statement for Mr. Bridges to use as an initial statement in the conversation.

## Helpee Situation 4

You are a principal and Mrs. Sanders is a teacher on your faculty. During the last month she has been late to work several times. She has given you a variety of reasons: "My car wouldn't start. The clock didn't go off. I had to call a cab and they didn't come. I thought I was going to be sick so I waited." Today she was an hour late. When she reported in she explainted, "The place where I leave my baby wasn't open on time. There just wasn't anyone there, so I had to wait for them to come. I couldn't bring Mikey here! I tried to call you but you were busy. Didn't you get my message?" You check with the secretary and she states that she had not received a call from Mrs. Sanders that morning. Later in the day another teacher inadvertently mentions that she had left her child at the same day-care center at 8 o'clock, the time that Mrs. Sanders indicated the center was closed. Describe what you would do and say.

## Helpee Situation 5

One of the teachers in your school, Mrs. Jenkins, has created problems for you on several occasions as a result of spreading inaccurate accusations about other staff members in the school. Today, she comes to you to talk about one of your most trusted and valuable teachers. She says, "I hate to be nosey, but it seems like Mr. Jackson is coming to school in the morning with liquor on his breath. Maybe that explains why he has had so many discipline problems in his class lately." Describe what you would do and say.

## Helpee Situation 6

You are in the teacher's lounge this morning when one of the janitors, Mr. Jones, walks in and begins pouring himself a cup of coffee. A first year teacher in your school is sitting in a chair next to the coffee pot and you overhear her say, "You can't use this lounge. It's only for the *teachers*. You have an area down in the basement." Describe what you would do and say.

## Helpee Situation 7

Mrs. Arlan was transferred to the school where you are principal. You weren't eager about her transfer to your school because of things you had heard about her. Her former principal told you, "If it weren't for things she says, she would be the best member of our team. It's just that she keeps things in a constant uproar because she is so opinionated. Actually she's *great* with the students."

You have wondered if Mrs. Arlan's problem in the other school might have been due to overreaction on the part of the principal, so you approved the transfer. Everything has gone very smoothly during the first few weeks of the school year and, from your frequent observation, Mrs. Arlan appeared to be an asset to the faculty.

Just now, two of your other teachers enter your office. One of them is crying and the other appears angry and says, "We just knew it wouldn't work out and it *hasn't*. That big mouth you brought in here just shot off her mouth to Rose. I told her to apologize to Rose but she just stomped off. There is *no way* we are going to put up with *that* stuff all year long. Something has to be done about it, and done about it now!" Describe what you would do and/or say.

## RESPONDING TO INAPPROPRIATE COMMUNICATION

There are five major categories of communication that we shall consider to be inappropriate. Regardless of the type, the alternative responses are similar. These responses range from being punishing or damaging, through silence or passivity, to the preferred response of a warm but firm refusal to engage in inappropriate communication.

The basic principle of effective responding to inappropriate communication is the same for each type: It is to communicate, politely and with caring, your preference for not participating in that conversation. This response may not appear attractive at first glance; it is difficult to deliver and it carries with it the risk of being rejected by the helpee. It is, however, the response style that will give the most favorable results over a period of time. Other response styles only perpetuate inappropriateness.

There is no answer you can give that will suddenly change the helpee's communication patterns. You can realistically work toward the establishment of a base relationship that may permit you, over a period of time, to influence the helpees' communication styles (through modeling of good communication, information, and instruction), to assist them in modifying their behaviors, and to encourage and support their seeking intensive help if that proves to be indicated.

Probably more than in any other communication situation, the way in which the response is delivered (the nonverbal component) is critical.

When you decline to continue an inappropriate interaction, it is easy for helpees to read an attitude of condescension, superiority, or arrogance into your response. They may want to do so to avoid feeling scolded for behavior that they know is inappropriate.

The suggestions below will help you formulate and express an effective response:

1. Give it your best effort. It is just as important to perceive the helpee accurately in this as in any other kind of communication situation.
2. Speak thoughtfully. Do not rush your response.
3. Communicate fully your warmth.
4. Include anything you genuinely can that is supportive of the helpee as a person or that supports appropriate behavior.
5. Determine to respond effectively, no matter how difficult it may be. If you can deal with an inappropriate communicator effectively one time, you may never again need to deal with that person's inappropriateness.

The five types of inappropriate communication are listed below with examples. While these situations may not occur in what we usually think of as helpee/helper relationships, we will use that terminology, referring to the person whose communication is inappropriate as the helpee. The person who habitually communicates inappropriately may not be asking for help—but probably is in need of it—and the potential may exist for you to become a helper.

## Rumor

Rumor, as used here, refers to an opinion or statement without known authority for its truth, and its emphasis does not center upon a person. Rumors are not necessarily spread with the knowledge of their inappropriateness or inaccuracy, but it seems inevitable that even "neutral" rumors quickly become distorted as they move from person to person. For example, the innocuous report, "There was a lot of talk in the staff meeting about vacation days, but I don't know if there is anything in it for us," can quickly become, "All the departments but ours are getting an extra week of vacation next year." Sound ridiculous? Perhaps, but if you think about it, you will probably recall actual situations that you know of in which an innocent remark quickly became absurdly different or, worse yet, vicious and harmful.

Rumors often begin without having any names linked with them. This soon changes, probably as a result of carriers trying to make the story more believable as they pass it along. This considerably increases the damage that can be done to specific persons, groups, or organizations. What is said in the section below about responding to gossip also applies to responding to rumor.

## Gossip

Gossip is a rumor of an intimate nature; the focus is on the character or behavior of a *person.* Gossip may open with lines as blatant as, "Did you hear the latest about. . . ?" or with a feeble attempt to be subtle, "You know, I'd be the last person to say anything against anyone, but . . . ." For most persons, the problem is not in knowing how to recognize gossip, but in knowing how to avoid becoming a part of it.

Nobody wants to become the victim of gossip, so we may be afraid of cutting off a gossiper because we do not want to make that person angry and thus become the subject of gossip. We may unwittingly reinforce the person by our silence, and we may even accidently become a "carrier."

The helpee situation below has five responses that illustrate ineffective ways of responding to rumor or gossip plus an effective response.

## Helpee Situation

Teacher to teacher: "Listen to this! You know that curriculum consultant who comes around once a week? The one who is so hostile to you about your lesson plans? Well, she's finally going to get what's coming to her! Guess what they found out she's been up to?"

INAPPROPRIATE HELPER RESPONSES

    A. Responses in which the helper accepts the opportunity to hear gossip.
- 1. The "helper" is eager to hear: "What?"
- 2. The helper denies interest but actually wants to hear: "Who cares? She's not worth my time."
- 3. The helper responds with passive acceptance, as though there were no possibility of influencing the nature of the conversation: "I wouldn't know anything about that."

    B. Responses in which the helper declines the opportunity to hear gossip but does so in a way that may damage the relationship.
- 4. The helper is disrespectful or punishing to the helpee, and the relationship between them is most certain to be damaged: "Thelma, you're always scraping up something and there's usually nothing to it anyway. If we gossip about her, it will be like putting ourselves on her level. I'd rather not even hear about it."
- 5. The helper is brusque or cool toward the helpee. This kind of response may not damage the relationship, but neither does it move the relationship toward constructive change of the helpee: "I'm pretty busy right now so I'd rather not talk about it."

APPROPRIATE HELPER RESPONSE

In the appropriate response, the helper attempts to be warm and respectful of the helpee, and tries to avoid sounding superior, but clearly declines to interact further on the subject, e.g., "I guess you want to help me keep informed about what's going on around here, and I appreciate that, but this seems like something I really don't need to know about." The helper seeks to communicate acceptance of the helpee as a person without condoning the helpee's inappropriate behavior. This is probably as demanding a communication situation as any, especially when it involves responding to a friend or co-worker.

## Inordinate and Chronic Griping

Inordinate griping is exaggerating a small complaint; chronic griping is continued complaining about something that cannot or need not be changed. Griping or complaining in any form is unpleasant to hear. It may signal a significant and legitimate complaint and, if so, it should be attended to with your best and most facilitative efforts. On the other hand, if the griping is found to be inappropriate, it should not be supported. It may result from deficient personality adjustment and, if so, be outside the scope of your help. In that case, your best option is to accept the person as a person, support his behaviors that are appropriate, and ignore as best you can the inappropriate and unpleasant parts of his behavior. If you need to respond, you may express your own opinion or findings on the same subject (situation 1) or gently challenge the helpee's assertion (situation 2), if this can be done without antagonizing the person.

## Helpee Situation 1

> Helpee: "Lousy, miserable, rainy weather again! This is the second rotten day in a row!"

> Helper: "On days like this, I'm glad to have an inside job!" Or, "I guess if we're busy with our work, we won't be affected by what's outside." Or, if the helpee's behavior is unusual for him, the helper may choose to open the conversation for further elaboration of the feelings by saying something like, "It sounds as though this weather is changing some of your plans for you."

## Helpee Situation 2

> Helpee: "We didn't have weather like this before they sent up all those rockets to the moon."

Helper: "You seem to think the rockets *cause* the bad weather. I'm interested in where you got that information."

You are not likely to be able to stop the inappropriateness, but you do not want to use behaviors that reinforce it. With persons with certain personality formations, punishing the inappropriate behavior reinforces it. Your goal should be to relate to the person in a way in which your good communication is modeled for him/her, your attitude toward his/her inappropriate behavior is clear, and neither of you has unpleasant feelings about the other.

## INAPPROPRIATE DEPENDENCY

It is easy, especially in lower grades, for teachers to allow students to become inappropriately dependent upon them. You may have students who have been in classrooms with teachers who encouraged and fostered weakness and dependency on the part of the students. The purpose of education is to teach competence and independence. It is the teacher's role to know how to assist the students in moving from dependence to mature independence and interrelatedness.

Inappropriate dependency usually arises from fear. Some students believe they will not be able to deal with an impending situation; therefore they seek to be sheltered by the teacher or to remain helpless so that facing the object of the fear can be postponed. Some of these fears are real and some of them are irrational.

Dependency also arises from a natural need for attention and for interaction with other persons, but it can grow into a neurotic dependence if persons do not have adequate options for expressing themselves. If students find that their ego needs can be met by being sheltered and cared for by the teacher, they will resist giving up their dependency, and their behaviors may regress to those of an earlier developmental stage.

Inappropriate dependency often results in the student's feeling hostile toward the teacher. The countermeasures for dependency are: (1) recognize situations that are likely to develop into overdependence and exercise prevention and (2) know how to deal constructively with a dependent person.

The process for helping the dependent person utilizes the communication skills learned in earlier chapters. Particular aspects are summarized as follows:

1. Find out, through facilitative communication, what the situation is. Assist the helpee in exploring and understanding that situation, its roots, and its implications.
2. If the helpee reveals exaggerated or unfounded fear, there is probably more fear that will be revealed after further facilitative communication.
3. If the helpee discloses "real" fear, an intervention program must be devised. Give the helpee support, information, and as many

success experiences as possible to restore his/her confidence in his/her ability to cope with the feared situation. Start with what the helpee can do and progress gradually toward the goal behavior. The helpee should be assisted in working toward change of the situation or in securing help in changing the situation, as indicated.

# INAPPROPRIATE ACTIVITIES

This category includes suggestions for avoidance of the encouragement of or solicitation of participation in activities that are potentially harmful to other persons or the organization. This would include acts that are illegal, unethical, of questionable judgment, risky to the safety of others, or that encourage an inferior level of performance. These situations may carry a high potential for serious problems.

You must decide if the talk is idle chatter, or something concrete, and estimate the effect it may have on others. This will guide the style of your response. If the inappropriateness does not significantly threaten anyone's welfare, you may deal with it by seeking to understand the helpee and trying to facilitate his/her self-understanding. If risk to persons or property is involved, protective action must take precedence over facilitation. Still, this can usually be done without alienating the helpee. You should deal with the helpee as warmly and respectfully as possible but express your views clearly and firmly. Your response may: (1) point out undesirable consequences that might occur and/or (2) offer alternative actions that are appropriate, and (3) it must clearly state or imply what behavior would be appropriate.

If you are aware of inappropriate behavior of a serious or potentially serious nature, you owe it to your organization, your co-workers, and students to take steps to prevent possible damage. This may mean talking with your superior about it, a step that may take courage and may carry with it the possibility of making you unpopular with the other individual or your co-workers, but for the long-term success of the organization there is no alternative.

## Situation:

Three teachers are working on a proposal for changes in the curriculum. They have been assigned this project by the principal and stay late after school two days a week until the project is finished. Suddenly the electricity in the building goes off.

> Helper A: "Well, the electricity is off. It's not *our* fault if the work doesn't get done. Let's go home!"

Helper B: "I'm tired of working too, but I think if we call the maintenance department they can fix this in no time. Let's try that first."

Helper C: "If they don't come right away, we'll *never* get home. Put a penny behind the fuse. Nobody will know the difference."

Helper B: "That's dangerous, so we won't do it. We'll call maintenance and then call the principal to report what's happening."

## ADDITIONAL PRACTICE IN RESPONDING

Write responses to the situations below in which the helpee's communication is inappropriate. If possible, role play the situations with another person.

### Helpee Situations

1. Teacher to teacher: "You were in the office talking to the principal for almost half an hour. Did he say anything about staff next year? There's a lot of talk that Helen is not going to be asked back."

2. Principal to student: "They expect me to be responsible for what my staff does, but when I need to reprimand someone, the Board of Education doesn't back me up. I don't know how they can expect me to do a good job when they tie my hands like that!"

3. Teacher to teacher: "You know Mrs. Thomas called in sick yesterday. Well, guess where I saw her last night? She was at the country club—and she was dancing! She sure didn't look very sick to me!"

4. School secretary to teacher: "The principal will be away all day at a staff meeting. If you need me today, I'll be back in the duplicating room doing some personal stuff."

5. Teacher to teacher: "Well, the principal has been here two years now. The last two only stayed that long—it's all anyone can take, with the crummy staff we have around here. I suppose we're due for a change of principals soon."

6. Teacher to teacher: "You spend too much time trying to do your job perfect. Why don't you just put in your time and enjoy life like I do?"

7. School secretary to teacher: "You can't trust her to keep a secret. She's the biggest blabbermouth I've ever known!"

8. Student to teacher: "I can't figure out what to do after I graduate from high school. You'll have to decide for me."

9. The person who team teaches with you says, for the third time in the last hour, "Look at that rain! All it ever does is rain! I get so sick and tired of it!"

10. Custodian to school secretary: "Take home anything you need—the school will never miss it. Besides, everybody does it."

# ACCEPTING COMPLIMENTS

Many persons respond to a compliment by denying or minimizing the achievement or characteristic that is being complimented. For example, the following compliment is given by one teacher to another teacher, "You did an excellent job in your presentation to the faculty this morning. I especially admired how you handled the question and answer period." The teacher who has been complimented responds, "Oh, I thought it was probably pretty boring. In fact, I felt pretty awkward trying to answer a couple of those questions. They should have had someone else up there." This kind of response to a compliment is rather typical, yet it actually punishes the person who has given the compliment. This kind of response challenges the validity of the perception and integrity of the statement of the person giving the compliment. It will probably leave him/her feeling rebuffed and unlikely to offer a compliment to that person again.

Many persons are suspicious of the genuineness of compliments. They may believe that the person who is praising them is fishing for a compliment in return, using flattery for some hidden purpose, trying to manipulate them, or is praising them as an introduction to giving criticism. However, compliments are usually genuine, and when they are not, it is obvious. Accept a compliment as you would accept any other gift from a friend; if it makes you feel good, say so.

For example, a person says to a co-worker, "Delores, it's hard to put this into words, but I want you to know I'm glad that we get to work together. You care a lot about the kids but also a lot about the rest of us. What you said to me this morning especially meant a lot to me." An appropriate response would be, "Thank you! It makes me very happy to hear you say that." The most meaningful compliments often come as a surprise, which makes them difficult to respond to easily. But, since the person giving the compliment has revealed genuine feelings, you can reveal yours in your response. Don't be reluctant to accept the compliment. Simply say something along the lines of, "That's really kind of you to say that," or "Wow, thanks! I appreciate that!"

In giving a compliment, remember that it can make the other person feel uneasy. Don't overdo it. Don't say anything that is not genuine, and try to make your delivery of the compliment simple, brief, and clearly sincere.

If your interpersonal relationships are consistent with the principles of this communication model you will probably earn and deserve compliments. When they come, accept them graciously, and enjoy them.

## DEALING WITH AN ANGRY PERSON

Each of us has had the experience of receiving an attack of anger from another person without warning and for no apparent reason. Even though the outburst is verbal, we generally respond as if it were a physical attack, and the body prepares itself for fight. You know the physical effects: increases in heart rate, respiration, perspiration, secretion of adrenaline, and so on. These physical reactions often occur even when we know the attack is misdirected or unjustified, and this "gut" reaction interferes with the process of responding.

At the same time, the perception of the angry person is not functioning accurately. *Anything* you say or do is *likely* to be distorted. This means that your communication must be particularly effective under those circumstances in which it is most difficult to perceive and respond with precision.

Two elements are present in most instances when an outburst of anger occurs: (1) a precipitating situation or incident and (2) a readiness on the part of an individual to become angry. This readiness usually results from prior conditions not related to the precipitating incident. Some of the reasons why a person might be prone to overt anger include:

1. Frustration; not being able to meet a goal. This is a condition many persons in our society experience every day.
2. Not feeling good about self; redirecting the anger toward self to others.
3. An immature attempt to show strength or individuality.
4. A defensive maneuver to keep other persons from getting too close.
5. A desperate effort to reach out to others; a plea for help.

Being aware that conditions such as these frequently underlie expressions of anger will help you respond to the person himself/herself rather than to his/her inappropriate behavior.

The information below outlines the aspects of communication that are unique to responding to an outburst of anger. Entries one through six describe considerations and helpee behaviors preliminary to implementation of the model in its "regular" manner. In other words, certain conditions must be met in order for the model to be used. When those conditions are met, interaction proceeds according to the basic model. The first six factors tell you how to create conditions in which helping can begin.

1. Know and understand your own response to anger. Anticipate the ineffective responses you might be inclined to give. Use the model as applied in the exercises dealing with an angry person, to respond effectively.

2. Remember the dynamics of anger; frequently an attack comes from a person who is unhappy because of unfulfilled needs not related to the precipitating incident. As soon as you show the angry person that you are trying to understand those needs, you begin to reduce the anger.

3. Let the angry person talk. Allow his/her angry feelings to spill out. When the anger is allowed to flow from the helpee, it will usually dissipate quickly. The angry person is not going to feel good or be receptive to your help until his/her bad feelings are communicated and understood. It is futile to try to force logic or information on a person who is filled with strong emotion—at that moment he/she simply does not have the capacity to utilize it.

4. Accept his/her right to be angry and accept him/her as a person of worth, even though you may not agree with his/her reasons for being angry. You must always allow the other person the freedom to be wrong.

5. Show nonverbally that you are listening. Nod affirmatively, pay close attention, do not crowd the person or give any motion that might be interpreted as anger on your part. React calmly but with clear meaning. If it seems appropriate to speak, you might say something like, "I'd like to listen to what you want to say," or, "This must be very important; please let me know more about it." Say only enough to show your acceptance of the person as he/she is now.

6. If there is a quick solution to the precipitating incident give it. If, for example, the person is angry because a fellow worker did not assist him/her with something, help out if your duties permit you to do so. This is "first aid" for anger, not a cure for the causes.

7. When the angry person is ready for you to speak, respond to his/her feelings. Communicate verbally and nonverbally to the helpee that you recognize how important the situation is to him/her. Show that you want to understand how he/she feels and why he/she feels that way. Do not be superficial or trite; communicate caring and concern.

8. If you have been part of the problem, admit it, fully and willingly. If you do not, no restoration is possible and the problem can only become more serious. Do not deal with the helpee's feelings when you should be taking action. If, for example, the person is

angry because you are not doing something that you are responsible for doing, do not sit around and listen to the anger, get up and do your job!

9. Seek something about which you can compliment the other person, or something about which you can agree, but do not use this as a "technique." It can bring you and the other person close together *only* if you are genuinely seeking to develop your areas of common interest.

10. Always communicate helpfully. Your good communication adds pleasure to the lives of others who, in turn, will communicate more helpfully with other persons.

## RESPONDING TO AN ANGRY PERSON

Part of the skill in responding to anger is being able to take it—to perceive accurately and respond calmly under complex and emotionally charged circumstances. These conditions cannot be simulated very well by printed helpee situations. If possible, ask someone to take the helpee role and together verbally act out the situations below. If that is not possible, write the initial response that you would give in a helper role. In responding to each of the situations, you are the teacher.

### Helpee Situations

1. Parent to teacher: "The school is supposed to offer band instrument lessons, but when I talked to the music teacher she said that only certain kids were eligible. She said a child has to make a certain score on some test. I don't know how any *test* can prove whether or not a child should have lessons! I'll tell you one thing, my Tony has talent! That music teacher wouldn't even tell me how Tony did on the test, but I know that he's as good as any kid in school. He's entitled to have lessons and I'm going to see to it that he gets them!"

2. High school student to teacher: "This whole society is a ripoff society! Everybody feeds off of somebody else! *You're* part of it! You may *say* you're here to help us, but you're just in it for the money. You have a union just like all the other ripoffs. You couldn't care less about the students!"

3. The principal, Ms. Jones, calls to you as you are walking to your car after school. She catches up with you and angrily begins confronting you about an incident that occurred that day. She said you sent a student,

Ray Smith, to the office instead of bringing him to the office yourself. Instead of going to the office the student wandered around the halls for half an hour. The principal ends by saying, "You know the rules. I don't want this to happen again!"

4. Custodian to teacher: "I wish you'd do something about these kids and their gum. It is everywhere—on the floors, on the steps, on the desks; and the cafeteria is covered with it. We've got more than we can do with our sweeping and waxing and emptying the trash and everything else without cleaning up all that filthy gum!"

5. Elementary student to teacher: "I don't like you! You never choose me to do anything special!"

6. High school student to teacher: "You have it in for me. You always make a fool of me in front of the whole class. You ask me the hardest questions every time just to pick on me. I don't think I've done anything to deserve this!"

7. High school student to teacher: "This class is a waste of time! There's no reason in the world why I should have to study this stupid stuff! How is this going to help me earn a living? As far as that's concerned, there isn't any reason for me to be in school."

# Appendix A

# vocabulary of affective adjectives

This list of adjectives was developed to help the user find the most appropriate description of perceived feelings. No attempt has been made to order these words in terms of their degree of intensity.

Note that by simply preceding many of these adjectives with appropriate adverbs, you can control the intensity of your communication. For example:

You feel *somewhat* angry with your instructor for embarrassing you.
You feel *quite* angry with your instructor for embarrassing you.
You feel *very* angry with your instructor for embarrassing you.
You feel *extremely* angry with your instructor for embarrassing you.

## PLEASANT AFFECTIVE STATES

### Love, Affection, Concern

| | | | |
|---|---|---|---|
| admired | dedicated | just | receptive |
| adorable | devoted | kind | reliable |
| affectionate | easy-going | kind-hearted | respectful |
| agreeable | empathetic | kindly | responsible |
| altruistic | fair | lenient | sensitive |
| amiable | faithful | lovable | sweet |
| benevolent | forgiving | loving | sympathetic |
| benign | friendly | mellow | tender |
| big-hearted | generous | mild | thoughtful |
| brotherly | genuine | moral | tolerant |
| caring | giving | neighborly | truthful |
| charitable | good | nice | trustworthy |
| Christian | good-humored | obliging | understanding |
| comforting | good-natured | open | unselfish |
| congenial | helpful | optimistic | warm |
| conscientious | honest | patient | warm-hearted |
| considerate | honorable | peaceful | well-meaning |
| cooperative | hospitable | pleasant | wise |
| cordial | humane | polite | |
| courteous | interested | reasonable | |

217

## Elation, Joy

| | | | |
|---|---|---|---|
| amused | exalted | humorous | serene |
| at ease | excellent | in high spirits | splendid |
| blissful | excited | inspired | superb |
| brilliant | fantastic | jovial | terrific |
| calm | fine | joyful | thrilled |
| cheerful | fit | jubilant | tremendous |
| comical | gay | magnificent | triumphant |
| contented | glad | majestic | turned on |
| delighted | glorious | marvelous | vivacious |
| ecstatic | good | overjoyed | witty |
| elated | grand | pleasant | wonderful |
| elevated | gratified | pleased | |
| enchanted | great | proud | |
| enthusiastic | happy | satisfied | |

## Potency

| | | | |
|---|---|---|---|
| able | durable | influential | spirited |
| adequate | dynamic | intense | stable |
| assured | effective | lion-hearted | stouthearted |
| authoritative | energetic | manly | strong |
| bold | fearless | mighty | sure |
| brave | firm | powerful | tough |
| capable | forceful | robust | virile |
| competent | gallant | secure | well-equipped |
| confident | hardy | self-confident | well-put-together |
| courageous | healthy | self-reliant | |
| daring | heroic | sharp | |
| determined | important | skillful | |

# UNPLEASANT AFFECTIVE STATES

## Depression

| | | | |
|---|---|---|---|
| abandoned | below par | defeated | despised |
| alien | blue | degraded | despondent |
| alienated | burned | dejected | destroyed |
| alone | cast off | demolished | discarded |
| annihilate | cheapened | depressed | discouraged |
| awful | crushed | desolate | disfavored |
| battered | debased | despair | dismal |

| done for | horrible | mistreated | ruined |
| downcast | humiliated | moody | run down |
| downhearted | hurt | mournful | sad |
| downtrodden | in the dumps | obsolete | stranded |
| dreadful | jilted | ostracized | tearful |
| estranged | kaput | out of sorts | terrible |
| excluded | left out | overlooked | unhappy |
| forlorn | loathed | pathetic | unloved |
| forsaken | lonely | pitiful | valueless |
| gloomy | lonesome | rebuked | washed up |
| glum | lousy | regretful | shipped |
| grim | low | rejected | worthless |
| hated | miserable | reprimanded | wrecked |
| hopeless | mishandled | rotten | |

## Distress

| afflicted | displeased | lost | swamped |
| anguished | dissatisfied | nauseated | the plaything of |
| at the feet of | distrustful | offended | the puppet of |
| at the mercy of | disturbed | pained | tormented |
| awkward | doubtful | perplexed | touchy |
| badgered | foolish | puzzled | ungainly |
| bewildered | futile | ridiculous | unlucky |
| blameworthy | grief | sickened | unpopular |
| clumsy | helpless | silly | unsatisfied |
| confused | hindered | skeptical | unsure |
| constrained | impaired | speechless | |
| disgusted | impatient | strained | |
| disliked | imprisoned | suspicious | |

## Fear, Anxiety

| afraid | fearful | jittery | shy |
| agitated | fidgety | jumpy | strained |
| alarmed | frightened | nervous | tense |
| anxious | hesitant | on edge | terrified |
| apprehensive | horrified | overwhelmed | terror-stricken |
| bashful | ill at ease | panicky | timid |
| desperate | insecure | restless | uncomfortable |
| dread | intimidated | scared | uneasy |
| embarrassed | jealous | shaky | worrying |

## Belittling, Criticism, Scorn

| | | | |
|---|---|---|---|
| abused | diminished | maligned | scoffed at |
| belittled | discredited | minimized | scorned |
| branded | disdained | mocked | shamed |
| carped at | disgraced | neglected | slammed |
| caviled at | disparaged | not taken seriously | slandered |
| censured | humiliated | overlooked | slighted |
| criticized | ignored | poked fun at | thought nothing of |
| defamed | jeered | pooh-poohed | underestimated |
| deflated | lampooned | pulled to pieces | underrated |
| deprecated | laughed at | put down | |
| depreciated | libeled | ridiculed | |
| derided | make light of | roasted | |

## Impotency, Inadequacy

| | | | |
|---|---|---|---|
| anemic | flimsy | insecure | unable |
| broken | fragile | insufficient | unarmed |
| broken down | frail | lame | uncertain |
| chicken-hearted | harmless | maimed | unfit |
| cowardly | helpless | meek | unimportant |
| crippled | impotent | nerveless | unqualified |
| debilitated | inadequate | paralyzed | unsound |
| defective | incapable | powerless | unsubstantiated |
| deficient | incompetent | puny | useless |
| demoralized | indefensible | shaken | vulnerable |
| disabled | ineffective | shaky | weak |
| effeminate | inefficient | sickly | weak-hearted |
| exhausted | inept | small | |
| exposed | inferior | strengthless | |
| feeble | infirm | trivial | |

## Anger, Hostility, Cruelty

| | | | |
|---|---|---|---|
| aggravated | belligerent | combative | dictatorial |
| agitated | bigoted | contrary | disagreeable |
| aggressive | biting | cool | discontented |
| angry | bloodthirsty | corrosive | dogmatic |
| annoyed | blunt | cranky | enraged |
| antagonistic | bullying | critical | envious |
| arrogant | callous | cross | fierce |
| austere | cantankerous | cruel | furious |
| bad-tempered | cold-blooded | deadly | gruesome |

| | | | |
|---|---|---|---|
| hard | insensitive | perturbed | severe |
| hard-hearted | intolerable | poisonous | spiteful |
| harsh | intolerant | prejudiced | stern |
| hateful | irritated | pushy | stormy |
| heartless | mad | rebellious | unfeeling |
| hellish | malicious | reckless | unfriendly |
| hideous | mean | resentful | unmerciful |
| hostile | murderous | revengeful | unruly |
| hypercritical | nasty | rough | vicious |
| ill-tempered | obstinate | rude | vindictive |
| impatient | opposed | ruthless | violent |
| inconsiderate | oppressive | sadistic | wrathful |
| inhuman | outraged | savage | |

# Appendix B

# communication "leads"

To understand other persons' feelings and experiences we need to attempt to enter their phenomenal field—their personal frame of reference through which they interact with their world. However, since it is impossible for us to be the other person, the best that we can do amounts to reasonably correct but approximate understandings. With this in mind, it seems desirable that we be continuously open-minded and cautious in appraising others, consider most judgments as tentative, and remember that at best we will have a limited understanding of the unique person with whom we are interacting.

Phrases that are useful, when you trust that your perceptions are accurate and the helpee is receptive to your communications:

> You feel . . .
> From your point of view. . .
> It seems to you. . .
> In your experience. . .
> From where you stand. . .
> As you see it. . .
> You think. . .
> You believe. . .
> What I hear you saying. . .
> You're. . . (identify the feeling, for example, angry, sad, overjoyed)
> I'm picking up that you. . .
> I really hear you saying that. . .
> Where you're coming from. . .
> You figure. .
> You mean. . .

Phrases that are useful when you are having some difficulty perceiving clearly, or it seems that the helpee might not be receptive to your communications:

> Could it be that. . .
> I wonder if. . .

I'm not sure if I'm with you, but. . .

Would you buy this idea. . .

What I guess I'm hearing is. . .

Correct me if I'm wrong, but. . .

Is it possible that. . .

Does it sound reasonable that you. . .

Could this be what's going on, you. . .

From where I stand you. . .

This is what I think I hear you saying. . .

You appear to be feeling. . .

It appears you. . .

Perhaps you're feeling. . .

I somehow sense that maybe you feel. . .

Is there any chance that you. . .

Maybe you feel. . .

Is it conceivable that. . .

Maybe I'm out to lunch, but. . .

Do you feel a little. . .

Maybe this is a long shot, but. . .

I'm not sure if I'm with you; do you mean. . .

I'm not certain I understand; you're feeling. . .

It seems that you. . .

As I hear it, you. . .

. . . is that the way it is?

. . . is that what you mean?

. . . is that the way you feel?

Let me see if I understand; you. . .

Let me see if I'm with you; you. . .

I get the impression that. . .

I guess that you're . . .

# Appenδix C

# scales for rating the helpee

All scales that have been presented up to this point have dealt with rating the helpers in their interaction with helpees. The three scales presented here are used to rate helpees. These scales look at the extent of the helpee's desire for problem solving. They are analagous to the commitment of the helper to the helpee, which is measured on the Respect Scale, except in this case it reflects the commitment of the helpee to himself/herself.

The three scales to be presented are Helpee Help-Seeking Scale, Helpee Self-Exploration Scale, and Helpee Action-Implementing Scale. These scales are designed so that helpees must be at high levels on the Help-Seeking Scale before they can be at high levels on the Self-Exploration Scale and, likewise, they must be high on the Self-Exploration Scale before they can be high on the Action-Implementing Scale. Thus, the three scales roughly form a continuum of helpees' commitment to the process of their own problem resolution or personal growth.

The action dimensions should be used only after high levels of self-exploration have been achieved. Therefore, you may use the scale of helpee self-exploration as an excellent indicator for timing the introduction of action responses.

The three helpee rating scales are outlined in the following section and the levels are defined.

## HELPEE HELP-SEEKING SCALE

The Help-Seeking Scale is a measure of whether or not the helpee wants to be involved in a helper-helpee relationship. Helpees are rated on this scale according to the strength of their desire for help.

Level 5—Helpee actively seeks help.

Level 4—Helpee accepts help when provided.

Level 3—Helpee is open to being helped, will consider entering a helping relationship.

Level 2—Helpee admits need for help but avoids entering a helping relationship.

Level 1—Helpee overtly refuses available help, or the helpee participates in helper-helpee relationships in order to qualify for benefits extrinsic to the aims of the helping relationship.

## HELPEE SELF-EXPLORATION SCALE

The Helpee Self-Exploration Scale is a measure of the extent to which the helpee is actively searching for new feelings and experiences. Helpees are rated on this scale according to the strength of their desire to self-explore.

Level 5—Helpee actively searches for new feelings and experiences (even if fearful).

Level 4—Helpee volunteers personally-relevant material with spontaneity and emotional proximity.

Level 3—Helpee volunteers personally-relevant material but mechanically and with no feeling.

Level 2—Helpee responds mechanically and with no feeling to personally-relevant material introduced by the helper.

Level 1—Helpee avoids all self-expression, is defensive, and provides no opportunity to discuss personally-relevant material.

## HELPEE ACTION-IMPLEMENTING SCALE

The Implementing Scale is a measure of the degree to which the helpee participates in the determination and practice of problem-solving or growth-directed behaviors. The course of action is defined as the steps helpees take toward solving their problems and includes training or psychotherapy, socialization, education, restitution, physical exercise, relaxation, or other efforts.

Level 5—Helpee follows the course of action to the extent that it exists. He/she does everything known to be done for that situation at that time.

Level 4—Helpee accepts part of the course of action.

Level 3—Helpee considers following the course of action as it is evolving.

Level 2—Helpee accepts helper communication that is high on action dimensions.

Level 1—Helpee rejects or avoids helper communication.

# Index